Memoirs of a Minotaur

Memoirs
of a
Minotaur

The Making of a Poet

Robin Magowan

 Story Line Press | *Pasadena, CA*

Layout assistance Vera Hines

ISBN 978-1-58654-050-0 (tradepaper)
978-1-58654-103-3 (casebound)

The National Endowment for the Arts, the Los Angeles County Arts Commission,
the Ahmanson Foundation, the Dwight Stuart Youth Fund, the Max Factor Family
Foundation, the Pasadena Tournament of Roses Foundation, the Pasadena Arts &
Culture Commission and the City of Pasadena Cultural Affairs Division, the City
of Los Angeles Department of Cultural Affairs, the Audrey & Sydney Irmas Char-
itable Foundation, the Kinder Morgan Foundation, the Meta & George Rosenberg
Foundation, the Allergan Foundation, the Riordan Foundation, Amazon Literary
Partnership, and the Mara W. Breech Foundation partially support Red Hen Press.

Originally published as *Memoirs of a Minotaur: from Merrill Lynch to Patty
Heart to Poetry*

Second Edition
Published by Story Line Press
an imprint of Red Hen Press
www.redhen.org

For Juliet, Felix, James, Samantha, Colin

Contents

Appendix

You can't take from me what I've danced.
No se puede quitarme lo que he bailado.
—Mexican proverb

MAT-RIDING

The first thing I remember about the ocean is my father. On several occasions, long before I was ready, I recall him yanking me by the waist and dragging me, screaming, into the surf. When I was seven the Beach Club lifeguard began teaching me how to cope with the waves. Before long I had a rubber mat equipped with a rope so I could haul it over the sand. We used mats, instead of a surf board, because of the way the waves broke upon the Long Island shore, not rolling so much as knifing down. To ride them I had to position myself out ahead of where I thought that big daddy of them all would come shattering down. Waiting, I stuck my chin in the middle of the mat's five cushiony rills. Then, when the right wave appeared, I kicked and paddled fast as I could.

Entering that world I would stand, green as that beginning when wave first flowered into child and I ran away, my home those white umbrellas out there among the tumbling casks. Those waves may not have been the night, but they came crying with the night's full fire and it was that fire I felt compelled to ride, hurtling onto foam, sand.

Best were the days honored by a red flag when the combers towered high as steeples, spuming into ashen stains. When they rolled me, it felt prehistoric: fish darted through my eyes, pebbles scraped me red, and sometimes my head bounced off the bottom, stunned. When I struggled up from the churn most likely there would be another wave bearing down and I'd have to gather in my breath and dive and make sure I stayed flatter than a shadow until the whole train's length had thundered by. By that time I'd be out over my head and fearful, lest the backwash and my diving momentum should propel me into the grip of a sea-puss.

In that sea-wrack insanity glittered, "Crawled out of you, wave, here I am crawling my way back in." I was under the breaker as I turned, lifted the mat overhead like a trolley, and hastened across the receding slack. My concentration was all on my voice squiring me out through the slits in the breaking wall. I was coming home, home where I once belonged. Ahead I saw a path opening. I must! I will! Chin down, I hopped on and, paddling furiously, flailed my way out of the vast dissolving cathedral.

Once out, a different fear surged as I found myself a whole roof higher than the shore. At first, though, I'd be too tuckered to do much other than savor the relief of being afloat in the froth mill, feeling the wind behind the shadow behind the wave blade. Everything was teeth, savage, distant, Saturnian. Mine, too, were chattering, but as I hung on, blue-lipped, I experienced something of what a ski racer knows, poised above a run's starting gate, the lover as he maneuvers his bulk until it locks onto that tumbling ecstasy when the waves parted and I shot forth alone into that chaos.

As a mat-rider I wanted nothing more than to be the arc in that fire spume and it was to that end I shivered until finally out of some faraway cave a breaker loomed, scary enough to ride. "If not for this, why have I been out here?" words to set me paddling ahead of the wave's racing engine. Then the breaker and I collided and it was "Diamonds out" as the mat catapulted forward and I took it, this wave house spattering me forth on a cushion of foam in a ride I never wanted to see end.

Robin on the beach at Southampton

SPEED INCARNATE

Before I ever waded, or got thrown in, there was Father himself. His weekend arrival seemed one continuous motion towards the ocean: the tearing out from Wall Street on the Long Island Cannonball Express; the change at home out of his business suit into casual polo shirt and shorts. Then, driven over with my brother Merrill to my grandfather's "Beach House," the long non-stop run down through the dunes and across the beach as he hurled himself with a great crack out through the first wave. There for a minute or two he would float, arms forward and head like a dead man down, and only then, when there was none of the city's work week grime left on him, would he wade towards us, shaking like a dog and happy. The beauty was all in the charge, the brusqueness of it, the sea spray moistening and feathering as it turned him green, gold, and white while the twilight curled around and translated him to us.

There was something superbly clean in that headlong running of his, that raging fire of his intensity. Speed incarnate, hardly straying out of the middle lane on a drive to Southampton; or, on an irresistible impulse, as a young man in Paris, grabbing the white nightstick out of a gendarme's holster and sprinting away with it into the night. Don Regan, his personal assistant at Merrill Lynch and later President Reagan's Chief of Staff, wrote that in all his working life he had never encountered a man who did everything so rapidly: clear a desk, pound a typewriter, fire off a memo in his trademark telegraphese. Working for "Boss," as Don fondly called him, you hopped—or else.

A natural force, like wind, like thunder and rain, unpredictable and more than a bit dangerous. To anyone encountering him even casually his presence intimidated. "The most frightening man I've ever met," an acknowledgment I've heard again and again. It took some twenty years before he relented enough to call his Safeway secretary, Jeanne Hickerson, by her first name. Bill Schreier, a Merrill CEO, remembers receiving, at an early stage of his career, a "smiling ram" memo of praise. (RAM were his initials from Robert Anderson Magowan. There was also a second set, with a scowling ram.) When Schreier acknowledged the memo gratefully, Father reminded him, "There's only a few inches between a pat on the back and a kick in the ass."

Tennis did a little to ease the whirlwind as long as a son crouched at the net on the receiving end of one of his lethal forehands. Booze worked better. Put the slow fire of his "Early Times" into a glass and he visibly thawed. Put another and add an excellent cuvee over dinner, and you might get someone confiding, intimate, companionable. But what about afterwards, in the next morning's white-out, clamped behind his triple-folded business pages, unable to utter so much as a greeting; or frantically looking for something, "Who stole my cufflinks?" as he thundered up the stairs. There was always the threat of not knowing when, or on whom, his volcano would spew its flames. In what manhole could a son hide, un-devoured by his all-seeing eye?

The importance of learning to live under such chaos, wave after fatherly wave ringing on my ears, cannot be exaggerated. Other people become paralyzed, stuck on a runway in an airplane that won't take off. Or disabled by an inordinate amount of hallucinogens breaking over them, one wave of thought heavier than the last. For them such havoc is exceptional. For me it seems my native medium, a fatality I'd been steeped in at the primal source.

FROM PEANUTS TO PEARLS

My father was born in 1903 in Chester, Pennsylvania, on the Delaware River, the son of the local railway station master. The first American Magowan had emerged in 1789 not far away in New Castle, Delaware, fresh presumably from the highland clearances. (In Gaelic we are blacksmith's sons, a caste accorded the peculiar powers, and consequent isolation, of those who handle fire.) Throughout the 19th century the family remained in the Delaware Gap, their marital horizons limited to the next lassie off the boat from Glasgow.

Robin on a swing in the park

Chester is a blighted mill town some twelve miles south of Philadelphia. Yet a rewarding life could be lived there and on my one visit, in 1960, I met my 94-year-old uncle, Orlando Cloud, a sprightly fellow sporting a green eyeshade; a man well-informed about the greater world, who had never in the whole of that long life spent a night outside the current city limits.

For my father, Chester was no Arcadia. As far as any of us knew he had no memories of the town in which he had lived until he was fifteen, none at any rate he cared to voice. Memories were always sealed in the bitter grime of his poverty, qualified as "dire," or "abject," leaving me to infer the circumstances: the wrong side of the river where they lived? The mockery of the shop windows, too tantalizing for people who went out only to church? The penny-pinching of those days made him frugal about dousing the house lights, or spending more time than necessary on the telephone. He delighted in a bargain, the senior citizen card he'd flash at a movie house, the social security check that might barely pay for a dinner at La Caravelle in Manhattan.

Back lawn with trellised roses, "Little Orchard," Southampton

If my maternal grandfather, Charlie Merrill, was the prototype of the flamboyant Wall Street tycoon, my father was the somewhat more traditional figure, a person basically formed by the Horatio Alger stories he read avidly as a boy. To him and his friends, he insisted to my brother Mark, interviewing him for a folklore assignment, "They weren't stories, but truth itself." Not only did he absorb a pattern of success from them—how you achieved it, climbed a slippery drainpipe, extricated yourself from one or another snake-surrounded pit—they also furnished him with his ideals, the equation of the pursuit of money with the pursuit of happiness, and of business success with spiritual grace. Likewise, the story of any white American male who failed to muster the combination of pluck and luck to achieve in this way counted as nothing less than a tragedy. When he met Charlie Merrill he could not help but see in him the epitome of all he believed, a man he would give heart and soul to serve.

Charles Merrill with his son, James, Palm Beach, 1931

As a small child, Father had contracted a bad case of mumps. According to the medical wisdom of the time, the way to reduce his swollen neck was to make him wear a spiked collar—bleed the fever out! The little boy wore that contraption for years, never getting any better, until a Christian Science practitioner made his parents throw it away. Thereafter he thrived, gleaning chunks of coal along the railroad track with his younger brother, Ned; hustling, at ten, his own ice business; anything to make a buck.

Like so many youths of the day, Father saw the World War as a possible escape from Chester. But it ended when he was fifteen, the year his father was transferred in failing health to Philadelphia. There through the generosity of a certain Mr. Cox (whose grandchildren he was to befriend when their father suddenly died), he got his first break: a post-graduate scholarship at the age of nineteen to the Kent School, an Episcopal academy in northwest Connecticut.

A miracle of a sort had happened. He had been lifted onto an unexpected plane. But he was not the free agent his classmates were. There was his family, whose one hope he had become. The responsibility can only have compounded his anxiety. "Where should I apply to college?" I can see him asking his adored mother, Estelle.

"To the very best—Harvard," I see her replying.

That must have occasioned a gulp. "All very well, but how am I going to pay for room and board? With my grades, Harvard isn't going to award me a scholarship."

"With this typewriter," I see her replying, unveiling the newfangled invention she had acquired for just this occasion. "You'll be the only freshman who has one and those Gold Coast guys with lousy handwriting will pay a lot to hand in something proofed and legible."

His mother could not have come up with a better graduation gift. The typewriter was the one machine he actually understood down to its tiniest spool. Before long Father was banging out, not only fellow student papers, but journalism as a paid-by-the-inch stringer for *The Boston Globe* and *The New York Times*. By senior year he was employing five student assistants and raking in the not inconsiderable sum of a hundred dollars a week while serving as Editor-in-Chief of the Harvard *Crimson* and manager of the Baseball Team. By then he was not only supporting his parents, but paying for his brother's tuition at Ohio Wesleyan as well. He was able to spend two summer vacations in Paris, renting an apartment and subletting to nine of his classmates. He even shipped over his brother, along with a red Ford.

It might be asked what time that left for studying. His college grades, as revealed in the transcript the Navy requested, were such it's remarkable the Navy made an officer of him. It's equally remarkable, my brother Merrill commented that, given his genes, we sons ever graduated from anywhere. This, though, was the Roaring Twenties and life at Harvard had its own "Gold Coast" aura: Boston deb parties to be crashed; un-crashable black tie social clubs; the infrequently attended "great man" lecture. For kids on the make, like my father and Charlie Merrill, that was pretty much the hierarchy. You went to college less for the patina of a liberal education than for the savoir-faire and the chance to make lifelong social connections.

By senior year Father had all too many juggling balls in the air. At the beginning of the term he received a long frantic letter from his brother describing his parents' situation. They had moved, for some reason—a retirement home? a treatment center?—to Asheville, North Carolina, and their father was threatening to bring the two of them down with him into the dust. As the transcript shows, Father obtained a leave of absence for the semester. What happened with his family he did not tell us, but it left him with a spring semester load of seven courses, if he was to graduate with his 1927 class. One of them, a not altogether surprising Psychology I, proved too much. And there he was in summer school finishing his B.A. while his classmates were regaling themselves on the continent.

Father at a table in Paris, 1934

Upon graduation Father took a job at *The Boston Globe*. When he learned that its star reporter was drawing down a measly $15,000 (multiply that by at least ten today), he decided journalism wasn't for him. With the encouragement of a classmate, my future godfather Jack Straus, he went to work for $30 a week in the management training program of the Straus-owned R.H. Macy's, the world's largest department store. At those wages he kept body and soul together dining out at the Automat and snacking on the free food offered on bar counters. But Father was a born merchandiser, and it wasn't long before he became Macy's chief European buyer, based in the mecca of his generation, Paris, seven months of the year.

How satisfying it must have been for a young man from so deprived a background to shop all over Europe on Macy's oversized pocketbook. Whatever he liked could be copied and mass-produced. Back on Herald Square, he made sure that every last one of those gloves and hats purchased in Berlin before Hitler's unexpected ascendancy was sold. As Jack Straus told me years later, "Your father understood merchandising, what you have to do to sell a product, better than anyone. Had he stuck it out, he and not I would be running Macy's." Doubtful, that. Running a company, getting employees to perform for you, requires other skills than sheer merchandising brilliance. To Father, even more intolerable than being one of the few WASPs in a Jewish concern, was having to sacrifice his weekend to work on Saturday. When Macy's failed to deliver the extraordinary pay raise he requested, he quit and became a rather unlikely advertising executive.

He was wealthy now as few people were in those highly depressed times. With savings of $250,000 he could think of offering himself as a potential mate. He proposed to a gorgeous Parisian couturiere, Yvonne de Peyrimhoff, a woman who was to go on to seven marriages of her own—ending up a duchess—and a distinguished career in fashion working for Dior and Saint-Laurent. But Yvonne, as she told me, had her reservations, about his anti-Semitism, for one. In softening the blow she told him to set his sights on someone more promising than a woman with no money.

Father was vacationing in Palm Beach when, through the good offices of Johnny and Audy Baker (my future godparents), he found himself attending a birthday dinner dance Charlie Merrill was giving at the Everglades Club for his 20-year-old daughter, Doris, a petite blue-eyed brunette with a figure like a swan's.

For a man who hardly danced, the highly poised beauty whirling away on the dance floor seemed unreachable. But when Ned's brother, as she knew him, showed up a week later on the same train headed back north, there was time to get acquainted.

At the time Mother was engaged to Johnny Slocum, a medical student and future psychiatrist. But such commitments never kept her from flirting with a handsome man. This 5'7" 32-year-old businessman was striking looking, with piercing, sapphire-blue eyes that flashed sincerity even as they blazed into your inner soul: a strong needle-fine nose; parted medium-short black hair; a compact slender torso set on legs that were, like his arms, a trifle short even for one of his height. They would have recognized a shared metabolism: two quick-flitting supremely intense hummingbirds. There may even have been a topic or two they shared: the spell of Europe, for one, which had transformed them both. All the same I wonder what, other than his irresistible self-belief, the prospect of great wealth he wore like a star, he had going for him. He was thirteen years Doris's senior. Then again it may have been these very differences that gave him the erotic fatality of The Stranger.

Father, 1949, Rapallo

Doris's destiny was enhanced when, several months later, driving to New York with a friend she had been visiting, Mother's car broke down in Dunn, North Carolina. The damage, fortunately, was minor and the garage assured them they could be on the road again in an hour to their next engagement, a party my Uncle Ned was throwing at Central Park's glamorous Casino Club to celebrate his 30th birthday,

That left some time for Doris and her friend to amuse themselves. Right opposite the garage, a placard advertising a fortune teller—tarot cards and palmistry—caught their eye. What fun, they thought. But it took on an oracular aspect when the gypsy woman, probing Mother's palm, prophesied she was going to marry the man on whose right she would be sitting that evening. (Mother's friend learned she was going to have a road accident later in the day: a flat tire, as it turned out, after they had crossed the bridge into Manhattan.)

Wedding photo, parents, 1935

Getting to New York on time, on the roads of the day, and locating a corsage to go with her evening dress kept Mother reasonably concentrated. But when, at Ned's party, she found herself seated on his brother's left, her wick ignited. Who was she to fight the inevitable? A mere six weeks later, they were engaged. Half a year later, on June 15, 1935, when most of the country was still mired in the Depression, Charlie Merrill tossed them a society wedding reception on the front lawn of his Southampton house, with a seated dinner for a thousand guests.

For all the rapidity of the events, or perhaps because of it, there is much that eludes me. Wasn't there still, at the time of Ned's party, the medical student to whom she was betrothed? If so, how was he disposed of? More incomprehensible, what appealed to her in the crass campaign of furs and jewels with which he promoted himself? Could she have indeed relished going to the highest bidder—was that the eroticism in which she had been nurtured? And what did Father promise her other than a Nassau honeymoon and a large, shallow, but very showy Cartier diamond ring? What, in other words, made her renounce her one genuine freedom—that of choice? Could the electricity, as it crackled between these two intensely wired dynamos, have been that sufficient?

As it was, her friends were far from pleased. "How can you be marrying a man with whom you have NOTHING IN COMMON!" one of them remembers shrieking into the phone. Others remarked on the "rough edges" that no amount of dance lessons could polish away. While recognizing that Mother herself held no such qualms (who else, after all, would eventually bestow on her Dutch lover, the former Shell CEO, a new swimming pool?), they deplored the invidious vulgarity of his gifts. Of her two suitors this mature man was clearly the more exciting; all the better in that, unlike Johnny Slocum, he did not want to live holed up in the country and actually looked forward to sharing the glitter of her social life. With Father, she knew, she would never be bored.

Her marriage, she always maintained, was her choice. But I see the decisive vote coming from her adored father. He did not need a doctor son-in-law to help him run his corporate empire. To Father, the prospect of becoming Charlie Merrill's right-hand man and dynastic heir must have been a Horatio Alger story come unbelievably true. One can see the two highly explosive men, with their not dissimilar backgrounds, conspiring, while the heiress was sold, or rather transferred, from one ledger to another.

NOB HILL

Back from their Nassau honeymoon, the newlyweds settled in what Mother described as the most beautiful apartment in the whole of New York, on luxurious Sutton Place with a stunning view over the East River. But as the final curtains and carpets were being fitted, Mother learned to her distinct shock that Father had accepted a position with Safeway in San Francisco. In the thirties, Safeway was Charlie's major business interest. Father assumed he would be learning the grocery business from the ground up in the same way he had mastered merchandising at Macy's. In a couple of years he would be running the entire show.

How was Mother to be compensated for all she had put into fixing up their Sutton Place apartment? A second honeymoon, a three-month tour of the great European capitals, proved the successful lure; all the more reassuring when Father, in the grand hotels where they lodged, kept being taken for that other sharp-featured fox, the Duke of Windsor. Their tour ended in Berlin where they suffered the embarrassment of watching Nazi thugs haul a Jewish friend right out of their taxi. Was he not wearing the Yellow Star?

In San Francisco they had intended to acquire an apartment within their means. But Charlie ruled otherwise and, with his help, they took up residence in the annex of the Mark Hopkins Hotel on the top of Nob Hill. Meanwhile Father drove to work across the Bay in seedy downtown Oakland. On Thanksgiving Day he arrived home too knackered from catching cardboard boxes thrown from a delivery truck to sit down for dinner. When the census man asked the box catcher for his address, his disbelief was so palpable that Father invited the fellow home for a drink and a gander at the panoramic view.

It was there I was born, three weeks early on September 4, 1936, a Virgo under Scorpio rising, with a moon in my grandfather's Libra. "We almost didn't make your birth," Charlie's second wife, Hellen, would remind me whenever we met; understandable, since it was a mere hunch of her husband's, signaled in a dream, that had brought them by rail in the nick of time. Charlie trusted his psychic hunches, as he had once in hastening outdoors when there was an uncanny stillness to find his 5-year-old daughter in flames, too terror stricken to scream—she had set her long hair on fire playing with Fourth of July sparklers. He staunched most of the fire by rolling her up in a carpet. But the part he had forgotten about went on burning and left a long scar that confined Mother forever after to a single-piece bathing suit. As for matches, she could never again bring herself to light one, much less turn on a stove.

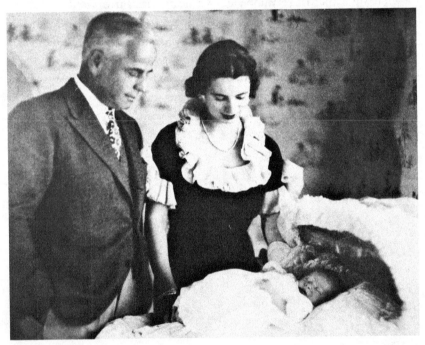

Charles Merrill, Mother, baby Robin, 1936

Now on the occasion of his favorite child's first baby—and his first grandchild—Charlie wanted to be present, a supernova emblazoning the event.

My parents welcomed the Merrills on the evening of their arrival with a big dinner party. Midway through the dinner the water sack containing me burst, completely drenching Mother's new evening dress. Another woman might have excused herself and left the table. Mother called on all her reserves to keep sitting through one course after the next, not wanting to disturb the splendid occasion. No one but Hellen noticed Mother eventually slipping away, in a panic lest I pop out on the floor of her taxi. A first birth, though, usually takes some time, and it wasn't until ten o'clock next morning that I emerged into their entrepreneurial labyrinth. "Look at that baby," Hellen cried, "all bald except for that one tuft of gray hair!" And the tiny old man opened his eyes and everyone agreed that this Robert A., Jr., as I was then and there named—but Robin for short as Father was a Bob—was the unmistakable heir to the old lock, stock, and barrel. To assist me in making my life transit a successful one between the sphinx of Leo and the narrow pyramid entrance leading into the Symphonic City of Libra, Charlie Merrill went down to his bank that very noon and set me up with a trust fund.

The birth of a male child enormously affected my father. Charlie recalled seeing him so overcome by the news that he had to excuse himself and step out of their waiting room onto the hospital balcony. For the first and only time in their marriage he took to driving home for lunch, all the way across the bridge, impatient to see how I had changed since breakfast. And he resisted leaving me with the servants and going away with Mother to the Peninsula for fear of missing out on some milestone event such as a first smile.

CHARLIE MERRILL: SOME SORT OF A CROESUS?

My mother's father, Charles E. Merrill, was the seminal Wall Street figure of his time. The founder of Merrill Lynch and the co-founder of the Safeway supermarket chain, he is generally credited with bringing the Wall Street casino into middle class lives. In one of its reappraisals, *Time* magazine called him one of the two greatest business leaders of the past century—the other was Bill Gates. Various tycoons have founded whole industries. But no one else managed to bring into being two huge sectors of the modern economy: the chain store industry and the myriad-headed investment business.

Charlie was also a genuine visionary. He may not have foreseen the length of the Great Depression, but he did foresee the October 1929 stock market crash and he did everything in his power to mitigate its effects. Rarer still for a businessman of his day, he possessed a social vision, a sense of what had to be changed if capitalism was to survive. Bringing Wall Street to Main Street was his formula for enlarging the base of the capitalist pyramid by giving the small investor a stake in the commercial churn; co-opting him as it were.

To me, my grandfather's legacy lay less in these achievements than in his adventurer's life as I came to know it through the stories he told about growing up in the rural Florida of the post-Civil War. And the women he pursued—and held onto!—with every jot of the same tenacity that went into his business ventures. That brio of his challenged me, as it did my father. But where Father saw the challenge as one of personal enrichment—can I make as big a pile?—I saw a legacy taking me down unexplored paths into new terrain.

In 1943, when I was seven, Charlie suffered the first of a series of near fatal heart attacks. The second of them kept him in St. Luke's hospital for four months. For the remaining thirteen years not a day passed without severe angina pain. Yet even in that unremitting agony a signal vitality pulsed. To a child, most elderly people that ill are distinctly scary. Yet the affection he entertained for me and the relish with which in his soft-spoken drawl he clued me in to his part in my genetic inheritance were such that I made a point of visiting him most summer days in Southampton and every spring vacation in Palm Beach where I, sometimes alone, was his guest.

A number of self-made men have possessed great wealth, but not everyone knows how to make it sparkle, ecstatically, convulsively. Charlie made sure he personified it in his Van Sickle tailored double-breasted suits, his wide Art Deco ties and two-toned handmade shoes. For him life, not business, was the paramount adventure and he was its *Roi Soleil*, Charles E. Money as I thought of him, as proud of his philanthropic activities as of his beautiful palaces and business creations; so proud that he died with a Carnegie-like front page splash, leaving nearly the whole $32 million caboodle to charity—an amount that in the 20 years of the Merrill Trust would turn into $120 million disbursed. He must have figured on us grandchildren being well enough provided for. If we needed more, we could go out like any other self-reliant American and earn it; we could build that better mousetrap.

Hervé Télémaque

My father liked to maintain that he and Charlie rose out of the same pluck-and-luck, work-and-win success myth. Charlie may have been poor as a child, but he didn't hail from the same anonymous penury as my father. The name "Merrill" derives from the figure of a blackbird—*merle* in French. After the 1572 St. Bartholomew's Day massacre, these Huguenot blackbirds fled to Switzerland and thence to rural East Anglia. Two farming brothers, John and Nathaniel, joined the Massachusetts Bay colony in Newbury in 1633. From there his people moved through western Connecticut, western New York, and finally Ohio.

Charlie's maternal grandparents, the Wilsons, oversaw a 4500-acre cotton plantation in the Mississippi delta: a spread Charlie would buy in 1930, unable to resist the lure of a family home with a commissary post office in no less a burg than Money, Mississippi. My great-great grandfather valued education enough to insist on inflicting Latin on his 17-year-old second wife, "one of the best read women I ever knew," Charlie said, "and unquestionably the most brilliant historian I ever met." Something of their love of learning passed on to Charlie's mother, Octavia, the only one of their nine children to attend college. It was there at Maryville in eastern Tennessee that the 15-year-old met and became engaged to the future Doctor Merrill. The doctor was the son of an Ohioan, Riley Merrill, a cashiered captain in Sherman's army—he had balked at burning down a young widow's house on the infamous march through Georgia. In the course of his soldiering he had fallen in love with the South and its people and had purchased a citrus farm in what is now the Jacksonville suburbs. After a by no means atypical seven-year courtship—conducted largely by mail—Octavia Wilson and Charles Morton Merrill were married in Green Cove Springs, a couple of hours southeast of Jacksonville, in 1883.

In our family we spoke of Green Cove, where Charlie was born on October 19, 1885 as if it were the absolute sticks. But Florida in those days stopped at Saint Augustine. There was no Palm Beach, no Miami. Saint Augustine was a glamorous watering hole. Socialites from as far away as Europe descended to spend the winter months there. They would land at Jacksonville, the third largest East Coast port at the time, and take the paddle-wheel steamer up the St. Johns River to Green Cove, from the deck popping away at the alligators sunning on the banks. Next day they might continue overland to Flagler's new creation, Saint Augustine.

Green Cove might have seemed the sticks to us, but Charlie never spoke badly about the resort, a pleasant town even in summer with the breeze circulating off the three-mile wide northward flowing river. Growing up there, water spoke to him. He believed in homes from which you could always see the horizon. The life there gave him a taste for bathing resorts such as Southampton and Palm Beach where he spent the better part of his adult years.

In a well-situated resort, famed for its three big hotels and curative waters, "the Saratoga Springs of the South," a Bellevue-trained surgeon could be forgiven for thinking a clientele might exist capable of sustaining him and his family; all the more if he doubled as its pharmacist and coroner.

The reality belied these expectations. For most of the time he struggled to make ends meet. A gentle, kind-hearted man, he found it difficult to collect a bill. And he was a patsy, willing at any hour to let himself be rowed across the St. Johns to deliver a baby for a $5 fee that might never get paid.

Throughout the 1890s, rural Florida remained in the grip of a prolonged post-Civil War depression. As my grandfather recalled, "Rough going was so much part of our existence that it was taken for granted, as though it was the normal condition of life everywhere. A silver dollar in those days was just about as big as the wheel on a truck; not literally, but relatively."

Of Charlie's early childhood there is the story his mother used to tell about how one evening, shortly after he had learned to speak, she had taken him out on their porch to show him the full moon. At the sight, this moon sign pointed his arm straight up and at the top of his lungs began to yell, "I want it! I want it!" When it wasn't then and there deposited in his lap, he launched into a furious tantrum.

Thereafter Octavia had this Libra believing that anything he wanted—even the moon—could be his if he wanted it badly enough. Again and again, seeing her despair over some unpayable bill, he promised her, "Don't worry, Mama, when I grow up I'll buy you rubies and diamonds." Arabian Nights stuff—from a man who always trusted his dreams.

Growing up on the river Charlie developed into a powerful swimmer. At twelve, he swam across the St. Johns, trailed by a pal in a rowboat to ward off alligators. But his main love, and one he would bequeath to my brothers Peter and Merrill, was baseball. In a climate where you could play year-round, Charlie developed into a crack shortstop. By modern standards he was, at 5'5" and 120 pounds, a trifle undersized. This, though, was the dead-ball era and, with his reduced strike zone, he made an efficient hit-them-where-they-ain't leadoff batter. Charlie believed he could have progressed to the major leagues but for a playground accident incurred when an enemy deliberately fractured his throwing arm at the joint with a jujitsu over-the-head hurl. His father, setting it, said he had never seen a worse fracture. Despite an arm shortened by half an inch, Charlie's baseball ability would play a major role in his upward rise.

A charming, gracious, and charismatic man, Charlie had a wide-mouthed smile that flashed from one ear to the other. A fellow "who could inspire a corpse," one college friend remarked. "Merry Merrill," his teammates called him, a moniker his natural reserve allowed him to treasure. Yet the merriness could be put on, along with the "happy" drum-major strut he showed me, as if it were something I could add to my repertoire. Shy, maybe, but theatrical to the core. And with an intensity that radiated into every scream on the phone, every slide into home plate. A person who played everything for keeps.

Behind the ready smile and the misty willfulness of his gray-blue eyes lay the more problematic aspect of a sultan not about to be thwarted. (In the whole of his adult life there was only one person who ever succeeded in standing up to him—his mother Octavia.) The effect on those who got in his way, or merely happened to blunder onto the road when his chariot came blazing by, could be devastating. To be sure, he'd do everything in his power—afterwards—to make a proper restitution: dusting off his victim and pressing a fat wad into the man's hands with such heartfelt regret that a surprising number actually became lifelong friends. For all his generosity—and Charlie never loaned, he gave—there would always remain those who could never be compensated, wives and children among them. Their views still haunt me.

His father's disinterest in the financial side of his practice offered some scope to a son with fewer scruples about making a buck. The 12-year-old, working as soda-jerk in their pharmacy, took it upon himself to spike the cocaine-containing coca cola with pure grain alcohol, to everyone's delight but his old man's. Now and then he even succeeded in pulling off a minor coup: buying up at a nickel apiece all hundred copies of the newspaper proclaiming in oversized headlines the destruction of the Spanish fleet in Santiago de Cuba Harbor and lugging them out to the fairgrounds where he sold every last one at a quarter each.

To a child of Charlie's bent, the big city lights beckoned, and his enthusiasm may have helped persuade the Doctor to move to Jacksonville in 1898, establishing a practice in the one area available, the Ward Street red light district. In this "no go" district the schoolboy secured a job hawking *The Florida Times Union*. For the Doctor's son the route might not have been dangerous and Charlie spoke of being "kindly received" (with tips? tea and cakes?) by his father's prostitute clients. Throughout his life Charlie felt more at ease in the company of women and, like Louis XIV, seldom concluded a major deal without consulting the reigning favorite. I see a devotion to female beauty in all its myriad guises—no love ever a replica of another—emerging from the demimonde he encountered at a susceptible age.

Could the Doctor have shared these same proclivities? If so, it might explain their continuing poverty, a man who was no match for his clients' advanced bargaining skills. It might also explain why the family left Jacksonville in 1903 for the rural boondocks of West Palm Beach.

Merrill's Landing, seen from Lake Worth, Palm Beach

The move to West Palm was anything but a success. It began badly when the Doctor caught one of Florida's last cases of yellow fever. Worse followed, when Charlie's baby sister caught diphtheria and died. Forty years later, in a letter to his son Charles defending his pursuit of wealth Charlie wrote, "Had the family been living in Jacksonville, my father would have saved her life, but there was no hospital then in West Palm Beach and he did not have available the proper tools of his trade. The fact that my father knew how to save his daughter's life and yet, because of limited finances, did not possess the equipment, crushed him. Money, of course, is not everything. But, my friend, emergency after emergency comes up in this world of ours in which for a few brief moments, money is the equivalent of everything."

Mary's death did not end the run of misfortune. Returning from a late night call the Doctor was held up right outside his front door by a pair of robbers who cracked his skull with a crowbar and left him for dead. After lying two weeks in a coma, he staged a remarkable comeback. But he was never the same man, and for the rest of his life he carried a silver plate in his head and suffered periodic dizzy spells. Not surprisingly, his better clients drifted away.

As a child, Charlie used to accompany his father on his rounds, a way of getting to know him in his professional aspect. But the current flowing between them never matched the warmth his mother generated. Symptomatic is the story of Charlie being summoned to West Palm in 1929 as the Doctor's health began to fail. Charlie was 44 at the time. When he entered the room where his father lay in a virtual coma, the blinds were drawn and the room seemed indeed very dark. Charlie sat there quite a while waiting for a sign of life. Finally he plucked up his courage and asked, "Do you know who I am?"

"Some sort of Croesus?" Chilling words, all the more in that they were the last the Doctor ever uttered.

Charlie did not tag along to West Palm. Instead he supported himself in Jacksonville with four different part-time jobs while attending public school. What time this left for studies worried his parents enough to send him to Stetson, a military school that advertised itself as "the Harvard of the South." He wasn't there long before he found himself sent to the headmaster for concussing a passing master with a water bomb dropped from his dorm's fourth floor window. In words that seem mild under the circumstances, the headmaster told him, "Charlie, I think your skills would be better appreciated up north."

Those skills, at this point, were mainly athletic, and Charlie copped a senior year scholarship to Worcester Academy. He was the quarterback, hurled in short yardage situations over the line, ball in hand, for a first down. He hated it, the gauntlet of town whores the football team had to run after practice, the black roommate maliciously assigned to him, the ridiculous outfits that, working as a tailor's representative, he had to model. But he stuck it out, and Worcester gave him a way to enter nearby Amherst College.

Charlie arrived in Amherst in 1903 with all the dice, as he saw it, loaded against him. He stood a pint-sized 5'5". He spoke with a Southern drawl. He had no money, and to top it off, his mother accompanied him. Much as he tried to stretch his scholarship by "waiting on tables, raking lawns, and doing every odd job that presented itself," he had a hard time remaining solvent. Even the considerable sum of $1300, earned in his sophomore year, was not enough to keep him plodding toward his B.A., a lost distinction and one he always regretted.

With funding raised from his Mississippi relatives, he transferred to the University of Michigan, where he intended to study, of all incompatible subjects, the law. By mid-winter Charlie was back in West Palm running a one-man newspaper, *The Tropical Sun*. It all unraveled when, playing baseball, he got into a nasty home plate collision with a certain Hackett. That escalated into a name-calling match with the catcher's father, a saloon and bawdyhouse keeper. When one of Hackett's boys told Charlie his days were numbered, he took his situation to his father. Charlie knew how easily he could be shot working in a one-room newspaper office opening onto the street. The Doctor saw no way out but to call on Hackett. "There's only one thing I'm here to say," he told the startled gangster, "if anything happens to Charlie, it's you I'm going to kill." With that he turned on his heel.

A serious confrontation was averted when his Mississippi relatives came through with a job in Shaw running the local paper's business operation, while playing a shallow centerfield for the local semi-pro team on weekends. The locals took their baseball pretty seriously. The betting was so heavy that, after one 9–2 victory over a Pelham squad reinforced with several minor league pros, they found much of the town lined up, bricks in hand, by the one bridge out. His Shaw team went undefeated in 27 games, and his teammates pooled together at the end of the season to present him with a railroad ticket to New York. "I must say," he told me, "I felt like a damn fool heading off to such a big city where there was only one person I knew, but with their ticket in hand did I have any choice?"

Brothers Robin, Stephen, Mark, Peter, Merrill, Southampton, 1957

The fall of 1908 thus found Charlie, like an Alger hero, plunged into the New York maelstrom. His first job came through the good offices of Marie Sjostrom, a Smith College student to whom he had become engaged while still at Amherst. Marie landed him a $15 a week job as an office boy for her father, the chief financial officer for a textile conglomerate.

During the two years their engagement lasted, Charlie picked up the near equivalent of a business school education. After it ended, another four months of pavement pounding elapsed before he was able to nail down an on-again, off-again job in George H. Burr's new bond department. How he survived during this time is not clear, but there are Amherst classmates who recall coming upon him sacked out on a Central Park bench.

Charlie had the job secured when Octavia insisted, in one of her flashes of intuition, on his taking her last hundred dollars and plunking it down on a made-to-order suit from George Burr's personal tailor. "You can't sell stocks and bonds," she told him, "if you are self-conscious, and no one can feel at ease in cheap ill-fitting clothes." When Charlie showed up to work in his new Van Sickle suit, he learned—shades of Alger!—that his prospective department boss, a Chicago banker, had caught a cold, developed pneumonia and died before he could take up his new position. Since he looked the part, the 24-year-old found himself heading the bond department with a $25,000 budget. As a result, the members of our family have all had the importance of being well dressed drilled into us. My brother Stephen even titled one of his plays, "See You When You're Better Dressed"!

Charlie's first act was to hire as a salesman his roommate from the YMCA, Eddy Lynch. Built like a bulldog, Eddy had tenacity to match. Sent once to collect an overdue $122.80 bill, the client told him he didn't have that much in the bank. Lynch insisted all the same on a check drawn for the full amount. When he learned at the bank that the account was $8 short, he counted $8 from his wallet and deposited them in the client's account. Then, at a second teller's window, he cashed the check.

The relationship between the two partners, Charlie, outgoing and optimistic, and Eddy dour and pessimistic, was never easy. There were times when my grandfather complained there should be some recognition—inscribed preferably on his tombstone—of the albatross he had to lug around for all those years. Yet despite the screaming fits my mother remembered, the two were close. When Eddy died in 1938, Charlie insisted on saddling my newborn brother Merrill with the middle name of Lynch.

On a Saturday night in those YMCA days Charlie and Eddy used to cruise the late-night clubs together. Too poor to date, they would return from work to their rooms, set their alarms, go to sleep, and then rise at ten to shave and dress. At that hour, the well-wined and dined ladies were more than ready to appreciate the attentions of two handsome young men who liked to dance. Every now and then Charlie managed to make off with a dame while her usually older beau was in the gents.

To what extent my grandfather's lifelong running after the ladies reflected a compulsive need is hard to say. In little men of his stamp, with their Zeus-sized egos, the urge to dominate can take any number of forms. And when Charlie wanted someone he pulled out all the stops. Knowing my grandmother, Eliza Church, even in her 80's an oval-faced silent film beauty, it is easy to understand his breezing into the office, a day after meeting her, and remarking, "What a beautiful girl that Eliza is! I think I'll marry her." A gracious, gentle, convent-educated lady, the daughter of Samuel Harden Church, a railroad and steel executive, a distinguished statesman and President of the Carnegie Institute as well as the author of a two-volume History of Oliver Cromwell and a number of well-received plays, she repeatedly turned down the future tycoon. After a final "No," she boarded a train for far-off Florida. But Charlie was not to be denied. At every stop there was a bouquet-laden Western Union messenger waiting to greet her. The storm of flowers went on until finally at Aiken, South Carolina, the poor woman capitulated and agreed to take him out of his torment.

Wedding photo, Marcia, Robin, 1958

This ill-matched marriage to a woman he had known a scant few weeks—she, mistreated by a cruel step-mother, needed security; he, adventure—was, like his two subsequent marriages, to last a somewhat improbable thirteen years, with the two children (my mother Doris and her brother Charles) born at precise six-year intervals. Curiously, their half-brother James was born six years after Charles. Was there an extra-terrestrial intelligence imprinting his mayhem with a more rational design? Knowing his son's Ouija-board epic, *The Changing Light at Sandover*, one is tempted to speculate.

To be sure, Charlie had his own sentimental code. "Tell a woman anything," he once advised me," but never tell her you love her unless you mean it." Not that such sentiments deterred him from marrying his third and sexiest wife, Kinta, a New Orleans belle, even though he was no longer in love with her. She through an emissary, had threatened suicide; he, for some reason, believed her.

The marriage to Eliza and the birth soon thereafter of my mother, Doris, substantially changed Charlie's financial horizons. He had reason to believe, after growing George Burr's $25,000 into a $750,000 portfolio, he could succeed on his own. He had no hope, he knew, of crashing the exclusive club and complete law unto itself that was the J.P. Morgan-run Wall Street of the time. Instead he had to find a clientele outside the elite Morgan served. And as a distributor of securities, he had to find a new order of risk to underwrite.

Charlie found the combination he needed in the emerging chain store industry. Whether he invented, as he once claimed to a friend of mine, this sector of the economy, is open to dispute. Nonetheless his wholehearted backing had much to do with the chains obtaining the needed capital to finance expansion. And by taking his fee in the form of stock warrants, he made most of his initial fortune. "If a stock's good enough to sell," he remarked, "it's good enough to buy."

All the same, Charlie almost went under in his first major deal, an underwriting of McCrory, a chain of five-and-dime stores. For a variety of reasons, the issue didn't sell and Charlie was saved, if that's the word—it seemed certain ruination at the time—only by the outbreak of World War I, which shut down the stock exchange for four months. That he spent the next nine months drawing up an iron-clad prospectus shows how much he still had to learn about the investment frontier he was opening up.

This time the McCrory offering was a success, as was the next, of Kresge, six months later. With an additional $30,000 from Eliza's trust fund which he now felt free to accept, he prospered with such dispatch that our family scrapbook contains a 1917 clipping of the newly enlisted "Boy Millionaire" in his tailored uniform. The picture doesn't show the fitted silk underwear worn beneath, a little Napoleon's way of demonstrating—to himself, at least—that he was both richer and more hedonistic than the competition.

The army didn't give him the chance to pursue the ultimate Napoleonic fantasy. Instead he found himself doing time in cooks-and-bakers school, learning the hard way the useful maxim, "Never do a job well you hate."

Looking for more action and hoping to be sent to France, he transferred into the Air Force. "Pop," as the 32-year-old was known, graduated top of his class from flying school. Once again he may have done too well, for he was appointed instructor and served out the rest of the war at a series of Florida bases. While flying there may not have been the certain death it was in the French skies, it was the rare biplane that stayed more than half an hour aloft. Charlie never knew in what ditch or hedge he might have to crash.

For the more adventurous there was stunt flying. Ordered to put his plane into a tailspin at 4,000 feet, Charlie demurred, because the ground looked all too close. At 8,000 he pulled out once again. Finally at 10,000 he let it rip. The plane immediately locked in a nosedive and it was only at 1,000 feet that he managed to gain control and pull out. By the time he emerged from the war his temples had turned a premature white.

To a compulsive workaholic, flying brought a serenity he had never known. He even volunteered unsuccessfully for the now notorious Allied expeditionary force to Siberia. On his first post-war vacation he traveled to California and hired a plane he flew every day. A crack shot who had hunted all his young life, he was never to fire at a bird again. And it was in his air pilot's uniform that he asked to be buried.

After all that soldiering, shuffling money back on Wall Street might have seemed staid. But those were the Roaring Twenties and Charlie and Eddy had progressed from underwriting new ventures to running them as well. Among them was Charlie Chaplin's Pathe films. Unable to compete with the major studios who could book their own theaters, Charlie sold Pathe to Joseph Kennedy, the President's father and the one man he genuinely loathed. Both Chaplin and the window-ledge comedian Harold were to remain close friends, charter members of that five foot six "everyone else is a son-of-a-bitch," club of his. Mother recalls Chaplin coming to our 72nd street apartment when she was ill with a high fever and playing the piano, not with the usual thumbs and fingers, but with an orange in each hand.

My grandfather plowed Kennedy's money into a trio of ventures: Merrill

Petroleum still in the early Fifties pumping away on tax depletion dollars on the Canadian prairie; *Family Circle,* the first supermarket checkout stand freebie; and the outfit we Magowans came to be associated with, Safeway, the West-coast based supermarket chain my father and brother Peter would both direct.

Already by 1927, the stock market was looking distinctly suspect to Charlie. It wasn't merely that his customers were overbidding with dubiously leveraged assets for which he was personally liable. It was more that the fundamental structure of the economy had come to seem little more than a house of cards. Since no one else felt this way, or wanted to do anything but make more money, Charlie began to wonder if he was losing his mind and consulted a psychiatrist. Perhaps the new Viennese science could shed some light? This, the first such consultation in analytic annals, ended with the analyst selling out his entire portfolio. "If you're crazy, Charlie, I am too," he said comfortingly. Encouraged, my grandfather took out a full-page public service advertisement in *The New York Times* warning of the coming debacle. He even journeyed to Washington to offer his fellow Amherst collegian, the retiring President Calvin Coolidge, a $100,000 salary to forgo the silence of a lifetime and speak out against the rampant speculation.

All this Cassandra-like prophesying accomplished was to make Charlie so unpopular that "no one wanted to be near me." Still with $47 million in personal obligations, he was not afraid to crank up the rhetoric:

> I do not like the situation; I do not like the outlook and I do not like the amount of money we owe. Most of all I do not like the apathetic and indifferent attitude that seems prevalent in the New York office at the time. What has gotten into you ... that you can close your eyes and be absolutely nonchalant to a situation which is packed full of dynamite? If prices in general were not so high, if our holdings didn't show us such gigantic profits, and if the financial clouds were not gathering, I would still want to liquidate and get our affairs in A-1 shape ... Why there should be any resistance to turning a very substantial amount of this profit into cash is an absolute, unending, insoluble mystery to me. What difference does it make to you and to me whether we pay 12.5% tax or 25% tax so long as we can turn our holdings into cash and have rest and comfort at night.

This time it worked and Charlie did manage the considerable feat of liquidating his firm's security holdings and transferring its business to the bond house of Pierce and Cassatt (owned by members of the family of the painter Mary Cassatt) by the time the stock market crash occurred.

The crash left Charlie atop one of the pinnacles of New York life, the tower suite of the Carlyle Hotel where he and his vivacious second wife Hellen, a 25-year-old magazine publisher whom he married in 1925, a few weeks after divorcing Eliza, were to spend most of the next decade.

When my son James asked Hellen at the age of 101 what struck her about Charlie when she first met him, Hellen replied, "Why, his good looks! He had plenty of those." Summing it up an hour later, she added, "The best years of my life were with Charlie. I loved him, loved him very, very much." A few years earlier, Hellen had confided to my friend Bob Lenzner her delight in the distinct privilege of standing naked out in the rain on their balcony overlooking Central Park. ("What sexual confidence!" Bob remarked.)

Wedding photo, Eliza Church Merrill, 1913

As a wife, Hellen was everything Eliza was not: sure of herself, socially adroit, witty and energetic. And she made, as both Mother and her brother Charles repeatedly attested, a personable caring stepmother. It's no exaggeration that my mother's closeness to her father was one Hellen brought into being. That did not keep Hellen from putting Charlie down in front of their company: at the bridge table where she was the more experienced partner; at the dinner table where she would interrupt him in the midst of a story, "You're telling it wrong." And she had her own notions of social position. "I can't invite your mother, Doris, to your wedding reception. What would Southampton think of me? (In one of his Henry VIII moods a chagrined Charlie told Mother, "I should have divorced Hellen then and there.")

For all their competitiveness, they shared a lot, not least a Jacksonville background where Hellen had run a successful weekly, *The Social Silhouette*. And for someone as gregarious as Charlie, her social savvy must have come in handy. Charlie may have bought on his own his mini-Versailles, "The Orchard," a Stanford White-designed antebellum house completed just before the architect's murder in 1907. But it was Hellen who stocked its 22 bedrooms with the likes of Helen Hayes, Hoagy Carmichael, Gloria Swanson, and George Gershwin. Hellen wrote of sitting rapt in the vast two-storied Music room with its four immense twisting brass columns, stained glass windows, red damask curtains and sofa, marble Milanese fireplace and wall-length licentious Flemish tapestry, while Gershwin and Gertrude Lawrence were knocking out the future Broadway hit, *Oh, Kay*!

It did not help their marriage that Charlie was on the road often for months at a time, fleeing the graveyard that was 1930's Wall Street. Much of the travel was out West where he was negotiating the merger of some seven grocery store chains into a reconstituted Safeway. His Seattle partner, Gus Ledbetter, told me he was a fly on the wall of the Portland conference room where Charlie was putting it together. "There were 33,000 stores and Charlie did it all, the evaluations, the exchanges of equity, in twelve hours. As a feat, I've never seen anything like it."

Time on the road added its lures to all the others Charlie was forever accommodating. How was Hellen supposed to react when he left on the top of his dresser an amorous note from his New Orleans tart, Kinta? Or when, responding to the repeated tugging of Charlie's favorite setter, Mike, Hellen followed the dog up the stairs and into her best friend Dottie Stafford's bedroom to catch her husband sprawled in flagrant delight, sheepishly looking up from the sheets.

Meanwhile from all over the country, a never-ending stream of business solicitations poured in. Charlie was saved from heading the new Safeway—a field, he felt, outside his competence—only by a telegram announcing his remaining sister's death. Two years later, in 1935, he came within a hair's breadth of buying the Brooklyn Dodgers from the Ebbets family for half a million. Had he closed the deal the Bums might still be in Brooklyn and not Los Angeles and my brother Peter might not have felt compelled to step in and save his boyhood idols, the Giants, for San Francisco, and revitalize China Basin with a privately funded baseball park.

Charlie's mother, Octavia, 1938

As it was, Charlie was left with that ultimate expression of his vision, "The Thundering Herd," as Merrill Lynch, Pierce, Fenner & Beane came to be known. For much of his life the daily adventure had kept him sufficiently enthralled. Now at 53, he wanted more. He wanted a place in the annals of his time. Self-recreation seemed the point of the four volume biographies I saw him devouring; manuals on how you carved out a niche and became Robert E. Lee. In the face of his bête noir, FDR, and the New Deal's perception of Wall Street as Public Enemy Number One, he wanted to mount a counter-argument. If the depressed economy was to be churned in Keynesian fashion into prosperity, surely professionals with their own livelihoods at stake could do it more efficiently than the government's brain-trust.

THE SERAGLIO

Merrill Lynch succeeded, but for Charlie, its success did not come quite soon enough. Like most new businesses, the firm lost money—$309,000 in the first nine months. At the end of 1941, as America prepared to enter the war, it was still in the red. As his partners' life savings were at risk, Charlie drove himself harder than he should have. The result was a series of near lethal heart attacks.

If ever there was an overtaxed organ, it was Charlie's heart. The booze, the chain-smoking, the artery-clogging Southern diet, the non-stop partying, all exacted a toll. But it was the attractions of Kinta des Mare (originally de Mario) that blasted him into the red zone.

Mother, Father at his 75th bash

By the standards of Kinta's three subsequent marriages Charlie might be deemed fortunate. None of his marital successors managed to stay alive as long as two months. "That Kinta has the worst luck," I recall Mother, in a mood of surprising forgiveness, remarking. But Kinta worked at her luck, plopping her breasts daily in a basin of ice-cold water "to preserve their freshness." While Mother and her chums were barbecuing themselves a death-defying mahogany at the beach with tinfoil reflectors, Kinta kept her gardenia-white skin successfully smoldering under elbow-length gloves and oversized sombreros. The effect when she swished into a drawing room—the sudden hush, the turning of heads—could not have been more noticeable.

The staggering enormity of her sexual impact was lost on this child. I only saw a ridiculous, haughty, peacock-voiced Southerner whom, for some truly inexplicable reason, my grandfather had married. My enlightenment would come several decades later at a dinner dance we held to commemorate my father's 75th birthday. There, in a flowered silk *decollété* was the Countess di Carpegna. Kinta still had it, a magnetism, an intimacy of approach, I never dreamed a woman in her late seventies could still possess. For the first time I fathomed why Proust's Swann married Odette. There are more imperious necessities than those of love.

For most of the Forties Charlie had been too ill to contemplate divorcing Kinta, who had proven to be very temperamental. As her stepson, Charles, put it, "Why be difficult when you can be impossible?" But now in 1952, at the end of another unlucky thirteen-year cycle, he did not want to die in the arms of a woman he had come to loathe. Kinta's final mistake was to complain about Leroy Johnson, the Negro valet Charlie had inherited from his partner Eddy Lynch. Except for the difference in skin color the two might have seemed twins. Leroy shared not only his boss's best suits, but his appetite for women. Often Charlie had to come up with the wherewithal to get Leroy's current flame out of town before his wife descended. When they traveled first class together on the Saturnia to Italy in 1950, Charlie presented him as a diplomat, Mr. Ali of Pakistan, traveling incognito, so he could enjoy the pleasure of Leroy's dinner table conversation. So when Kinta delivered her ultimatum, "Either you fire that rascal or I'll divorce you," Charlie retorted, "Leroy may be a rascal, but I can't get along without him and I can get along without you."

Now at 65, not a great age by today's standards, came an all too miraculous final blooming. Not anticipating our era of pacemakers, bypass operations, and open-heart surgery, and feeling he had nothing to lose, he consulted a cardiologist, Sam Levine at the Harvard Medical School. For most of the previous ten years he had suffered from angina pains brought on by the series of heart attacks he had undergone; as many as a hundred episodes a day—the child of a doctor, Charlie counted them. He had heard that radioactive iodine could ease angina pain; could he offer himself to medical science as a guinea pig? Ever the optimist, he was convinced some human good could come out of the technology that had led to Hiroshima and Nagasaki.

The transforming effect of Doctor Levine's radioactive cocktail reads like an episode from "The Amazing Hulk." Visiting him in his lead-protected room at Peter Bent Brigham Hospital—even the wall pipes were sheathed in lead—I remember his pointing in awe to the two-inch increase in his shirt collar size. But along with the wider neck and damaged liver from which he would die five years later, came a startling renewal of sexual potency.

One need not have seen *Volpone* to conjure the galaxy of ladies that now orbited around him: the candidates for anything, everything; a place to the right or left of his chair; a bath in his river of gold. If an attractive woman was available, he pursued her. And he was more than willing to contemplate a "green bride."

Mother, 1932

My mother, seeing only harpies out for his money, did her utmost to restrain him, provoking the incident that would feature in the opening of her brother's novel, *The Seraglio*: the slashing of the Brockhurst portrait of herself in a formal Chinese jacket that she had given her father for a recent birthday. The police had detected signs of entry in the winter-boarded Beach House where the portrait was. But it was Mother who, in discovering the furiously slashed portrait, on top of a row stacked in a closet, felt the murderous power of the gesture. She burst into tears on the spot, as if she were the one stabbed.

Three divorces, a large number at the time, could leave a certain residue of scarred family tissue. To our parents, Charlie may have loomed as a financial potentate, an all-knowing prophet and philanthropic saint; but we were never allowed to see an oriental pasha. And any attributions of libidinous motivations were likewise taboo. We five sons, collisions of sperm and ovum, had not been produced by any sort of sex, but, putative adults, had apparently sprung like Athena from the dynastic godhead.

Symptomatic was my father's effort to delete any mention of Charlie's womanizing from the commissioned biography "so as not to cast him in an unfavorable light to his darling grandchildren." That's how Charlie, highly amused, reported it to his ex-wife Hellen. It was as if Father knew that the dynastic labyrinth he wished to design, one generation flowing seamlessly into the next, contained an inherent sexual flaw.

Charlie refused to be thus bowdlerized. "You can imagine to what extent I would ask any author to "soft pedal" some of my weaknesses and foibles which have become dearer to me as the capacity to repeat them becomes less and less."

Were Charlie's erotic adventures "foibles?" Were Zeus's? Wasn't there, both for him and any bedmate, considerably more at stake? Anyone witnessing, even in his final days, the transformation a girlfriend of mine entering his bedroom brought about had to acknowledge the depth of his susceptibility. The lengths he would go to stage an amatory coup were impressive. Turn your apartment over to him for an assignation, as his son, Jimmy once did, and you could find yourself endowed with a lifetime supply of percale sheets.

That eagerness remained to the very end. I spent the last afternoon before returning to college for my junior year waiting with him for his dear love of those final years, Lady Constance Saint, who had flown up from Barbados to discuss the financing of a beach cottage. A few days later he would pass into the coma from which he would die. That afternoon I couldn't possibly have guessed that the sword, poised over him so long, was about to descend, so buoyed was he by the prospect of her arrival.

To pass the time I told him some of what I had gleaned from his son's *Seraglio,* due out later in the year, a portrait even its sitter might relish: "How many septuagenarians get to play Zeus?" I asked. From there the emphasis must have shifted to *Huckleberry Finn,* his favorite book as a boy. In full stride now he told how, as a 12-year-old, in imitation of Huck, he had lit out for the fabled North. "I got as far as Waycross, Georgia, 75 miles away, before they found me. When my Dad finally arrived all he said was, "I'm glad, Son, you didn't get any further."

"Did he punish you when you got back?" I asked.

"Having me back was enough after I promised never to run away again. "But," he went on, nodding reflectively, "He did whip me once after catching me like a damn fool smoking in a hayloft. Worse than the pain was not being able to go swimming. I loved my Dad so much I couldn't bear to have anyone see the welts on my back."

The reminiscences were cut short when his chauffeur returned from the Westhampton railroad station without Lady Saint.

"How long did you stay?" my grandfather asked, wanting to salvage a degree of hope.

"Long enough to know she wasn't there. Maybe she missed the train?"

By now it was six o'clock, and I was due home for a farewell supper with my parents. Like any amorous man, Charlie couldn't bear to see me go before I had met this Prudence Good, as Jimmy was to call her, in pursuit of whom he had bought "Canefield," a winter residence perched on the top of the highest hill on Barbados, with wrap-around porches and commensurate views. I don't recall the remainder of our conversation, only the deepening gloom in which we sat. A half hour later the Lady herself swept in, out of sorts from a ride in a hired taxi and grimly determined on a restorative bath. Grandfather presented me as a grandson who could stay no more than a few minutes. But no invitation of a cocktail was going to deter her from her soak.

As I was saying good-bye, Charlie put his arms around me and told me he loved me as if I were his own son. Little suspecting this would be the last I ever saw of him, I hastened home. In the next month I received two letters from Lady Saint: of condolence, but also of remorse that she had passed up the opportunity of meeting me; a woman, clearly, not afraid to reach out and who knew that she had missed the moment.

When my grandfather died, Jimmy was already halfway around the world, in flight from his novel's devastating portrayal of Charlie and his social circle. I wrote to him that the funeral for which he was tempted to fly back was just another Southampton gathering, conducted behind the elegant black gates of the Church of the Ascension in Greenwich Village. Mistaken once again. There were people there who actually mourned, among them Charlie's valet, Leroy, whom my uncle Charles found sitting by himself in a shadowed stairwell, head on his knees, fully aware that a huge chapter of his life had come to an end.

SERGEANT BOB

Before the age of five, I have only dim memories: a room's feminine décor, white lace reflected on a wall. My mother's room? My nurse's room from which I totter forth to my ablutions, this water I feel running over me, this formal baby's dress I must put on for some reason. I want so much to be good, to please all these people who shower me with attentions. Yet I also feel repelled by them. Why do they insist on treating me like a doll?

Robin, 1939

Focusing I see the lady of those early memories, holding me at her knee's white-laced edge. In contrast to the males of my family, she represents another, softer, way of being. This may be why I've always resisted her. What doesn't declare itself, doesn't push, seems suspect to me. Precisely because there must exist, behind all the caring and tenderness, a motivation of which I'm part. But what part? A puppet looking with rapt gaze upon its creator? Yes, that summons not only Mother, but so many prospective Ariadnes. All the same I can't help but feel fortunate now. The life befallen me has been so much richer than the one to which as a child I felt sentenced, hemmed in as I was by my preoccupations, my lessons, my duties, my staring eyes and clumsy hands.

Hemmed. Penned. The various playpens in which I spent so many formative hours? The verbs may seem opaque, but not to a two year-old in his terrier-like harness traveling from San Francisco to New York. With me in one train compartment were Mother, my newborn brother Merrill and my minder, my father's mother Estelle; in a second compartment, all our luggage. It was the summer of 1938, and we were returning for good to New York.

Mother, baby Peter, Merrill, Father, Robin, 1942

My parents had led a charmed life during their three years in San Francisco. When during my boyhood they spoke about it, it was always with a pronounced nostalgia for the beauty of the city and the warmth of the reception that as a young couple they had known.

Still, a man as ambitious as Father had his timetable. How frustrating it must have been to find himself at an age when others were rapidly ascending their corporate ladders stuck as the personal assistant to pompous narrow-minded Ling Warren—a Jacksonville crony of Hellen's—who had no intention of stepping aside for the owner's son-in-law and would strut at the company helm for twenty more years. So now, after the birth of my younger brother, Father was returning to New York to work for Charlie Merrill and to do what he could to persuade him to start up a business in which a son-in-law could figure more prominently.

Father sat in on the discussions with the various merger candidates that would result in the new Merrill Lynch, a complete financial service organized on chain store lines and catering to the small investor. And his merchandising expertise was acknowledged in the post he was given as Head of Sales. Then, as the firm was approaching solvency, along came World War II. To some extent his wish to enlist represented a gamble; at 39 he was, for the moment, draft exempt. But, like Charlie, he was intensely patriotic, proud to buy his cars from Detroit and pay his full 90% share of the marginal income tax. The great point of America, as far as he was concerned, was the chance it gave a fellow to better himself. He was willing to pay and fight for the continuance of the opportunity.

I was six at the time, but I clearly remember Father, as he drove into town in our red leather-seated Buick convertible, telling me of his decision to join the Navy—the gentleman's service—as an Air Intelligence cadet. "It's not been an easy decision, but after weighing what I owe you and Merrill and Mommy, and what I owe our country, I've decided to enlist. I want you to know I'm not deserting you. There are a lot of people who can't afford to volunteer. We're fortunately well off, so I can. But I promise I'm not going to do anything foolish and get myself killed."

What did I feel—tears? That would come later, bidding him goodbye after a leave. Rather, pride. How I wished I was old enough to be out there too on a carrier in the South Pacific. The war was being fought far away across the seas, but it was always with us, in our rationing cards, our Southampton victory garden, the drills we school children carried out and the shades we had to keep drawn at night after a German U-boat was spotted off Amagansett. I learned to read following the advancing Allied campaign in *The New York*

Times, noting the pincer-like arrows of a tank attack, the star-like spread of the Solomon, Gilbert and Marshall Islands. Like every other American I know exactly where I was when Japan's surrender was announced: stuck among the deliriously honking cars of the white-tiled East River tunnel. That evening, standing in Times Square among the celebrating hordes and masses of plummeting confetti, I remember the feeling of a new chapter that possessed us all. America, once so isolated, had come center stage.

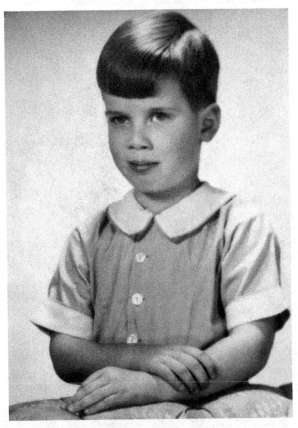

Robin, 1943

However two years on the USS Cowpens was war enough, and Charlie Merrill's second near-fatal heart attack in April 1944 had the welcome effect of bringing Father home before the dreaded assault on Japan would have taken place.

I was glad to have him home. I was at an age when I needed his presence: the distinct acrid taste of his cheeks; the scarred neck that bled under any but an electric razor; the antediluvian nightshirt in which he slept, always on his back, hands crossed atop his shoulders, feet even on the coldest night pointing out from the bottom of his bed. Incommunicative as he could be at times (mornings especially, clamped behind his *Times,* unable to utter so much as a greeting), he took the guidance of a firstborn son to heart, sacrificing time to be with me on a tennis court, or huddled among the masses at a ballpark. Such companionship brought out the generosity of a man who cared enough to see my boyhood and its aspirations as an extension of his own.

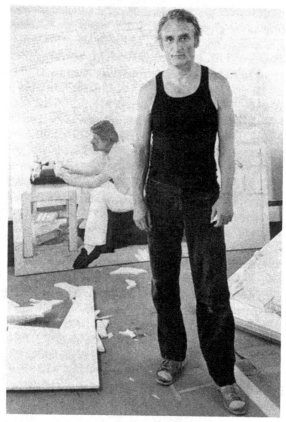

Larry Rivers, photo Allen Ginsberg, 1970s

For Father the social bench marks defined achievement and each meal at a "good" restaurant, each team I made, added its sum to his achievement. While any boredom he felt at the fatuousness of the business day was defined by a rapid-fire execution that left most bystanders gasping, if not terrified. Father typed all his letters just as he answered, often to the caller's distinct shock, his own phone. He rarely brought home a file or envelope and no financial discussion ever blighted the cocktail hour. For him management was not, as it had been for my grandfather, a matter of planning so much as one of performance; the master gamesman who made it look as if held all the right cards and the right employees to carry the day. Team logistics, only it was crucial to him that the teammates regard themselves as separate adjuncts competing for a pat on the back and, ultimately, a raise. In his book, loyalty was paramount. He stood by those he picked. And woe to the fellow who forgot to whom he owed that first fateful foot in the door.

Father had, as Don Regan said, "Boss" stamped all over him, he knew how to lead men. What he lacked was a sense of the complexity of the arena into which he was directing them, the interdependency between a business and the surrounding society. Charlie had possessed a vision of the symphonic whole, an orchestra always capable of taking on new personnel, new roles and assignments. He once confided that my father was an excellent sergeant for marshalling the troops and driving them from one campaign post to the next. By the same token he might not be the one to whose judgment you entrusted the reins of state. Charlie was in the last year of his life when he resolved the succession between Father and the capable operations manager, Mike McCarthy, by flipping a coin before a stunned Jim Boswell (the head of the world's largest agribusiness). Heads would get Safeway, tails Merrill Lynch. Thus Father landed Safeway, a company that suited him better than a more number-oriented Merrill would have. Boswell wrote that in all of his business life he had never seen anything so decided.

Father's instincts, in the difficult position he occupied as son-in-law, served him well. He never set up a tennis game, or arranged a luncheon date, without first checking with his boss. "Well, Pop," he'd say, when he checked in Saturday morning, "what's the schedule?"

Investing in the stock market is, of course, gambling; there are so many imponderables. Even Charlie maintained he wasn't right more than 60% of the time. But he could narrow his margin of error by seeking impartial advice. Here the two diverged. Where Charlie was forever commissioning market research reports, Father could not countenance throwing good money away on an item that did not show up on the bottom line. He did not devise policies as much as alliances, man to man against a common foe. Asked the secret of his success, Father invariably replied, "Decisiveness. I decided to marry the boss's daughter."

Rising from peanuts to pearls, Father made clear, was less a matter of talent than of how you sold yourself; or, as he used to say with understandable revulsion, what ass you were prepared to lick. His friend, Ricardo Sicre, rephrased it a little more broadly: "I've never made a business deal with a man whom I hadn't first met with my hand around a cocktail glass."

Father's own emergence from Chester's blue-collar depths was so unlikely that he could never imagine an alternative to that straight vigorous upward climb. He could work hard, and when his father fell ill, he had to—there were his mother and brother to support. As an American, was he ashamed of the crack in the middle-class floor his family had fallen through? He never discussed those hard times and any hint of curiosity found him reeling in an amnesiac blank. No one else I knew was so driven and so concealed. This muffled person, one felt, had never experienced a sustained moment of unambiguous pleasure, nor would he have wanted to. It would have smacked of decadence, a mockery of his consciously assumed self-creation. A complex man and yet one curiously forgiving, boyishly spontaneous and, when the chips were down, deeply loyal.

When Father came home from the Navy to find his job taken and Charlie unwilling or too ill to stand up for him, he came close to chucking his dynastic ambitions and heading out on his own. Mother intervened, trying to instill the patience and fortitude the situation required. Trusting her, he stuck it out, and by 1949, he was back in his old job as number two in Merrill Lynch, presiding over the Wall Street to Main Street expansion. "The only real fun in business," he once admitted to this prospective underling, "is running your own show."

All the same resurrecting Safeway from imminent bankruptcy took considerable skill and gumption. It was one thing to believe, as Charlie did, that shaving a penny off the price of milk in Los Angeles might be just enough to get him to heaven. Twenty years later, it was something else to sell every week a range of goods below cost with the consequence, if not the intention, of wiping out hundreds of smaller, weaker competitors.

Father wanted Safeway run from the ground up. To that end he spent much of his weekends visiting stores. He'd drop in unannounced, walk up and down noting the conditions of the shelves—couldn't they be more crammed?—and introduce himself to the often stunned manager to find out what worked and what didn't. The fodder came in handy at management meetings where he would confront the bureaucrats with the very different views he had gleaned from the store managers. They were the ones closest to the shoppers and inevitably more believable.

Not every regional manager was equipped to live or die by the results-oriented autonomy on which Father insisted. Nor did his shake-'em-up style make Father popular with the Oakland bigwigs who reacted as people do who find themselves threatened. In a palace revolution the Board upped and fired this anything but laid-back New Yorker. What could a Wall Street fellow know about the food distribution business?

Shaken maybe, but undeterred, Father flew back to New York and presented his case to the banks that were Safeway's creditors. They furnished him with a letter spelling out in no uncertain terms the consequence if he was not immediately reinstated as both president and chairman. Father repaid the banks' trust very quickly. In less than two years Safeway was completely turned around, a considerable feat for a company of its size. During his 15-year tenure a single share of Safeway stock grew to almost six times its original value with the help of two stock splits, twelve dividend increases and an adjusted 38% rise in market price.

BARON SAFEWAY

The public arena found Father poised on his achieved pinnacle: the recipient of two honorary knighthoods, two doctorates, his photograph gracing the covers of *Fortune, Business Week* and *Forbes*. On that eminence, like a fire-breathing dragon, he now sat, unable to deal with those who did not buy into the illusion of unlimited power he projected. Deep in his cups at his 64th birthday dinner, he was heard confiding, "I'm more powerful than President Johnson." All he may have meant was that, unlike the President, he had instituted mandatory retirement at 65 for everyone but himself at Safeway.

Stephen, Merrill, Father, Robin, Peter, Rapallo, 1949

For us sons there was one "final solution" now—money. Rather than reason with us we were sent scurrying down one or another silver-lined path. Brother Merrill was paid to stop smoking and, until the end of his life, Father firmly believed that a wad of banknotes had cured the boy of his filthy habit. But what to us was a couple of grand? Devils of any number of stripes might well seduce me, but not one wagging a fistful of bills.

At times his intensity verged on the histrionic: "Do this, or I'll throw a fit." No doubt such threats kept the office personnel hopping; among those not seeking a promotion, all it drew was a raised eyebrow. Father was forever presenting issues in black-and-white either-ors, and any attempt to suggest a measure of equivocation found him pressing his personal panic button, the high blood pressure—hypertension –from which he suffered and which killed both his parents. Without his world-class earning powers, how would we manage? We'd attempt to explain that we couldn't be constantly springing into action because he had caught us on a sofa curled up with a book. In reality, he so little believed in the family edifice, except as an expression of his will, that when one of us slipped up he was thrown into a panic, as if our errancy would send him sliding down the drain from which he had arisen.

What kept the inner man from calcifying was the faculty he had of admitting surprise, and even mistakes; unable to recall the next morning over whom his fiery kettle had exploded. His doghouse did not hold permanent residents.

On a country outing nothing so thrilled him as the spectacle of acre upon acre given over to one monocrop. That was the kind of gamble he could applaud, whereas a neighbor's field grown wild, a child's long hair, rightly bothered him. His response was to grab hold of a pair of clippers, a power mower, and level it. One of my brothers featured in his college room, under the obligatory Mao poster of peasants scything a rice field, a blown-up photo of Father attending his farewell Caterpillar board meeting. Picture an outsized green baize table with tiny directors seated all around. In front of each was a toy product of that immense earth-moving concern. Father's was a bulldozer.

This baronial right to rule unconstrained was at stake in the grape worker-organized boycott against Safeway, one that would last, off and on, fifteen years and make Safeway, next to Bank of America, the Left's most hated corporation. Cesar Chavez, the charismatic union leader, had targeted Safeway: crack the biggest and you'd crack them all. What he hadn't reckoned on was an equally resolute Father intent on holding the anti-union line for a host of suppliers, among them the Boswell Company, of which he was a proud director. What would be next, Father asked, Polish hams, Cuban cigars? And why Safeway, when the union's larger battle was with the growers? The struggle between Father and Chavez, two men who personally liked each other, became increasingly fraught. There was even a shaming march up to Mother's Pacific Heights home, undertaken without anyone in Chavez's office bothering to inquire whether she was in residence. She wasn't.

The loyalties enlisted by the grape strike were not all on one side. My family were all surprised when old Ernest Gallo, by no means a personal friend, showed up in a black suit at Father's Grace Church funeral. On a bitterly cold December Saturday, you'd think he had better things to do than drive all the way from his Modesto winery. Not only that, he contributed $10,000 in Father's name to the Children's Hospital Heart Fund. Because of the stance Father had taken twenty years earlier? Yes, probably, and there in a back row, silently on his knees was Mr. Gallo.

Stephen, Peter, Merrill, Robin, Rapallo, 1949

How lonely he must have found it poring over *The Wall Street Journal* when there was a houseful of us sons with whom he could be sharing his fascination with the daily mood swings and gyrations of his stock exchange all-stars. "At what price would you trade Winn-Dixie? With what would you replace it?"

Over cocktails one evening when he had all of us assembled he announced the "deal of the century." "I want each of you to pick ten stocks to invest in. At the end of the year I'll turn over to you whatever profit you've made."

For some reason we older brothers demurred. Maybe we didn't share the vision of a league, each with our own Big Board squad competing against the others and then Father himself in the finals. Or it may be that writing some corporate names on a scrap of paper required more energy than we could summon. But Stephen, the youngest, fell for it. He did a little research and picked his ten stocks. Twelve months later he had lucked out on every one of them.

"I picked them, now can I have the profits you promised?" Stephen asked Father who, impressed by his selections, had bought them for his own account as well.

In a bid for time—perhaps Stephen would forget? Father promised him the $33,000 profit "When you reach your majority."

Stephen understood. A 14-year-old is a minor. But his totem was not the elephant for nothing, and he remembered. On turning 21, he asked Father to deliver on something he believed he had rightfully earned. "I've reached my majority. Now can I have the profit on those ten stocks I picked?"

Father was not about to turn over a nest egg of that size, let alone pay the gift tax Uncle Sam required. Instead he decided to stonewall: "Your majority is when I decide it is."

Gullible to the end, Stephen persisted in believing this man of his word would make good. He had reached the age of 30 when Father decided the time had come to expunge this so-called promise from the family balance sheet. "It's all in your imagination that I'd hand over the profit from your ten stocks. I never said any such thing."

All the same, Father still wanted to appear generous. One evening, a year or so after Stephen had graduated Scholar of his Class from Yale, he offered to buy him a new car as a delayed graduation gift. By now, Stephen was aware that any such money would come, not from Father, but from his own undelivered trust fund. Responding carefully, Stephen replied that, living in the city and with such means as he had, he could ill afford the insurance, garage fees and general upkeep of a car. "Why not instead," he countered, "buy me a bicycle? I could really use one in Southampton."

Father wholeheartedly embraced Stephen's proposal. "But I want you to shop around and buy yourself the best possible. Remember I'm paying."

Stephen took Father at his word and canvassed the two local bike shops. When they didn't have what he needed, he got a ride to Easthampton, 40 minutes away. There he bought a ten-speed, state-of-the-art machine and pedaled it the whole traffic-laden highway home. That evening, with considerable pride, he showed it to Father, "A beauty, isn't it? Thank you very much."

Father gave it his once over. Then, pausing a moment reflectively, he asked Stephen how much he had paid for it.

"$175," Stephen replied.

"You paid too much," Father declared and, peeling off a hundred dollar bill from his wallet, he handed it to Stephen.

So much for the offer of a car.

I SANG IN MY CHAINS

The wealthy, as Scott Fitzgerald remarked, inhabit a country all their own. The fences are for the most part invisible ones. They come with the terrain, the clubs, the schools, the clothes, until that's what you are, unable to function in any other milieu. The acculturation usually proceeds gradually. Were a son to perceive the privileged sports, the defining hobbies for the entrapment they are, he might throw up his hands and flee. Instead it has to look as if you are the one, with the huge world stamp book you inherited from your uncle, the leather-bound classics you are acquiring in imitation of your parents, initiating yourself into opulent penury.

The older I got, the more pronounced the moneyed frame became, since pleasure wasn't clean unless bought. And it was most clean when most costly, rarity having ensured against contamination. Hence those French restaurant meals that irrigated my childhood. "On the expense account!" Father would toast, referring to his tax bracket, more than happy to shell out (always in cash, out of respect for the restaurant). It was as if Le Pavillon were to Father what a woman's eyes and thighs were to Charlie Merrill. From the most commanding of tables he would beam forth to the restaurateur, convinced he had reached nothing less than the arriviste finals, "The Provençal murals are great, Soulé."

"Tell that to the artist," the restaurateur surprised him, "he's sitting at the next table." Thus began the negotiations that would end in the Beach House's two Bernard LaMotte murals. To the same end he buttered up the two headwaiters by serving as their personal broker, while they responded with post-soufflé Dom Perignon and cooking lessons for Merrill's wife after he inherited the account. Yet I must say I responded to the colored sensualities of a reality so erotically purveyed in the still life paintings of Matisse and Bonnard.

The earliest form of the initiation into wealth Father proposed was tennis, a game synonymous with his own aspirations: the ability to maintain grace under pressure and the winning by which he saw himself validated. From the age of eight, he taught me himself: patiently from a basket on the clay Beach House court doling out the balls I'd be implored to hit. And, oh, the *mea culpas* I had to deliver if a ball I struck was not returned straight to him.

As I reached adolescence, the inculcation shifted to an arena more appropriate, the family dinner table. To Father I had no other identity—none, that is, he cared to acknowledge—than a pint-sized Robert A., Jr. Since this tabula rasa could not possibly entertain a belief on his own, any sign of independence I evinced was bound to be misread and laid at the feet of some corrupting genie: a maternal uncle, an ill-chosen school's history teacher.

Whenever I sat down to dinner now—out of lingering affection always on his right—he would set out to demolish my new friends: "I don't want you hanging around with a bunch of kikes and fairies," he'd start in, referring to the local art scene that had taken me up.

"How about that kike godfather of mine, Jack Straus?" I'd retort. "Your Jewish friends aren't kikes, but mine are?" For a moment, maybe, I'd have this shape-changing Proteus clutched in my grasp. Just as I was about to wrest a recognition of sorts out of him, he would lash out at a "pinko" prof of mine. No doubt, the slurs gave him a way of consolidating his personality, one banner after another proudly fluttering in the racist wind.

On this score my former sister-in-law Jill Tarlau remembers Father visiting Houston where my brother Peter was directing the Safeway operation. Jill is Jewish and, during their courtship, Father had done his "damnedest," pulling every nasty trick in his book to keep his 22-year-old son from marrying her. With time, however, he had grown fond of her and their two daughters. Now that she was carrying a third, he wanted somehow to make amends. It was late in the dinner and Father was in his cups, waxing sentimental about his family, the one he had married into. The Merrills, he was explaining, had a lustrous pedigree. They were even on the Mayflower (the Alden in Peter's middle name, shared with a million other descendants!). As for the Magowans, he said, throwing up his hands, who knows where they hailed from, there were scarce any records. "Maybe," he said, addressing Jill as if the notion had then and there struck him, "they were Jews—how else could I have been so acquisitive?"

For the wretchedly poor, as Father had been in his formative years, anti-Semitism can make a convenient scapegoat for the capitalist oppression they can't or don't dare acknowledge. All the same, it was hard for me to fathom how a person of his obvious intelligence could voice such inanities. Was he doing it to put me on, or, more incomprehensibly, did he actually believe what he spouted? Either way I wasn't about to let him ram his beliefs down my throat. My study of history pointed to another reading of the long struggle for equality and social justice. But at this stage of the dinner any defense of my new values was only so much kindling thrown on his raging fire. "Who's going to pay for this Left Wing society of yours," the taxpayer bellowed from a seat away. "Tell me how," he added, changing tack with his usual swiftness, "you intend to support yourself, let alone me in my old age, as all sons should?"

These horrible screaming Sunday night confrontations left Mother fatally torn between her maternal instincts and the loyalty she owed her husband. Within minutes of sitting down to the cold borscht soup we'd see her reeling upstairs with the beginnings of another three-day migraine. Because any argument was taken as a challenge to his paternal authority, he responded by taking it out on me personally. As with tennis, his forensic tactic was to so rile me with a line call that I would forget myself and make an exaggerated claim. Then, from a seat away, the master of the self-fulfilling prophecy would pounce, delighted to show me the dolt I remained for all my high-toned schooling.

"Just look around you," Father would propose.

"At what?" I'd ask, bewildered.

"At all the no-goodniks, the scroungers and pinkos this New Deal of yours is supporting. Do you think, given the chance, they'd want to live in Russia?"

"I don't know," I ventured, "some might find it appealing." I was about to reel off some of the positive features of collective life—the shared purchases, the way one sits down at a restaurant table with strangers—when I was zapped again.

"Do you think I'm paying for the best possible education so you can become a goddam intellectual? Shirt sleeves to shirt sleeves in three generations! Well, I don't intend to let that happen in my family."

"Education?" I snorted, horns lowered now, unable to abandon what I saw as my values.

"Well, a college degree," Father retorted, backing away. "It's the same thing in the end."

"If words are only things to twist." Oh, to be allowed to crack a joke!

And there might be Mother jumping in. "Don't be rude to your father. Remember the fourth commandment."

What choice did I have but to reject their thought control? "The two of you would make a fine pair of Commissars. I'm just to toe your party line?"

Mother had heard enough. "I think you should leave the table."

With a slight bow to everyone the comedian would slide back his chair, knowing this was by no means the end of it.

Next morning, I'd be summoned into her bedroom to hear once again how I had ruined Father's farewell supper. "I wish you'd see there's a time and place for everything and it's not the family dinner table. That was Mother at her conciliatory best, harmony at any price. Fine for one who had her bedroom in which to legislate, but what other venue did I have to let them know who I was? Or was it dutiful nods they alone tolerated, coat and tie, clean fingernails, the shortest possible hair?

"I'm not the one causing the storm, he is. Can't I discuss anything without his taking umbrage and gunning me down? I wouldn't mind being persuaded; Father knows so much more than I do. But when my friends are being maligned—Jews, homosexuals, all that—it's me, my values, that are being attacked. What would you do if you were constantly being chopped into bits—roll over, turn the other cheek, go on piling up brownie points for the kingdom to come?

"I won't stand your being irreligious," Mother retorted, aware she was the one now under attack.

"There you go, pulling down the curtain. Am I to be allowed a voice of my own, or is his every word gospel? Even God Almighty would not claim," I added, punctuating the remark with as direct a look as I could muster, "that the world was created by money alone."

"Perhaps not," Mother replied, pausing until my eyes had shifted away from her and onto the bedroom upholstery, the china bowls and alabaster lamps, and the rest of a considerable moneyed creation. She continued, "But whatever your opinions, your father is entitled to your respect and you're staying grounded until you apologize to him."

"For what?" I asked indignantly. "I haven't done anything wrong. You yourself admit I'm right."

"Still, you must apologize and, until you do, you're not going anywhere."

Wonderfully two-faced, yet her conduct fit a marriage in which the dynastic emphasis was assumed from the start and the fundamental disagreements were never allowed to surface. To keep the vital tension and their own liberty of action going, they had instituted early on a policy whereby one or another of us children—selected, it seemed, almost at random—would be sentenced to the doghouse. That way, each had the other to blame: "He's your son!" And the son, caught in the crossfire, could only hope to ride it out somehow.

THE DYNASTIC VESSEL

My parents may have disagreed about whose son I was, but I knew—Father's. Even at college he was all I talked about. Yet my mother, Doris, was in many ways more remarkable and to this day I know a small army of fans for whom she was that genuine article, a real lady. For all her unflagging concern for me and my entire family, and a generosity that to this day takes my breath away, ours was a somewhat murky relationship. Father was someone I believe I understood. He was a bull and he charged. Mother was considerably more complex, a woman of innumerable pockets and not a few secrets.

The most important person in Mother's life, as in so many others, was Charlie Merrill. Since he passed, she once confided, not a day slipped by when she hadn't thought of him. For all their closeness and mutual respect—she was his favorite child—it could not have been easy living under the thrall of a man so mercurial; one he could at a moment withdraw, as he had in divorcing Eliza when Doris was twelve.

The divorce had come on the heels of a key childhood event—her Roman Catholic first communion. It had taken place while Charlie was away on business in Chicago. On learning about it, he flew into a fiery rage; not that it had happened, he told Eliza, but that she had done it behind his back. On and on he blazed until Eliza, a timid woman who had scheduled it for that very reason, pronounced the words whose consequences she had clearly not thought out, "I want a divorce, I can't stand, Charlie, these rages of yours."

On the spot, granted. Mother recalled the two of them at the dinner table barely an hour later, Charlie still shaking and Eliza looking "absolutely awful, as if her life had come to an end, which," she went on, gathering herself after a reflective pause, "in truth it had." As she spoke I saw the lonely penthouse from which this claustrophobic lady, unable to step by herself into an elevator, rarely emerged during the forty years in which I knew her.

Her father hadn't spent the better part of his life laying siege to an array of luscious women without seeking to turn his daughter into one, a sparkling gem set as the very diadem of his empire; a control all the more insidious in that he seemed to know the styles, fabrics and colors that looked best on her and bought, as she acknowledged, her most stunning outfits. Before sending her off to school, or letting her go to a party (never in less than the family sedan and always called for by both a chauffeur and a maid), he would inspect her from head to toe. If so much as a wrinkle was found, she'd be sent upstairs to change.

Her father was famously soft-spoken. But as her brother Charles remarked, he had no need to raise his voice to "cut you into a thousand pieces." Admonishments all the more humiliating in that they were nearly always imparted over the dinner table before an assembled entourage. Failure to eat whatever lurked on your plate and you were summarily banished, plate in hand, to your room. "Popeye," her brother Jimmy once lamented, "would be astonished at the amount of spinach I've flushed down the toilet."

The fear of displeasing such a 'heavy father' meant playing a role. Mother had it in her to be the "It girl" he desired: pretty, popular, successful and good. But at key moments the strain of being Princess Doris showed its insecure face. She took unflattering pictures not because her nose was slightly too large, or her lower bite overcrowded, but because she had too much at stake to be relaxed and genuine. Blessed with an excellent spatial sense, able without measuring to tell exactly how many rolls of wallpaper she needed, there was no reason why she should draw a blank in geometry, much less fail the same algebra class two years in a row. Or was there? A woman who was always shifting in a chair, who could never sit still enough to read for very long, clearly had problems listening, paying attention, and concentrating. As for math, she had what one would now call a learning disability. Years later, on shopping trips to Europe, she would ask my 17-year younger brother Mark, still a child, to calculate for her the dollar equivalents of foreign currencies.

The crowning blow was delivered by her father. "Don't worry, Doris. I feel confident your future husband is not going to want to see your report card when he proposes matrimony." Words of consolation, maybe. For the poor girl one can see the book of possibilities slamming shut. She wasn't going to make it to college. She wasn't going to pursue a career. And she was going to get married. To whom, it might be asked, a man of whose choice?

Mother grew up disadvantaged by a society that did not encourage women to pursue a professional career. Medicine fascinated her, and if born a man, she probably would have been a doctor like her grandfather. "You're going to be locked up for practicing without a license," Father once remarked, recognizing the quality of her obsession. Though Charlie did not approve of women "who knew how to dissect earthworms," he recognized that most men in distinguished positions sought an informed, well-educated wife and consequently urged her to apply to college. Mother, for her part, aspired to the social celebrity of a debutante. Eventually, the compromise of a year at a Florentine finishing school was reached, where she would be exposed to languages, art, and a different culture.

At seventeen, there she was, removed from the attentions of a fop who drove a dazzling fire-red Bugatti, and dispatched to a school in the hill town of Fiesole, above Florence. This change worked a remarkable transformation. There were, it seemed, subjects she could excel in: Italian, for one, useful in ensuring the privacy of certain moments in her diary; and art history, which inspired her lifelong admiration for Italy and its culture.

There followed a pre-debutante year studying silver connoisseurship at the Metropolitan, and doing volunteer work in the children's wing of Bellevue Hospital. Her diary speaks of her concern for the children: "most of them absolutely deformed. One child dying of spinal meningitis, their little limbs so pitifully skinny. Made beds, told them stories, did jigsaw puzzles, cleaned out linen closets, gave them cod liver oil, went on errands and, as there wasn't a chair in the whole ward it was a rather exhausting day."

In what time remained she pursued a social life that could include as many as five events in a day, each with a change of outfit. Mother's diaries show that she responded to every crammed minute of it: the lunches, the tea dances, the squads of handsome young blades dropping in on their Park Avenue triplex, the college weekends and proms that took her up and down the East Coast.

Another might have shrunk at the size of the dollar princess price tag, the coming-out party with its seated dinner—served at 2 a.m.!—for a thousand guests at The Orchard where marquee tents covered a half-mile of front lawn. It was 1932, after all, the nadir of the Depression. But to Mother her debut meant precisely that—emergence from a childhood chrysalis—and it never occurred to her to question her set's values, their excesses of wealth and heartlessness, their avid pursuit of trivia at the expense of deep feeling. School had been reasonably satisfying, especially in the group of life-long friends she acquired. But in trying to earn her teachers' approval, her own human yearnings got short-circuited.

Then again, if being a gorgeous butterfly is everything your 18-year-old heart is set on, why not spend a glittering evening fluttering about on a packed dance floor if you have been trained in ballet and absolutely enjoy the succession of beaux holding you in their generous arms. As for deep feeling, she was lucky enough to end the year by falling in love with Johnny Slocum, a Princeton senior on his way to medical school and a distinguished psychiatric career. They became engaged and, despite her wish to enter marriage a virgin, she made the *supremo sacrifizio*, as she called it.

Much as Mother exulted in the surprise, the astonishment of their love-making, "*i più perfetti momenti della mia vita*," she did not relish becoming pregnant by a man who still faced three years of medical school. A New Year's Eve diary note, in the Italian she used to express private thoughts, remarked, "*ho paura per il futuro . . . Come voglio avere un bambino, ma dobbiamo aspettare così lungo tempo.*" (I'm afraid for the future. I'd give anything to have a baby, but we've got an awfully long time to wait.)

Reading over the newly discovered diary, almost a century later, I find Mother's scruples hard to grasp. Why couldn't they get married, if that's what they both wanted? Didn't she have funds saved from a generous allowance and didn't he command an income of sorts? Could it be that marriage for her meant maintaining an establishment in a certain style and not the indignity of student housing? I wonder also about Charlie's veto power over a daughter who hadn't reached her majority. What did this son of an M.D. feel about a medical son-in-law, let alone a psychiatrist? Mother's diary speaks of her step-mother Hellen "trying to poison Daddy against me. I love Daddy so much," she goes on, "it would almost break my heart if she should bring a breach between us. She tells him things that aren't true just to upset and worry him." Could it be that a woman as status-oriented as Hellen had her sights set on a more prominent son-in-law? The prospect of three years of waiting, with their risky sexual encounters, must have become more and more intolerable. How else explain her falling for a jumped up working class fellow with whom she had so little in common?

I suspect Father must have appeared at a vulnerable moment. Freedom is always temporary. However much we may relish independence, most of us run out of the courage needed to sustain it. And our controllers, who see a prize there for the taking, know exactly how to appeal to our regressive instincts, the need some of us have to replicate the patterns we only think we are trying to escape. Marriage is a deeply conservative institution. In embarking upon it we are, often enough, seeking a partner who can reconnect us to the sundered past, a domain all the more appealing if we have somehow forgotten all it entailed. Freedom is daunting precisely because we have to change so much to accommodate its spaciousness. Whereas our jailers always carry a reassuring conviction.

Mother's wedding pictures supply their own evidence. Where Father is radiant, basking in what is clearly the supreme moment of all his striving, Mother is serious, unsmiling, grave. This is a marriage, we understand, chosen with her head, not her heart. Was her choice of Father a fatalistic one? Romantic? Compassionate? In the "excitement" he generated, what part did that bogey of hers—boredom—play? Or was the campaign of over-the-top gifts he mounted exactly what this narcissist needed by way of confirmation? Too frequently, we are willing to escape the trammels of freedom. In marrying the man she did she became, not so unwillingly perhaps, Father's and Charlie's pawn. Yet there may well have been compensation in finding herself the subject of an ongoing duel between these two jealous lovers.

Mother's bridesmaids, Southampton, 1935

Doubts there may have been, but I never heard them voiced. In marrying, Mother had scrupulously chosen, "Not until death do us part." Since her irascible husband was as capable as Charlie of throwing up his hands in a moment's exasperation and breaking with everything—us progeny included— it was up to Mother to be the good sport who kept our brittle show on the road. For this thankless role she paid with a lifetime of afflictions: cramps, ulcers, hives, hay fever, migraines, twitches, itches, rashes, mouse eyes, back problems and a constant allergic cough. Whatever miracles she achieved never lasted, since the chaos and violence and sheer nastiness never let up, fueled by the alcohol with which Father medicated himself to ward off his own inner demons. Mother was too cowed, too guilt-ridden, to realize she was not the one at fault. And Father, perhaps because he owed her so much, put his own considerable energy into subjugating her.

In a no-win situation how do you survive? Do you gratefully thank him for a birthday brooch, a sable martin coat, when you are the one footing the bill for the palaces, their staffing, the whole glittering life style? Do you think of fleeing with the kids to Charlie's? On vacations, yes, that's where we went, but she couldn't see worrying a very sick man with her marital troubles.

She must have recognized, early on, the futility of standing up to the monster she had married. With controllers of his sort, you don't win, you just get nuked. All you can do is try to tame him, to smooth over those sharp edges. In her dealings with us it was only natural she should emphasize the surface values of family harmony, courtesy and agreement at whatever price. If she could score straight A's in the dress, hair, speech and deportment that mattered to Father, why couldn't we do the little—everything?—it took to please him? Was it that difficult? That reprehensible? Before any descent of Father's on Southampton, she made sure we were all properly accoutered. For one such event my brother Stephen reported, "Father was due. So the mother thought, if I was to be invited, I ought to be suitably armored. Therefore she told me the shoes would be on her, but I must provide new slacks, sport shirts, bathing suit and a haircut to fit the helmet. A full Everything Card later, I arrived in Southampton to do battle with a pink, a green, a brown and a blue combination: an elegant G.I."

For all her nervous twitching at her too tight skirt and the occasional anxiety of her drawing room conversation—silences were not tolerated—the results were stunningly effective. Parisian evening gowns, soft as sherbet, floated down the stairs with an éclat all the more telling in that they were more a sign of social distinction than anything sexy. Her tanned skin gleamed, her scented shoulders were bare. At 30, the square-cut "angel" hairdo of her debutante photographs (never pictured smiling and thereby all the more soulful, a woman with a hidden mystery) had grown into a hip-length chestnut mane carried coiled in a chignon. Most petite women want to lengthen themselves with dark single color dresses, but Mother preferred clashing, dizzying effects, the brighter, the gayer: acid turquoises, lemons, greens; stripes, zigzags, bold prints, big hats, and had few qualms about mixing fabrics. From within her get-ups she radiated a style always featuring some detail: an opulent moonstone, or even a set of buttons could become the pretext for an outfit. The more relaxed she became in later life, the more the soft milky blue of her deep-set eyes added to the picture of intense aliveness she conveyed: one of those pert, small-chinned women who sparkle in a wild hat.

Not for her were long *tête-à-têtes* on a corner sofa. Instead, she sought to amplify a wife's presumed decorative role with volunteer work: ace fund-raiser; board member of several national foundations; a doer, summoning meetings, notifying commissioners, changing zoning laws. The war gave her activity a patriotic glamour. When it was over, the attention involved in overseeing the various Magowan-Merrill consulates—thirteen at one point—took up much of the slack in her schedule. To others, the demands of running so many houses could seem a problem. "Doesn't it bother you," a friend once asked, "not knowing in which house you are spending Christmas?" Mother understood her concern perfectly. "But I have boxes of ornaments in all my houses." And a room in each, I might add, set aside just for wrapping the Christmas presents purchased, in all likelihood, the previous January. A woman highly organized.

Occasionally one hears of a grande dame going to great lengths to get right a certain feature of house décor. But it's Mother who decides one day, as we are all sitting on the verandah of her newly acquired Southampton house, to move the swimming pool.

Swimming pool, Merrill's Landing, Palm Beach

"Move it?" we exclaimed, aghast.

"Yes, we'll fit it in." And she built another, of exactly the same dimensions, but turned at a right angle and placed 50 feet to the side, where it would not spoil the view of the creek.

More "Mother" still, was what she did to her Pacific Heights home. She had viewed over a hundred houses before settling on her elegant palazzo with its Italianate loggia and breathtaking views of the Bay, fronting on Octavia Street (a steep winding red-bricked roadway featured in many films, with the unattended baby carriage about to rattle down it). She hadn't been long in her house when she noticed it lacked what was for her a necessity—a cozy nook where she could lunch with a friend. So she acquired the villa immediately below her on the hill and had it razed. That allowed her to tack on the ten extra feet she needed for an intimate nook off the dining room. My father could not believe it.

The scale of her activities, viewed through the foreground of her nearly daily migraines, could give rise to genuine perplexity. "Why," her sister-in-law Mary Merrill once asked, "are you running yourself into the ground?"

Surprised by Mary's question, Mother reflected for a moment before venturing, "I'm afraid, I suppose, of being bored."

"But when was the last time you were bored?"

Mother thought again, scratching her head. "I don't remember."

"You could," Mary suggested dryly, "give it a try."

But slowing down and adjusting her personal clock wasn't Mother. Life had stacked her deck with valuable cards, but moral courage wasn't one of them. Without it she kept getting stung. The Gershwin song, "I've Got You under My Skin," received a new gloss as her flesh erupted in hives and rashes that stung "like a thousand jellyfish." The "quacks," as the man under her skin referred to them, gave her what balms they could. But they could only treat the symptoms, not the tension brought on by the perfection she required of her every transaction, her every golf swing, almost it seemed her every mot. There were a number of less demanding activities she enjoyed, such as painting and playing the piano. But she wouldn't commit herself to anything in which she couldn't excel. For her, as much as for Father, life was performance. And part of winning was bluffing, not being a bad sport about her migraines, never admitting to being less than right.

Our family motto reads, *Qui patitur vincit* (the one who suffers, triumphs). By those weird standards Mother deserved an alp all her own, innocent of novocaine, toughing it out in a dentist's chair. Her migraines became more frequent when the canvas-roofed Buick convertible she was driving, with me in the front seat and Merrill and a friend in the back, skidded on some black ice and rolled some 350 feet down an embankment. (I remember the father of the girl in the back seat, who was driving behind us, tearing the roof cover apart with his bare hands and pulling us out through the roof one by one.)

Just as serious could be her allergic reactions. A dish of scallops at Proust's old standby, Lapérouse, was enough to keep her from ever again tolerating seafood. On another occasion, the ripeness of the odors, as she threw open the doors of a large barn in the California Central Valley, brought on a fit of sneezing convulsive enough to rupture a spinal disk. More recently, a hospital I sent her to for testing confirmed that she was allergic to 241 different substances. They had never encountered such hypersensitivity and were adamant in refusing to let her pay for a two-week stay. Hers was, they told her, a rare learning experience.

Not so long ago, in a newspaper column, Mother came upon the question, "Which would you rather have—health or wealth?" After a broken hip and three spinal disk operations—including a life-or-death one on her cervical vertebrae—she was sufficiently troubled to run downstairs and consult the Latvian maid. The maid, a sensible woman, replied, "I've never had any wealth to speak of, but you're nothing without your health." Mother was less than convinced.

I remember the "little dynamo," as a magazine article fondly summarized her, coming down the stairs gleefully holding up a caption, "REST IS RUST." But what else but rust was her lividly red skin? Tensions never addressed have to erupt somewhere.

HURRY HURRY

Growing up in the inner city, it was difficult to savor the adrenaline rush provided by the scurrying, heads down, pavement-oriented throngs, the delicious prospect of danger lurking behind every garbage can, every fire escape, the Mondrian boogie-woogie of pulsating lights and energies. To a child, the city could seem a vast set of tunnels. You were conveyed into Manhattan by one or another such subterranean passage and, once emerged, a consciousness remained, formed by all that kept you tip-toeing about, afraid and small at the bottom of so much rectangular life.

Then again New York may not be the kind of city one encourages a child to explore. For my parents the great merit of St. Bernard's, the British-staffed school we attended, was the way it kept us fully occupied until five o'clock doing the whole of our homework. From there, on the fringe of Harlem, we were bussed home by way of Gracie Square and the tough tenement kids waiting on their brownstone stoops, pea-shooters and saliva poised, for the bull's eye of an open window. A reminder of how, even within the confines of our upper East Side district, there lay another milieu of burnt, gutted tenement housing, of kids roaming in packs through the park, armed with clubs of pig iron and razor-sharp umbrellas, while we schoolmates huddled in a circle, protecting a precious leather football.

If we escaped that time, thanks to a passing police car, there was a day when, in too much of a hurry to change out of my jodhpurs, I tried to make it from the Squadron A Park Avenue Armory to the Lexington bus stop a block away. That, even I knew, was a bit daft, and two knife-wielding urchins spotted a prize calf and prodded me into a basement alley. They then proceeded to relieve me of the $2.25 in coins I had squirreled away. When, still shaking, I arrived home and told my father what had happened, he was appalled—why couldn't a son of his stand up to a mere knife—"At your age, they wouldn't have done that to me!"

Hurry. Hurry. In another family a time piece might represent an heirloom on a wall, or a jewel on a wrist. In a business family like ours, time was nothing less than Mammon himself, and we were always amazed that others—doctors notoriously—did not share our respect for the ticking word. And word is exactly what it was. If I wasn't home on the dot, they'd start wondering if something ghastly had happened, "It just isn't like him." As a child, I seemed to be always in a rush, hearing the appointment clock ticking, bomblike, as I hung on a strap in some fuming bus, or ran, dodging in and out of the stalled traffic. (Miscalculating now and them, like the time when jay-walking across 57th, I forgot about the lanes of traffic hurtling eastward and landed, shaken but unhurt, atop some terrified man's hood.)

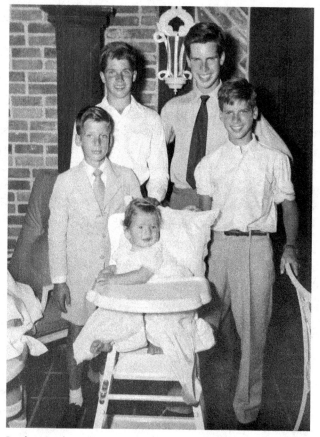

Brothers Stephen, Merrill, baby Mark, Robin, Peter, Beach House, 1953

Our fourth floor retreat, above my parents on the third, below the servants on the fifth, was dark, gloomy. Perfect for the night wolves that, slithering like fishes down the chimney, used to run around the precariously poised island of my bed. Perfect, too, for the burglar apprehended in the depths of the playroom closet and who allowed himself to be taken by the elbow by the maid into the elevator and shoved out the front door.

In our playroom I had my Uncle Jimmy's enormous world stamp book, the maps from Volume XXVI of *The Brittanica* I would trace for hours on end (as if by committing their outlines to memory, I might possess something of the labyrinthine life, the courtyards, the forests, the antediluvian reptiles), as well as the cupboards crammed with those legions of stolidly parading tin soldiers and the clumsy building blocks to which I would be directed when Mother's planning left me with an unstructured hour. But did her planning fail? No, she was good at providing opportunities, as she called them: riding lessons on big frightening steel-mouthed horses at Aylward's across Central Park; skating lessons at Rockefeller Center; dancing lessons at the ballroom of the Pierre. When lessons flagged, there was the orthodontist to rectify my rabbity overbite, the eye doctor so I wouldn't see everything double in each Madison Avenue window.

In our fourth floor quarters life was close, four brothers, less than eight years apart, kenneled two to a room. Fortunately we had a young, warm, wonderfully spirited peasant nurse, Eileen, and her fellow household servants to insulate us. For a couple unable to pry the lid off a can, servants were a necessity. The only item Mother cooked was toast, while Father's culinary talents barely extended beyond boiling water for spaghetti.

One day Stephen was doing the cooking, and in the midst of culling the bottom third of the asparagus and discarding them into the waste basket, when Father popped into the kitchen. The grocer protested, "You can't do that! They cost $1.69 a pound." Stephen, born with a quick wit, rejoined, "We throw away the dollar, we eat the 69 cents," and stormed out of the kitchen, not to be seen there for a week.

What held for the kitchen applied equally well to the nursery. Conceiving and giving birth to a dynastic heir was one thing; taking care of the little guy was, like everything else, best left to a trained professional. One hired the best possible—a couple of years off the boat from Europe—and let her get on with it, the feeding, the burping, the changing and washing of diapers. Then at the designated hour, dressed in his finest skirts for those maternal kisses, those popping paternal flash bulbs, Nurse brought him in, the living doll. Mother still spoke about the panic she felt on Nurse's first afternoon off. What if she broke me?

In my grandfather's houses the help were "colored," as they were then called. That's whom this Southerner felt comfortable with. In ours, they were Irish. Cook was something of a battle-axe, reluctant to serve us wartime rations in the quantity Eileen desired. For the more visible roles, Mother preferred having young nymphs about, and our Gaelic-speaking maids with their intense white skin and mischievous eyes could not have fit the bill more voluptuously. To a child, such beauty was not particularly unsettling. They were my pals, smuggling me off to mass, and teaching me the jig steps they danced at the Tuxedo Ballroom in Yorktown. Most people's servants tend to come and go, but Mother ensured that ours stayed until it was time to marry their inevitable policeman.

Stephen, Robin, Peter, Mother, Merrill, Rapallo, 1949

DAMAGED GOODS

If anyone stitched me together and put me on my own two feet it was Eileen Phelan, a round-faced intensely blue-eyed young farm girl from embattled Fermanagh, a majority Catholic county absorbed into Ulster as Protestant Lebensraum. I was a physical mess, at six, when she came to us. Along with rabbity teeth, crossed eyes and a perpetual sniffle—my tonsils hadn't been extracted yet—I had a pronounced stammer, the result of being switched from a leftie to a righty by her Swiss predecessor, Soeur Ami.

To a mother overwhelmed with two little boys, one can imagine the godsend a disciplinarian may have seemed. Here was a specialist pledged to turn the two of us into the dynastic props they desired. By what methods, one may ask? No one did, and Soeur Ami was only dismissed when Mother became aware, three and a half years later, of the welts up and down my left arm.

Obedience training works best on a child too young to remember, much less hold anyone accountable, for the evils inflicted on him. My left-handedness gave the abuse a focus. Just why everything I did instinctively—picking up a toy, spooning a morsel of food into my mouth—was now wrong, wrong, wrong, must not have been clear to me. I reacted with foot-banging tantrums that still, years later, were remembered with awe. These bouts of insurrection had to be squelched—hence the welts.

In looking over a family album I'm struck by the difference between the beaming bright-eyed lefty of the San Francisco snapshots and those taken after I passed, at age two, into Soeur Ami's hands: puzzled, distant, withdrawn. Nor does the change in nursery dynamics posed by a new brother's arrival provide an explanation. One has only to look at my younger brothers, Peter and Stephen, and then at Merrill and me, to spot the difference. They were not abused; we were.

The enforced switch took all too well. While I still start every gesture instinctively with my left hand, only to correct it, there is hardly anything I do that's not right-handed. But there is a missing person I keep trying to revive. Batting left-handed, playing tennis ambidextrously, choosing always the left side of a hockey rink, a soccer field, were ways of trying to reconnect with that awkward, sweet-faced lefty.

It was not only my self-trust that took a blow. When a child gets whacked every time he reaches out his paw, and when any toy he loves can be taken from him—I was a child without a teddy bear, without even a security blanket—his responses change. He learns to make do with less, with what might seem nothing at all. But I have paid an emotional price for such forbearance. When the woman of your life decides to walk out, do you throw a fit of convincing astonishment? Or, having foreseen even this moment of moments, do you kindly help her into her coat, into the taxi, a gentleman to the last? The tears, after all, have the rest of their days in which to flow.

Looking back at those pre-Eileen years I realize how frightened I must have been. Frightened by my loathed Soeur Ami whom I remember nonetheless mourning after she was dismissed—she was, after all, my proxy mother. Frightened, too, by my peers. My face felt so vulnerable with the corrective lenses I was beginning to wear, my first instinct was to run away. "Don't run," Eileen insisted, "stick up for yourself and fight." In her battling Irish way, learned surely from her seven brothers, she had me down on the floor, wrestling and tussling with her. Of the many school fights I later got into, I didn't win a single one. But the fact that I had stood my ground, waving my fists about, somehow counted. My classmates may have had their reasons for wanting my blood—the nervous energy, for one, I exuded. But every one of those who pummeled me thereafter accepted me as his friend.

My newborn brother Peter was Eileen's principal charge. Despite his demands on her time, she treated me with warmth and respect. Whenever I asked a question, no matter how banal, she always answered it truthfully. Some, like her explanation of how babies were made, ran through me like water. But much of the rest sticks, her fervent Catholicism, her love of all things Irish and contempt for the British. My affection for the countryside and for those who gouge a living from it stems directly from her. She was the first to suggest, seeing me engrossed in Kenneth Roberts' *Northwest Passage*, that maybe I should think of a career as a writer. Being Mother's assistant cannot have been easy. Shouldn't she have paid more attention to my wretched table manners? But for all her cavils Mother told me she had never known a finer servant. As for me, I'm eternally grateful.

Eileen's charges, Peter and Stephen, six and eight years younger than I, were each other's best friends until adolescence set in. But Merrill and I were intensely competitive, because our parents insisted on stirring up, if not provoking us, two little terriers squabbling for their scraps. As the older, I believed that seniority carried its perks: new togs, a shiny bicycle, all that. Mister "Me Too," as Merrill was known, naturally resented the hand-me-downs he had to wear, the rusted bike he pedaled when I graduated to something fancier.

To Merrill, little Stephen must have seemed a new kind of dormouse. He didn't dip him in a pot of tea when he became obstreperous, but he was not above stuffing him away in a drawer, or, better yet, dangling him by his little heels over the great well of the staircase from our fourth floor banister.

The railings surrounding the stairwell vortex exerted a fatal attraction over Merrill. He was always perfecting, extending to a greater height, his imaginary stairway toboggan run. Inevitably the moment came when, arms out, he leaned too far into the second floor turn by the library and fell in a pool of blood and shattered teeth on the entryway's marble floor below.

At this point who should open the front door but Stephen's hated piano teacher, Miss Rooks, she of the enormous mole on her breast. She took one look at Merrill and promptly keeled over in a faint. When little Stephen emerged from the dining room moments later, there were his two greatest enemies, both collapsed on the foyer floor. By what miracle had he wrought this? Not too long thereafter, the doctor came by, as doctors did in those days. He picked up Merrill's scattered teeth and wedged them back in his gums. To our astonishment, they re-rooted themselves.

The two year difference was enough for Merrill and me to grow up on both sides of the television divide. Looking up from a book, I'd find him crouched before our new black-and-white set watching the dyed blond wrestler, Gorgeous George, in hopes of coming up with an unanswerable hold. But when Merrill started to take piano lessons, I insisted on learning as well, even though I lacked Merrill's fabulous ear. He was able to identify by name any ten notes I struck, or play back a melody heard at a Young People's concert.

To our mother, though, we were two chips off the same dynastic block, to be poured into matching sailor suits and marched down to 70 Pine Street where we inspected the ticker tape and, in tribute to Father away on his carrier, sang "Anchors Aweigh." Or, for our school's mid-winter Pierrot show, because of our extraordinary resemblance to one another, made to act out the Stevenson ditty:

> I have a little shadow
> That goes in and out with me;
> But what can be the use of him
> Is more than I can see.

How humiliating for Merrill all that must have been!

Robin, Merrill, on Robin's tricycle, Southampton, 1941

The trouble with Merrill, as with me, lay in the inflexibility of our assigned role. We had our blazers, our short pants, our closet of suits and were expected to be always properly turned out, as if in training for some adult 'best-dressed' award. In our forest of conformity we small apples could not fall far from the family tree. In time, with greater upper body brawn (Charlie Merrill's basically), Merrill would become the better athlete and better game player. And he was more physical, as he gloriously demonstrated night after night banging his head outside our new governess's bedroom wall until she finally caved and quit.

In those days Merrill's tactic was to provoke me into smacking him so he could exact some sympathy from our parents. In their book, though, what counted was performance—grades, trophies, teams—and their system of rewards ran my way. Like many an older brother, I got to go places and try out things. And they talked to me. After a meal Merrill had alone with Father at Le Pavillon, I remember his saying as he lay weeping in his bed, "You know, he talked to me. For the first time in my life he actually talked to me." Merrill was sixteen at the time.

SOUTHAMPTON

New York is where I lived and went to school nine months of the year, but Southampton, a fashionable resort on the south fork of Long Island, is where the life I would make for myself began. In the city I was one more kid acquiring the smarts he needed to make it as a grown-up. In Southampton I lived each day in its marvelous fluidity. To see a friend, all I had to do was hop on my tricycle (with gas rationed there were few cars to be feared). There seemed nowhere we couldn't play, out in the wind and along the margins of what was then one of the Atlantic's whitest beaches.

What defined Southampton and stamped my young dreams was the presence of water. With less than four miles separating the ocean on one side and Peconic Bay on the other, Southampton was a virtual island, a maze of ponds and brackish creeks. Wherever I swam, I paddled, I sailed, I encountered a mirror; one that, try as I might, I could never breach. For a small child, water is always suspect and I never knew whether any of the creatures it teemed with, the snapping turtle the size of our coffee table, the swans whose wings could break a grown man's back, the hammerhead shark lurking out at a sandbar, the U-boat reported 15 miles down the coast, might up and spirit me away. Scarier still, were the storms bringing it to a boil. Did any force pack the wallop of the 1938 hurricane which created the inlet where I sailed?

It was more than the mists and the amplitude of bathing possibilities that made Southampton a must on a socialite's calendar. Arriving from the flat potato fields and bleak pine barrens of central Long Island you were struck by green barriers: the elm and maple-lined lanes and, most Southampton, the privet hedges. A friend called the village, "Big Hedges." Nowhere else have I encountered hedges so high, so defining.

Behind the hedges, buried in a blur of green at the end of a gravel driveway, lay the houses. The structures might vary from low-ceilinged shingle cottages put up as long ago as 1640 to the block-long mansions that dominated the dunes. You never thought of them as having contents, only windows: views out over perennial gardens and lawns; the vivid green of a cattail-fringed marsh; the cobalt blue of a late summer pond.

In the old world the oligarchy barricaded themselves behind iron gates, moats and high stone walls. In the new, we defended ourselves with terrifying vacancies of lawn. Against it the intruder, the child with his bike and binoculars, the visitor in his sedan advancing up the gravel driveway, couldn't help but feel conspicuous. On what business could he be challenging the right manifested everywhere—in the raised glance of a gardener, in the yelping of Labradors and the barrage of "No Trespassing" signs—of a family to its own privacy?

The big estates hailed from a time when a mercantile prince's house was a self-sufficient island. Charlie Merrill's pile, "The Orchard," was of this order. To my enchanted eyes it had just about everything: an old-fashioned icehouse, extensive chicken and turkey coops, a pair of cows keeping us furnished in milk and ice cream; a great kennel of yelping flame-colored setters, the progeny of "Mike," whose life-sized portrait adorned the entrance hall. Behind the house, classic columns led the eye into a huge three-sectioned garden, flanked by wisteria-hung pergolas and ornamented with Roman goddesses and copper fountains bubbling within a labyrinth of formal boxwood. Until I came upon the Alhambra in my twenties, I had never seen anything more paradisiacal.

Charlie's Southampton house

It was the lawn off the lateral wing's card room that stunned visitors. In a society that worshipped lawns, not leading anywhere, just extending between you and the others, this was the greenest vacancy going. Broad as a ballfield, the lawn ran the entire length of the 16-acre property before ending in a row of maples and a containing hedge. The problem, of course, was what use to turn it to, and with a mischievous smile Grandpa would encourage suggestions—a driving or archery range? Eventually his third wife, Kinta, installed, in line with the card room, a croquet court. Against the immensity of the lawn, the white hoops stood out like a wondrously distant sailboat regatta.

To the casual visitor a house like Charlie's could seem the last word in opulent beauty. But beauty on such a scale is rarely pure, and to me now, it all seems part of the non-stop charade our family lived. In a working-class family a man sells his labor, indenturing himself so many hours a day. But once the whistle blows he is free to lead something that may be called a life. In a mercantile family the pretense never stops. You are at it 24 hours a day. Everyone is constantly playing a role of appearing successful and therefore credit-worthy. Some, of course, do it better than others. They become the company chairmen.

Behind the household name there may lurk little more than a man and his word. For some, that was enough. They took in the sincere blue eyes, the firm handshake and the made-to-order suit and staked the 26-year-old Charlie Merrill to the two-month personal loan he needed. Usually, though, bankers require more: guarantees, hostages. That's where a firstborn son fits in. You serve as a kind of guarantee.

In a family business the notion of permanence—"you're going to be dealing with me and my brood until the end of time"—can never be true over the long run. Among all the debts, the divorcing wives, the competing children, there is much that can and will go wrong. But as Minos of Crete discovered long ago, you can create much of the needed illusion, of acres and acres of greenbacks rolling away to the near horizon, through the device of a showpiece palace.

Somewhere below his palace at Knossos lay the sacred labyrinth where Minos's adopted son, the Minotaur, spent his days and nights. Many have pictured this prison-sanctum as composed of a maze of paths, intersecting and spreading out like fans or twisted like a ball of twine. But not all prisons are walled; as André Gide maintained, so far as appearances went, the labyrinth did not differ from the rest of the palace grounds. What kept the monster from wandering off and scaring others was an invisible barrier of carefully vetted smells, tactile sensations, and sounds. He was drugged, Gide claimed, by the sensual beauty of his surroundings.

The essential, for his minders, was that the son and heir of a family concern should look happy; or, if that was asking a bit much, wondrously idle. To a visiting grandee, the appearance that the young man reveled in his gilded confinement constituted proof enough that the family enterprise was that miracle, an enduringly sound investment. To this end the master of pleasure was encouraged to take up a variety of pursuits, one more consuming than the last: court tennis, skiing, polo, falconry, grouse shooting, motorcar and sailboat racing. The great number made it all the more unlikely he would ever excel in any one. Rather a certain proficiency was expected—the perfect weekend guest.

By the time he came of age the son and heir may have grasped that the promised succession was a sham and that he was effectively immured. Wherever he turned, he came up against a wall—of money—the vast amounts needed to maintain him in his accustomed finery, hobbies, houses, divorces. To be sure, there was a generous allowance, a harbinger of what might one day be his outright. But no capital was actually forthcoming. It was to be controlled, in his "best interest," by experts in the matter, the lackeys in service to the mercantile potentate.

When the time came to seek gainful employment, the potentate made a point of reminding the son and heir that his talents were such that there was only outfit able to pay the inordinate wage his life style required—the family firm.

"But it's the same old labyrinth!" the son and heir protested.

Still all the power lay on his father's side, including access to the money tap. Not that the potentate ever expected anyone to succeed him, much less his son. He merely wanted him tethered to a desk where he could be pointed to as the upcoming generation. Not only did it keep the lad out of harm's way, but the princely wage could be read as a sign of corporate solvency, one only the most prosperous of firms could afford. There, for as long as directed, the Minotaur remained, effectively immured.

In the middle of nowhere there was reason enough for a dinosaur-sized country estate. As transportation improved and land values soared, the burden of providing labyrinths shifted to a new institution, the Club. The more elaborate the club life, the more exclusive the resort. The ability to afford it all—golf, polo, tennis, bridge, yachting—became as good an indication as any of a mogul's status.

Father understood this quite well. In our cost-conscious household where there was never a light bulb left ablaze, everyone was always after Father to cut back on his memberships. Did he really need a hundred, since he only set foot in a few of them from one year to the next? But Father felt about clubs the way Imelda Marcos must have felt about shoes, and my refusal to join at his expense a Harvard social club flabbergasted him. For what else but making connections with the right "brothers" was I attending that august university?

During my childhood Southampton looked, for five days of a week, like a rural village. Land values were still low enough that there remained a scattering of farms, barns, potato fields, duck-breeding ponds, and even a horse-riding stable with trails through the woods. Other than mothers, nannies, Polish gardeners, domestic servants, and the usual beachside bunch of Labradors and Setters, there were few people about. Nor was there all that much to do, as far as organized activities went. Sometimes all we did was sit around a radio's play-by-play ballgame, imagining us as fellow players, cleverly sliding base-stealers, touring tennis bums.

Then after five days of rural peace, if that's what it was, the Friday "Cannonball" train would arrive and the superstars of the Business and Society Pages would troop in with their weekend guests, bringing their inevitable Big City excitement, tension and fear. It was for this all week long we had been mowing lawns, practicing forehands and backhands and all the rest of it. For the next 48 hours an intricate and sometimes newsworthy social life sprang up, since who entertained whom and what they wore concerned seemingly everyone: from the lucky participants themselves to the shops and fashion emporia they patronized, and even finally the man or woman in the street poring over the gossip columns to deduce what they could of the glitterati's shifting alliances.

For the first two summers, after returning east from San Francisco, we rented: the cottage that's now the village museum, dating from 1644. With its low ceilings and tiny windows, I remember it as insufferably hot and dark. A summer later, we took a picturesque windmill on the ocean end of Lake Agawam, well situated between the Beach and Meadow clubs. But transporting the household gear we needed in a big moving van back and forth from the city could come to seem counter-productive and in 1941 Mother acquired the house on Cooper's Neck where we would live until I was twenty-one.

Deferentially, she called it "Little Orchard." Only in respect to my grandfather's pile could a 12-bedroom house with 8 acres of surprisingly varied grounds be deemed little. The house stood in the middle of the property, but it was so surrounded by privet, by stands of towering *Cryptomeria,* ancient maples and beeches, that you were not aware how very large it was; unless you could see the peaked roof over its third story, visible from the Beach Club a mile away. It accommodated all of us generously, but I always felt it was more a house to escape from, than to be in. Each outside door seemed to open onto a different lawn, another thickness of turf.

Felix, Robin, Paros, 1970

I knew those textures because, from the age of six, I had to work an hour a day in the garden for a 25-cent wage. Nor could I go anywhere until I had put in my hour's work. For Father it was a way of imprinting his work ethic: a boy lucky enough to be born with certain advantages should not allow himself to become lazy. And the property, with the big "victory garden" we maintained during the war years, was more than the single gardener we employed could manage.

At first my work consisted of helping John, the Russian and German-speaking Pole who lived with his wife and black-and-white schnauzer in the cottage-garage fronting on the road. I raked leaves and smoothed the gravel driveway, picked vegetables and berries for the table and cut flowers for the house; anything so as not to have to weed, or pick dandelions and crabgrass out of the lawns.

When I was nine, I graduated to the power mower, which had a starting cord I was not strong enough to pull on my own. I remember the pride with which I bent and pulled and figure-eighted towards an ever-diminishing center so the lawn would look perfect for Father's Friday evening inspection. Those words of praise were the high point of my week.

Among my playmates each of our parents' properties had its function; the size and varied mystery of ours suited the games of hide-and-seek tag we played. Home and prisoner base were at the bottom of the lily pond a few feet from the lake. Those defending home base counted to a hundred while we fanned out. By the time they opened their eyes I'd most likely be out by the back of the house and on one of the two gravel driveways. The idea, as in guerilla warfare, was to lure our pursuers far from the lake and home base, Then, while they were chasing a will-of-the-wisp from one hedge hole to the next, the rest of us would infiltrate through the shrubbery until, at a signal, we all converged on an undermanned home base.

Of the two driveways I preferred the service one, as I had only to crawl through a hedge to be in the Rose Garden. There I could melt into the dense *Cryptomeria* that flanked the lawn's sides, crawling further and further in until everything around was black. Nearby feet would rustle, voices would call, and I would go on gaining back the breath I had expended running until I could feel my way out by one or another tunnel and down to home base.

I subjected the property birds to endless hours of hide-and-seek. I had first become aware of them when Mother placed a chart of the 20 most common birds on our bedroom wall. Another child might have closed his eyes and allowed them to fade back into the surrounding wallpaper. I couldn't, and before long I was completely fixated. The radiator would squeak and I'd rush outside, convinced some new wonder had alighted.

At first I birded on our grounds. But other than the usual robins and grackles there wasn't much to see, and I soon found myself, Alice-like, crawling through a gap in our hedge into an overgrown 8-acre lot. The lot was infested with tick-laden brambles, with stumps and clumps of ragged vine maples here and there. To a child, though, it seemed a magic wilderness. I never knew what I might find next.

To identify creatures as small and elusive as birds, you normally need binoculars. But my parents must have felt that expensive prisms weren't to be entrusted to a child. Their chromosomes, however, had resulted in two mismatched eyes: the right slightly far-sighted and the left so myopic it had no way of telling what was about. Squinting with my good eye, I would do my best to assemble the elements of the flitting mosaic—rump, wing patch, eye ring, lores, mandible—into a memorable pattern. Then with my reading eye I would pore through the folio-sized *Birds of America* I had retrieved from my grandfather's Beach House library, comparing the vivid tones I remembered with the plates Audubon had painted from shot specimens a century earlier.

I would press forward in my dripping sneakers and short pants, feeling my shadow sticking close, my breath's hushed pointing toward a silhouette, the size of a nugget, gleaming in a far treetop. Without binoculars, how was I to identify it, while all but invisible, the bird twittered and called? How but by imagining I could become myself that bird flitting from leaf to light to song-lit perch? I saw, no, I was the ripple on the lake where a pied-billed grebe dove and surfaced, stretching it to silk again. Then I was off to the next bush of waiting cardinal flame. "Nowhere to go but up!" I'd exult, flat on my back atop an ancient root as I scanned the treetops for a vireo eye-stripe.

What could my quarry have surmised as this crashing child blundered about? Hard to persuade them I was not some oversized cat, or a new form of bulldozer. As their pursuer I sensed my own intrusion; I had no business disturbing their efforts to feed. Eventually, this sense reduced me to the thinnest quiet as I crept along—a dime in a vase of wind. Only one aspect counted—color. Above, color shifted, color sang. Color may even have been me crying out in mute submission, "Let me be you, little gem, in my next life, just stay put until I've named you." Was that the gold my wings glistened with, as if by craning my neck a degree more I'd no longer be this robin-named boy, but a new bit of ore on a bough?

Out in mid-lake we children had our own island. For an exploring child, the island was quite scary, wondering at each step whether I was going to disappear down a quicksand quagmire and never be heard from again. At the end of our first summer, Mother had the island's shrubbery levelled and erected a plank bridge with guardrails so we and our friends could wheel our bicycles over to the Meadow Club on the far side and onto the Beach Club in more safety than the road at the far end of the lake encouraged. With the bridge came a log cabin out of the F.A.O. Schwarz toy store on 57th Street in Manhattan. We shared it with a nest of hornets who never once stung us as we sat directly beneath them, playing board games on a little table.

On the island we maintained a vegetable garden. With Eileen's considerable help we turned it over, spade by heavy spade. For fertilizer we harvested the swan droppings, left that year on the tip of our island. We grew strawberries, carrots, and soil-improving beans, as well as Irish potatoes in honor of Eileen. By then I was reading gift books from my Uncle Charles: Douglas Fairchild's *The World was my Garden* and Louis Bromfield's *Malabar Farm*. The dream of a tiny farm corresponded more to a need of Eileen's than mine. But the island did give a base on which I could project a longing for the kind of rural satisfactions Eileen had known in the "old country."

Merrill, Robin, in their rowboat, named after Father's carrier, 1943

COMING OF AGE ON THE CONTINENT

The great divide of my childhood occurred in 1949 as I was going on thirteen, when Mother took us to Italy for the summer. Before going abroad, I honestly believed there was no better place in the whole globe in which to grow up than Southampton. Its skies were me, its ocean waves, me, its hundreds of grasses, me. By the time I returned, 13 months later, something new had altered everything. It was as if I had stepped by a magic causeway from a country island into a vast treasure chest of century piled upon century, one maze after another of stairs, squares, peekaboo arches, all leading back, back, into worlds of otherness and difference.

The chameleon in me felt challenged by how people lived: could I make myself into a peasant, a fisherman, a café waiter? I studied how they went about it, their hands fluttering earnestly as they jabbered, their almost gliding gaits, as if a walker could be the ripple of a line thrown forward. To that end I outfitted myself with phrase books and verb manuals, as if the ability to claw my way inward on the ladder of the language would allow me to penetrate to the spoken heart of a new reality.

In the cities to which my parents took me, Florence, Rome, Venice, I was free to ramble wherever I wished. And I, that hyper-alert Manhattan child, sticking out uncomfortably in a subway seat, or birding in the Bronx's Van Cortland Park, was now someone almost invisible, a tourist. With the lightest of baggage I proceeded from one marvel to the next, never knowing what I might stumble upon. After being confined in Gotham, running an errand, making an appointment, here was historical space and, like a bird released, I flew singing away.

The further I flew, the more at ease I felt. Gone was all the twisting and untwisting of a necktie, hands flailing in every unlikely direction as I stammered. I was not deracinated so much as starting out anew, in a different culture, yet one that allowed me to remain that same open-mouthed child, startled by a flash of wings, a squeak hiding in the branches, craning my neck towards a name newly alit.

Like everything Mother undertook, our summer abroad was meticulously organized. She wanted it to be the same complete seduction Italy had been for her as a 17-year-old studying in Florence. The previous November, she had sailed by herself all the way to Genoa for the sole purpose of renting a suitable villa. This turned out to be the first three floors of the Contessa di Robilant's lemon-colored palace, rising from a rock over the sea in Rapallo. Leaving the staffing to a friend, she returned to New York to prepare for the great removal. By June, the last props in place, we sailed off: Mother, four boys, a tutor, and 13 steamer trunks. One of the trunks contained nothing but medical supplies; a second bulged with pink toilet paper—Mother did not trust the Italians in this department; a third, cigarette cartons, a form of barter. Immediately, at the Franco-Italian border the cartons came in handy in placating the *douaniers* who wanted to confiscate an item they had discovered in another trunk—yes, the pink toilet paper.

To transport our gear we brought a behemoth De Soto station wagon. It aroused virtual awe, if not downright worship, wherever we stopped. Nothing in my experience had prepared me for the sensuous bombardment of post-war Ligurian Italy: the terraced grape-and-olive heights rising out of the sea; the creamy azure skies; the pink, raspberry, apricot stucco of the tenements; to say nothing of the beauty, the well-being the people themselves exuded. All the same, the effect might have been less consuming had Mother not been so present, guiding, pointing, exclaiming. Before long I, too, was smitten.

Why my heart couldn't contain both Southampton and Rapallo—as Mother's did—I can't explain. Inexperience is the best I can offer. And Rapallo in 1949 was still the Rapallo that had enchanted Pound, Yeats, and Beerbohm, not to mention Mussolini, whose gutted palace overlooked the adjoining cove.

We swam right off the villa's rock, climbing to a projecting pinnacle and plunging headfirst from there, over the hissing brine and the spines of the clinging sea-urchins. For sport there was tennis on the Casino's red clay, with high bouncing balls and ball boys to retrieve them. Across the bay at Santa Margherita we kept a starfish sailboat, now and then anchoring it off our rock. Out at the point, two villages further west, lay Portofino with its red and green fisherman's dinghies and horseshoe-shaped jewel of a harbor. From there we would climb up and up a several hundred-step staircase cut in the rock to an unbelievable restaurant with views stopped only by the opposing headland.

With Mother as guide we traveled to Florence, a city I came to know site by site in a way I had never known New York. When at the beginning of August Father arrived, our expeditions extended to Rome for fittings with his two tailors; to Milan, Bellagio, and across the Dolomites to the tapestry in stone that is Venice. Everywhere, buoyed by a dollar then at its acme, we shopped: silk ties and dress shirts; calf-bound books for me; brocade fabrics, antique gilt chairs, inlaid marble coffee tables and, of course, the leather suitcases to cart it all home.

Not all our treasures reached home. There was Father's white gabardine suit. He had just collected it from his Roman tailor and was wearing it next day in Orvieto when he made the mistake of lunching next to me at a trattoria. A particularly expressive flash of my hand and a glass of Chianti spilled, ruining the suit in a way he was never to forget, much less forgive. To him the spill was tantamount to a bloodstain. A Minotaur had gored him. Whenever afterwards we sat down together, he and I knew the fate we were tempting. What we didn't know was that in Italy a spilled glass carries magical properties. "Si porta fortuna," our waiter remarked, a consoling smile on his face as he deftly laid out a new tablecloth and steered Father, salt shaker in hand, to the gents. As even Father ruefully acknowledged, from that time on he was a fulfilled man, number two and heir apparent at Merrill Lynch or Safeway, as he wished. Our summer in Italy was for him, indeed for all of us, the high water mark in our life as a family.

Our Italian summer, unrepeated miracle as it proved (Mother would always regret not having taken advantage of the high dollar to add a Tuscan villa to her string), had come into being as a solution to my graduating from St. Bernard's at the age of twelve, not too young to attend Phillips Exeter Academy, which had accepted me, but too young, Father knew, to stand a chance of eventually earning a varsity letter. Realizing how vital to a boy's self-esteem that could be, he decided to "redshirt" me for a year by sending me to Le Rosey, a privately owned Swiss school for boys aged nine to eighteen. There I could make a start at acquiring the language skills that had eluded him. And the school, alternating between Rolle on the Lake of Geneva and the Bernese Alps of Gstaad in the winter, with a cast of princelings drawn from some 27 nationalities, sounded as if it might stretch me in some of the right directions.

Yet there was, Mother felt, such a thing as being overstretched. A boy who had never been away from home for longer than two weeks couldn't be expected to land in Geneva and make his own way with all his luggage to Rolle and his new school. If I had to be accompanied, why not make the transition easier by renting a villa on the Italian Riviera for the summer?

Robin, Marcia, Marcia's mother, at the Sounion temple, Greece, 1962

Ingenuous, yet perfectly compatible with the "Let's move the swimming pool" side of Mother's character. Better yet, she did me the kindness, after the rest of the family had departed, of taking me by train to Lausanne and, after an overnight stay at the Beau Rivage Palace, depositing me at Le Rosey. For Mother, the prospect of not seeing me for another six months unleashed a flood of tears far worse than what had flowed after launching me at six on my first school bus. Some friends took one look at her, propped on a bar stool at the Beau Rivage, and prescribed a very stiff dry martini. For once, she confided, it helped.

Of anywhere on the globe, Switzerland with its 700-year history of glittering neutrality might seem one of the safer places to deposit a child. But in 1949—the height of the Cold War—the country felt awfully close to the Iron Curtain's Russian tanks. I remember Father advising me how, should the Soviets invade, I was to strike out for the Pyrenees. (To the end of his life Father was convinced war with the Soviets was inevitable. When my brother asked why he remained on the board of the Naval PX stores, a chore he clearly despised, he replied, "When the war breaks out, I want to have some influence so you and your brothers can be officers in the Navy.")

Before sending me off, Father had taken advantage of a car ride into Genoa—for a fitting, of course—to explain what sexual intercourse involved. I, who still believed babies were things created under cabbage leaves, could not have been more dumbfounded. If Father set sex on an impossibly remote pedestal, a risk a man submitted a woman to only when both wanted a baby, I, at least, stood forewarned.

Their misgivings were well founded. For the first weeks I was homesick enough to unleash a torrent of letters to godparents, family servants, a head gardener's wife, anybody. It did not help that my Italian roommate took a disliking to something about me—the different suits I donned each day?— and started popping away at me with his BB gun. I coped easily enough by ducking under the covers. When he began threatening me with a belt, I requested a transfer. That landed me with three fellow Americans, not what I had come for, but hard to avoid in a school dominated by our imperial dollar. More sexually mature, they spent much of their free time secluded in their respective closets.

I don't know quite what it was, the temptation presented by our pretty Italian maids, the nearness of Geneva with its prostitutes, or simply the hothouse atmosphere generated by so many as yet un-crashed, un-burned stars of the Almanach de Gotha, but the student body exuded a randiness the likes of which I've never encountered elsewhere. I learned never to stoop over a drinking faucet, or a foosball machine, without first cupping a protective hand to my parts. We all moved with a karate-like readiness, lest a paw reach out and, with a chortle of triumph, claim a prisoner.

On the academic side our teachers were as memorable for their eccentricities as for any wisdom dispensed. The curriculum ran on the continental model, a dozen or so courses a term. But it could include such useful oddities as a yearlong history of the French revolution and its imperial aftermath. And the best teacher I ever encountered, Signor Mastelli, combined intimidation with a stingy marking system, "Good work, you've earned a 3.8 (out of a possible 10)" to such effect I was eventually competing with native Italians. It might have been worth staying on a third year just for his Dante.

STRANGER IN A STRANGE SOUTHAMPTON

In going abroad I had crossed one kind of threshold. When I returned 13 months later, I learned that my friends had undergone a more telling transformation. They still convened every afternoon at the Meadow Club. Only now it was with their girls among ashtrays, pop bottles and overstuffed couches in a plush sitting room. In the evening the scene transferred to a dune and became a "party," a word pronounced with a sacrosanct intonation, as if it would not do to arrive all by myself on a bicycle.

I had barely settled in when I found on my doorstep a delegation of my old playmates come to welcome me back. They told me about the summer of mat-riding I had missed, the sand bar extending out from the Beach Club barrels for several hundred yards, giving the kind of rides you see on Hawaiian postcards. On calm days they could see, looming beneath them, the rusting farm implements of the previous century, a sign of how far the seas had risen.

A kind and impressive gesture, but would they have come if they had not sensed how dislocated I felt? Yet, even alone, I might have been welcomed among the blankets and cigarettes of a dune could I have found a way of downplaying what I had undergone. Of course my old friends would ask, "What's it like over there, tell us!" But as I rattled on about the radiant skies, the plunging views, the narrow cobbled scooter-loud streets, I could see their eyes glazing over. They didn't want to know; just being a teenager was difficult enough. Yet it was precisely those comparisons, of place, of style, of attitude, I wasn't willing to renounce. They constituted the one distinction I had.

All the same it might be wondered what, in a year of foreign schooling, I had learned. Certainly not the French for which I had been sent. Before coming home I had persuaded my parents of my need for a second year. Those two years, along with the traveling and people I met on the month-long vacation breaks, rather disoriented me.

Among the disorientations were the sensationally divorced and now married Ingrid Bergman and Roberto Rossellini. We had been taken to their Roman home by some producer friends of Mother's. I was too young to appreciate the rarity of Ingrid's beauty. But I did get on with the director of "Open City." He told me how he had filmed it, walking, camera in hand, among the retreating German tanks. The next night, they invited me back—by myself! Was it a way of allowing my parents a romantic night out on a Tiberian dance floor? Probably. But for a gangly, acne-pitted 14-year-old, dinner with them could seem rather special.

Robin, Greece, 1965

One year abroad could be discounted by my friends; not a second. Where before my dreams had been exclusively American—to see all 650 species of our native birds—now I found myself straddling a more problematic divide. Would I ever wake from the enchantment of Europe? Or was that earlier existence a dream and these new girlfriends the reality? If so, what had brought about these changed circumstances? Was it I by taking too big a bite out of Mother's Mediterranean apple? Or my pals who now found me hopelessly immature? Either way, the verdict registered.

Compounding my bewilderment were the changes Southampton was undergoing. Up to then life had been relatively low-key. The cars were jalopies you didn't mind seeing rust away in the salt air. The big houses were strictly for summer occupancy and the dress style was informal—sweaters with holes, baggy slacks, sensible shoes.

Now, after twenty lean years, came the 1949–51 stock market boom. There was no way, as Father said, not to make money. But some fared better than others. What brave new world were they to conquer? Southampton was a mere three hours away from Manhattan and here they were muscling in on our life. They came in droves. Where I had my eight friends, my younger brothers commonly attended parties of forty to fifty.

For all our efforts to barricade ourselves behind new five-acre zoning, village life changed. Out went all that spoke of country life—the potato fields, the duck farms, the riding stables—and up went the mansions. Much of the development took place on the periphery, but it affected us too. When the next door eight- acre lot where I birded came on the market, Father bought it "to preserve our privacy." He could have left it the thorn-riddled, tick- infested wasteland it was. But that wasn't Father. He had been bitten by the English bug of lawn, Capability Brown's rolling immensities, and wanted a green sward stretching into the ocean mists.

By the following summer everything had been bulldozed. My grandfather's gift of a maple-lined *allée*—to commemorate a 15-year "wood" wedding anniversary—lined a new formal entrance driveway. Where before our house, shielded by a long hedge and towering trees, had come as a surprise, now it loomed head-on in all its 12 bedroom pomp. To accommodate the added acreage, our grounds changed as well. The future knight wanted the five shrubbery-filled fingers of lawn that reached from the house down to the lake fused into an immaculate palm. Mower in hand, like a battering ram, we sons obliged, blasting forward and hauling back until the last vestige of shrub had been liquidated. A green vista may thrive in England's moist gardening climate. But on sandy loam, a quarter mile from the sea, all that sprouts is crabgrass. Where before there was a mystery of shrubbery separated by secret lawns, a book with no end of pages to flip through, now there was only the great eye of the sun staring in on our vacancy.

After buying the Beach House from my grandfather, my parents decided to sell our Cooper's Neck house. They saw no point in maintaining two estates, and the Beach House had the two essentials we lacked—swimming pool and tennis court—on a highly prominent site next to the Beach Club. "You are selling my childhood," Stephen, all of eleven, lamented. But we older siblings understood. The grounds we had romped in were gone. There was no way of restoring what we ourselves had destroyed.

What applied to us, our failure of character as it was, held for Southampton. To a visitor from the city, the village, with its ever-changing play of water and sky, its shingled houses picked out in the seaside light, may have looked pastoral, an embodiment of the good life. But it wasn't pastoral, because it remained so exclusive. And exclusivity brought a buzz none of us succeeded in silencing. It made us adolescents restless, unable to countenance being alone another minute. It sent wives in their pastel outfits scurrying into town where they might meet outside the post office and confer. If nothing was going on, hopefully their very eagerness would create something, a party, a foursome for golf or bridge. Ours was a society in which conspicuous activity had to be maintained from morning to night.

The energy fueling the frenetic activity was money, money, money. By the end of a weekend I'd be hearing it in my sleep, dripping off the tongue, a little wave rolling over and over up the driveway. It was as if everything—the lawn you were standing on, the landscaped trees that framed it, the wives and their children—was quantifiable and, among us natives, an appraising eye sharply assessed the going values.

THE MINIATURE MASTURBATOR

In my isolation I became a young animal in rut. The adolescent shore loomed and, as I hurtled down toward it, a buxom pillow in lieu of a surfing mat wedged between my thighs, I felt a new male identity hardening under me. Who was I? In my need the straddled pillow became hope itself decked out in feminine allurements. As the invoked goddesses multiplied—no earth mother too vast, no witch too skeletal—I became aware of something uniquely my own: an imagination, wondrously compliant. Surrounded as I was by family males and all-boy schools, I could not help but see women as a distinct species, with different goals, habits, ways of being, talking and communicating. Much of my later life would be spent trying to assimilate the otherness they represented; to become, through their agency, a more rounded person.

At that stage I was reduced to narcissism; to knowing them in myself. One way was to paw through Mother's drawers in search of her magic accoutrements: chignons of hair, douche bags, nylon stockings, lace panties, girdles, garter belts, the variously lifted and cupped bras, and most embracing of all, the transparent couture negligees. Then, a pair of tennis balls inserted in a bra and head wrapped in an androgynous towel, I would stand in her mirror-walled bathroom contemplating a new female self somehow predisposed to love me and no one but me till the end of my days. In bed later, that mirrored image became Aphrodite of a thousand shapes as I straddled the bed pillow, imploring it to do no more than gently canter while I prolonged things as best I could.

As a boy of ten, I had felt suspicious of girls and their ways. I was bent on becoming a man, and felt it was with my fellows I should associate. My bias was so pronounced that Mother decided to enroll me in dancing school. "Girls, yuck," I protested, "only sissies like girls." Over my protests I was buttoned into a blazer and tie and bundled off to the ballroom of the Pierre. Of all my city activities, dancing school is the one I still think about: the Lolitas in their blouses and flaring skirts, scented flesh within an inch or two as I steered. The lessons brought a new unsuspected way of moving—and being with. Not that I was particularly adept at the steps, the box that, arms extended and raised, I had to convert to a round fluency. As if the quick-quick-slow of the fox trot were a wave and there, on its crest, right hand in the small of her back, were the two of us, a couple gliding ever so slightly ahead of the next looming beat. The steps, so restricting at first, conferred a freedom within which all illusions were encouraged, even that of flight itself. For a moment, maybe, held, sustained in the rhythmed flow, a female consciousness took me over. I understood what stepping backwards permitted—the gaining of a welcome leverage from which to sail out past all the surrounding congestion. I felt like a primitive who, having spent all his days on a single plane propelling him forwards, suddenly discovers that going backwards offers a delicious alternative. As does swaying between the two, neither of you quite knowing what will happen next, but nonetheless balanced, supremely with each other, ready.

The intimacy I knew on the dance floor was not one I could translate into my dating life. I was at the acme of my powers, exuding semen from a seemingly encyclopedic fount. But between the opulence of my fantasies and the meager village reality lay a considerable divide. A Minotaur might be greeted with open arms at a cotillion, especially one who adored waltzing. But he might not be whom you wanted pawing you in the black of a movie theater. Add the hazards of petting, the female obstacle course of straps, buttons, hooks, and one might understand—barely—why I spent the better part of two summers sprawled in the dunes besides one future fashion Woman of the Year without ever embracing her for fear of shattering the experienced image she allowed me to think I was projecting.

In a milieu where even the grass articulated greenbacks, a would-be rake could wish to reverse the Midas touch. By reaching out and breaking through the sexual chasm, couldn't I restore the disorderly wilderness? That was my question as I glided in my new Italian walk, a knowing smile on my lips, round and round the Beach Club porches: past the swimming pool's cleavages, up into the guzzling, tippling, half-naked terraces and down onto the baking, body-by-body outlined, strapless sand. It was all there, the most paradisiacal of weekday feasts spread before this one lone male and for some inexplicable reason it was unavailable. Why? Why? Why?

Does a kid finally grow out of a town? Or is breaking with it something that just happens? You look one day and it's no longer there. Or it has becomes so crumbled up and revolting you can't bear to take part in it. There were times when I even dreaded going to bed—getting out so much more exhausted than I had gotten in.

In the circumstances it does not seem odd that my frustration should be vented on a milieu that had so misled me. Anywhere else, I knew, there would be a maidservant, an older woman, a specialized prostitute willing to accommodate my voluminous urges. Nor was it exactly a desert I was living in. If Southampton was famous for anything, other than the sheer wealth packed into it, it was the allure of its women. Pick up a fashion magazine, a tabloid's society page, and there they all were, that voluptuous figure, those million dollar legs, faultlessly moving from one diamond ring, one divorce to the next.

To come of age in a town where every touch disclosed money, bought at one auction and unloaded at the next, was deceptive enough. To find that the promise which kept an adolescence throbbing—that boat with the seven edible maidens—was never going to dock, could find a Minotaur questioning his part in the ongoing charade. For what had I spent my youth preparing if no *volupt*é was ever going to alight my way? Nor did it help to be told that the real marvels are not those revealed by the lowering of a horn, the pawing of a pair of hooves; that coitus is not an act, an emission, but a dance of two bodies; or rather an emotional fusion of act and person. For my part I could not help but feel something had gotten monstrously out of hand.

HIC VENITE PUERI

"All boarding schools are prisons," I remember my youngest brother remarking as he headed off to Father's alma mater, Kent, "but it's only three years, so I'll make the best of it." Would that my three years at Phillips Exeter could have passed in an instant, or maybe a blast of wind, off the New Hampshire coast. It may have been the shock of re-entry to American life that was still affecting me, but from the moment I arrived I felt lost.

There were reasons enough. Any 700-boy boarding school might be a struggle to accept. And a rundown mill town did not offer much escape. After a brisk 3-week burst of autumnal glory winter would descend, not to let up for another half-year. There was, to be sure, black ice on the Squamscott River. You could skate upstream through otherwise impenetrable forest, clambering around little waterfalls and peering down into pebbled transparency. But soon lumpy snow would pile up, confining you to the school hockey rink.

For a while I escaped on my bicycle in the hope of finding a wintering Alcid out among the whitecaps at Hampton Beach. I even enlisted a creepy friend to take me into the forest to observe the warbler migration. He had the kind of ear that could distinguish a Tennessee from a Blackburnian. But he wouldn't stop to let me glimpse whatever name he called out. He took his birding so seriously that, a year later, he would be arraigned on a charge of garroting neighborhood cats. Not much of a crime unless you suspected people might be next. Another 15 years passed before I resumed watching birds.

Yet it was I, as Father kept reminding me, who had chosen the Academy. To an ambitious 12-year-old the country's top-ranked prep school seemed the right scholastic choice. And Exeter was competitive. With seven applicants for each place, you crammed just to stay in, while working to become one of the "wheels" around whom extra-curricular life revolved.

Old-line schools like Exeter don't acquire their endowments by educating free spirits. Rather they put you through their particular version of teenage hell. The school motto sums it up nicely, *Hic venite pueri ut viri sitis.* (You come here, kid, to be turned into a man.) As for the kind of man, you need only note the three debating societies (four, if you add the PEA senate) to see a distinct cast of mind. We were all prospective cynics, determined to avoid the embarrassment of being surprised, or, worse, astonished. It got 90 of us into nearby Harvard. At what cost, it may be asked, to our development, our understanding of styles and complexities? Yet, by not appearing to believe in anything, we remained masters of the occasion.

For myself, I was so put off that all I did the first year was to play bridge in the cellar "butt room." What drew me, I can't imagine. I didn't smoke and my rabbity concentration rarely extended beyond a single 200 point rubber. Yet there I was hanging out among the white buck shoes, khaki trousers and swept back "duck" haircuts. "How are they hanging?" one ringer invariably greeted me. A not impossible koan. Yet no response seemed to suffice. I was too daunted to fling back the "Up your ass!" he evidently required.

To my parents, bridge offered a social diversion where guests could compete without having to venture onto a conversational reef. At a high-pressure school a boy could stand out by wasting what little study time he had; at least, I wasn't being a 'greasy grind.' I may have needed a pastime that filled the hours the way tracing maps from the Britannica had as a child. Then, during the winter of my upper-middle year, my grades in English started to plummet: C+, D+, D, on successive papers. Not being a grind was one thing; flunking out, another. In some anxiety I called on my teacher, Darcy Curwen, a tall, imposing, ruddy-complexioned Englishman, with a great shock of white hair whom we regarded as the reincarnation of his much-quoted Doctor Johnson.

At Exeter teachers tended to be unapproachable outside the classroom or sports field. Recognizing this, Curwen sought to put me at ease. "I'm glad you came by, I've not had a chance to talk to you. What brings you?"

"My grades," I blurted out. "I've always performed well in English and I don't understand why I'm doing badly in your course."

"What have you been reading on your own?" Curwen asked.

I looked at him, trying to remember a time when I never went anywhere without a book in my pocket. *Freddy the Pig, Northwest Passage, The Mysterious Island, La Chartreuse de Parme, The Count of Monte Cristo.* At Exeter, the only outside books I cracked were my roommate's Mickey Spillanes. I didn't tell Curwen about Spillane, I just replied, "Before coming here I used to read every free moment I had. I guess I've gotten out of touch."

"Why don't you try this?" Curwen offered, taking *Barchester Towers* down from the shelf. Trollope's narrative pulse had me reading it compulsively. When I finished I asked Curwen for another. That turned out to be Mathew Arnold's verse novel, *Sohrab and Rustum*, lines blowing across a page. But my truancy was cured, and by the year-end I was doing well enough to be allowed two senior tutorials: in classical political theory and in French, where I read Anatole France and then Andre Gide.

As important, was the awareness I developed during a yearlong course in American history taught by Colin Irving (the novelist's father). Before taking it I was, like my parents, a little Republican. I subscribed on my own to *Barron's Monthly* and, while writing a term paper on the fateful 1952 New Hampshire presidential primary, I was rooting not for Ike, but the arch-conservative Robert Taft.

So far as exams went, the course turned on the twin hinges of the Civil War and the FDR New Deal. In a question that troubles me to this day Irving asked, how inevitable was the Civil War? Did the Union need to be preserved at horrific cost? I could fathom the cultural separateness underpinning secession—why must distinct regional entities be yoked together when they might evolve far better governed in smaller, more responsive units? More graspable was FDR's patrician response to the horrors of The Depression. I walked out of American History a convinced Democrat.

Rooming in an old shingle house on the edge of town—the setting for the play *Tea and Sympathy*—and with only two daily courses to attend, along with the tutorials, senior year proved bearable. Better yet, I had in Blaise Pasztory, a Hungarian refugee with whom I was to room for four of the next five years, a remarkable person who remains a close friend.

I did not feel close to the main currents of campus life. A boy can opt out. Yet in the course of three years I would never want to repeat, I had discovered not so much who I was, as who I wasn't: a newspaperman-turned-merchant like my Father; a leader of organizations like my mother. I didn't have their social instincts and administrative abilities. I had always loved books, but the bedazzlement of my arrival had drawn me away from them and towards activities for which I was ill-suited. Then at a crucial moment a master's perceptive interest had proved just enough to draw me back to reading and the kind of work the rest of my life would require.

VERITAS

After Exeter, Harvard seemed freedom itself. I could drop in on any course that took my fancy, attend or not attend a class. Yet, for all the midnight oil burned on their behalf, classes comprised only a fraction of what I was learning from my classmates and the Cambridge community. To be in a town where you could not ignore anyone who might address you was a distinct privilege. As was the variety on offer: foreign films at the Casablanca, perhaps 20 plays available on a weekend evening; galleries, taverns, museums, specialized bookstores, vistas opening everywhere.

There were also, for the first time in my school life, girls. Compared with the meagerness of Southampton, Radcliffe was a meadow replete with flowers of every possible distinction, one prettier, more intelligent than the last. By the end of the first week I had fallen in love with almost the entire freshman class. I memorized their yearbook photos and, despite the competition, dated as many as I possibly could.

At most universities, it is the field of concentration that matters and a student progresses gingerly from one stepping stone to the next. At Harvard it was the professor who counted, not the canvas he deigned to draw upon. From the globe's far quarters our wise men had been procured, solely, we were told, for our edification. Some departments were said to be crammed full of them, lectern upon lectern of beaming, gesticulating sages. It was these reputations we were checking out, enrolling in a major almost regretfully, because it so circumscribed the course catalogue's 200 page banquet.

Such concerns about courses, condiments, flavors, paled before the more imminent choice of a career. Each day that carried me closer to graduation only increased the panic I felt, surrounded like Tarzan in the pit, with the crouching business snakes on one side and the Southampton vacancy on the other. College, in my father's eyes, primarily existed to prepare me for a business career. From the day I was born it was assumed that I would not only go to work at Merrill Lynch, but eventually head the firm as well. While still a child Father had me propped next to him, teaching me his beloved tennis and, through it, what business itself—WINNING!—involved.

I'm not sure how well I absorbed his earnestly imparted lore. But Father thought I could fulfill most of his expectations. I could hold my liquor, don a tuxedo, and play, after a fashion, some exclusive sports. Not that he had forsaken his dream of a dynasty, of the realms five sons, working in tandem, might conquer. But such a succession had to be taken one son at a time. If he succeeded in coaxing me into my invisible cage, my brothers would presumably follow. All the same, before being handed the partnership keys, I would have to prove myself before all those corporate eyes gauging the aplomb, the studied nonchalance, with which I approached my career fences. If I could stick it out, a substantial world awaited my beckoning.

The catch lay, of course, in sticking it out. For every achieving Tartuffe, there must be thousands who, for one reason or another, disappear along the wayside. Their failures, though, may say something about the nature of money. For the scions of the rich, money makes both for an enviable luxury and a distinct uneasiness, since wealth is a toxic substance which poisons those who misuse it. In a society of image, what you resemble you become, since others can't help but treat your image as your creation. To accept my birthright I would have had to feel I was someone special. My mother could summon such princely pride. I couldn't.

To my entering college class, my dilemma was far from unique. And the gloom, not to say the fear at what awaited us in that post-McCarthy era, conditioned our choices. Asked on our freshman registration forms what professions attracted us, an amazing 70% put down "doctor." Perform a respected task and be well remunerated for it? Or had they somehow foreseen the extraordinary advances medical science would make in the next half-century? Feet thus firmly planted, the "best and brightest" went out to survive Chem 20.

Harvard's great legacy, from its ministerial beginnings, has always been one of public service. But in those gray-flannelled times, government service had come to seem the exclusive preserve of businessmen and generals. Not surprisingly we enrolled in subjects that catered to our nostalgia. Was it only by stretching, as Sontag put it, our "thin highly elastic band of irony" to something like its breaking point could an intellectual make his compromise with a culture that insisted on treating him like a stranger? That may be why, when the counterculture exploded, a number of us overaged Silent Ones rushed in. Here was an unheralded opportunity and we weren't about to let it slip by.

That a solution to career quandaries could involve recasting myself as a writer would have seemed improbable to any teacher who encountered me as a freshman. My convoluted grammar and tortured syntax struck my social science section man as positively Germanic, "worse than Carlyle," he remarked. His comment went on to note a "tendency to pontificate to the point of error; a persistent habit of making too much of too little, and too little of too much." After several more such remarks he concluded, "Don't succumb to the temptation to rest on bright insights alone (and the way they sound). Nobody has ever become a scholar that way. If I can help you in this respect, let me know."

At the year-end he provided a summer reading list. Among the items was Stanley Edgar Hyman's introduction to the New Criticism, *The Armed Vision*. There I found a chapter on William Empson's "ambiguities." Up to then I had plodded along in prose, not unlike Monsieur Jourdain. With the revelation that puns, like sex, could pop up anywhere—the more outrageous, the better—poetry opened, words aglow on a page. I no longer parsed sentences, but words in their prismatic contours.

That fall, I enrolled in a close-reading course directed by my Uncle Jimmy's thesis advisor, Reuben Brower. I still remember how I felt when, for our first assignment, I found myself confronted with the Gerard Manley Hopkins sonnet, "God's Grandeur." As I scanned its analogies, "like shining from shook foil," "like the ooze of oil/ Crushed" it looked as if the poet had let fly with a stick of dynamite. As I put together the fragments of alliteration, assonance and rhythm, a jigsaw puzzle emerged of what Hopkins depicted. Language was gesture; gesture, language.

A second Hopkins poem, "The Windhover," and a third on the metaphor of the wheel in *King Lear* helped build up confidence. We were next asked to trace a strand of tidal imagery through *A Portrait of the Artist as a Young Man*. I found Joyce's summons to write irresistible. After briefly fulfilling the assignment, I used the remaining pages to give vent to the mat-rider I had once been. Though my knuckles were properly rapped—"This is NOT a creative writing class!"—something new had broken free. I had jumped the boundary separating reading from writing.

MARCIA

That autumn I made another leap. At a get-together for new History and Lit majors I met Marcia Taylor, the woman who would become my first wife. The previous year we had shared a large lecture class and often enough I'd find myself walking across the quadrangle behind this large-hipped, swiftly striding Cliffie. I thought of her then as Scandinavian, a chaff-haired blonde with a striking face set off by high cheekbones. I was all the more intrigued when, after being introduced, she spoke of herself as Romanian. I did not grasp that she was referring to her Bucharest birth place, the daughter of a MIT-trained engineer who had returned to the States with the outbreak of the war.

Though we had chatted at some length, it took a month before I summoned the gumption to arrange a date. No sooner had she, in a red and yellow Mexican blouse, slid into my Bel Air than I, backing out all too casually, sideswiped a parked car. As we assessed the damage, the shyness vanished and we found ourselves talking sincerely, even intimately. The Europe that had my old friends rolling their eyes was for her, too, a desired world. Her foreign birth, reinforced by the furnishings her parents had brought back from their seven year stay, had been the one flame sustaining her in the monotony of Summit, New Jersey.

Marcia was five years younger than her sister, who had bloomed after college into a Miss Suburbia. This left Marcia to develop a wildness her sister shunned, never happier than on some Brontean moor. "My stormy petrel," her mother called her, fondly throwing up her hands.

For the remainder of the term Marcia was all I could think about, and any time from her studies she granted me was so much manna. I had no need to suggest going anywhere, I just wanted her company. Before long I was prevailing over both her beaux and her studies. What class could compete with a young woman's self-discovery of her flower-like body that would remain unknown but for another's mouth and fingers, his bee-like intuitions?

There came, though, a time when Harvard's unique post-Christmas "reading" period came to an end, and we each withdrew to repair as best we could our dereliction. In this I was the more fortunate in that my exams fell late. But while I crammed, Marcia was free to enter the dating waters. I did not take to this well. My first meltdown occurred during a performance of *Don Giovanni* at the Boston Opera. Could it have been the algae-green dinginess of the second floor balcony in which I was stranded? Or the way I identified with the rake, everything a grandson of Charlie Merrill aspired to? But the picture of Marcia enjoying the company of a determined rival, on top of the female havoc the Don was undergoing on the stage, had my nerves in such a state that I was up and gone before the Stone Guest made his final appearance.

Eliza Church Merrill, 1912

A few days later, on a friend's advice, I took some Dexedrine so I could stay up and study for the next morning's exam. I had no particular yen to enter a cerebral fast lane. But I thought a fresh reading of Schumpeter's *Capitalism, Socialism and Democracy* might be what I needed to bring the course together. Schumpeter's advocacy for an entrepreneurship had done much to soothe my social conscience when first encountered in my Exeter tutorial. Now, two years later, Schumpeter looked indefensibly reactionary. Why was I wasting sleep on him?

Then again, Dexedrine is not an optimal choice for a metabolism that needs to be slowed down rather than stimulated. I took the exam next morning in the pounding mental din of an air-raid shelter undergoing a major bombardment. When the exam ended I remember walking, as if on eggs, back to my room, where I proceeded to write "The Wanton Current," the prose poem that allowed me to see I could become a writer. Then I repaired to my bed to wake, some hours later, in a no less strange pool of bodily drippings.

A warning sign? Was my body trying to tell me I had trespassed into alien territory? Yes, probably, but what was this forbidden territory? Sexual, my worried uncle thought, commenting on my haggard mien. Certainly I was under a lot of pressure, not all of it self-inflicted, but then most students are. Wasn't that the point of college: to be in over your head and learn how much you can handle? As for this episode, my flipping out was perhaps no more irrational than that of the next overly possessive man. Whatever it was vanished when classes resumed and Marcia began favoring me once more with her undivided attention.

Marcia's kissing career had begun at 15 when a steward on a cruise ship told her she was beautiful and, reaching out, took her upturned face in his hands. "Please," she exclaimed, beside herself with delight, "do that again." For hours afterwards she found herself traipsing about in a delicious haze. But in the pre-pill era, getting pregnant was frightening, especially to one who regarded her virginity as her sole dowry and wanted it bestowed on the man she would marry. Was I, a callow 19-year-old, such a prospect?

Unlike most of her classmates Marcia did not want the independence of a career, but the old-fashioned security of a marriage. Whereas for me, on the threshold of my adult life, marriage could only be a damming of something essential. A sea of women, island upon island stretching into the mists, was what my upbringing had denied me, and therefore what I craved.

UNCLE JIMMY

What caused "The Wanton Current," the piece of prose that would sweep me into a writer's life, to burst forth? I have only one person to thank or blame, my uncle James Merrill. Jimmy was Mother's half-brother, twelve years younger and Hellen's only child. In our family album there is a photograph of him, all of eleven, dressed in his Knickerbocker Grays uniform and holding me in my baby dress. He knew instinctively, Mother reported, how to play with someone not quite two years old. Not long thereafter, Charlie plunged into his marriage with Hellen the sword of divorce; a blow from which neither Hellen nor Jimmy ever quite recovered. (Jimmy told me that, when his mother learned of Charlie's intent, she offered to take a trip and retire into the background for as long as it took his fires to cool. With sadness, Charlie turned her down. Being with Kinta and having to suffer the guilt he was inflicting on Hellen was more than he could bear.)

In the divorce proceedings, the two provided the tabloids with an unfortunate field day. When Hellen named two correspondents—Kinta and Dottie Stafford—Charlie trotted out a preposterous five. When he sought a quick Reno fix, she socked him with an injunction. Not to be outdone, Charlie made their 11-year-old a pawn in a custodial battle with his "unfit" mother. He even planted a housekeeper spy—Mother's nurse, Emma Brown—in their tiny house on 57th Street.

The divorce, product as it was of willfulness, was the biggest event in Jimmy's life, as it had been in my mother's. And it broke him in two. In the immediate aftermath, his grades at St. Bernard's plunged to a row of F's and, instead of going to Lawrenceville as planned, he had to repeat the year. Needing consolation, he began to stuff himself. By the time he was 16 he had bulked into a 200-lb. blob. Jimmy took charge soon thereafter, but the damage at 30 was still visible: pulpy Tiresias-like breasts and fleshy high-slung hips that hung over the bone.

The divorce took Jimmy out of our family orbit, and I have no memory of him in his "fat" period. All I remember is a glimpse of him walking onto the clay court with a borrowed lady's racquet, or defending Walt Whitman in our 69th Street library, "Prose poetry is so much more difficult to write than verse."

Father in his Pine St. office, 1953

Until he was offered at 22 a teaching job at Bard College, Jimmy may not have known he was going to work anywhere but Merrill Lynch, but it would be hard to conceive of a more considered literary progress. One glance at *Jim's Book*, printed by Charlie as a surprise 16th birthday present, with its array of verse forms, its faultlessly rhymed Baudelaire translations, its tribute to the now forgotten Elinor Wylie, and one can see a poet born to sing in his chains.

By the time he embarked on his first novel, he had read Henry James's *The Ambassadors* six times. A winter abroad went into devouring Dickens, a second, Balzac. He kept a full diary. Clearly he aspired to be something more than just a poet—a Jean Cocteau, an Oscar Wilde, leaving his mark on every medium.

The consistency of his son's progress, with prizes from *Poetry* Magazine, a summa cum laude degree from Amherst, was such that when Jimmy decided on a writing career, his father did not bark out a thousand threats. Disappointed he may have been to have no son rising within Merrill Lynch, but what counted was Jimmy's welfare. To that end, Charlie fired off missives to the editor of *Poetry*, to President Cole of Amherst, and to three of Jimmy's college professors, asking about his son's chances of succeeding in such a problematic career. Their positive responses led him to support Jimmy unstintingly.

What Charlie privately felt is unknown, but Jimmy remembered watching with him a polo match at Delray Beach. It must not have been the most stimulating of matches for, at one point, Charlie put his arm around Jimmy and confided, "I'd rather have a poet as my son than a third-rate polo player."

My acquaintance with my uncle took a turn in 1950, as I started my second year at Le Rosey. Jimmy had gone abroad for an indefinite stay, determined to make himself into "A Different Person," a feat more easily accomplished in a setting that did not include stamping bulls and Wall Street dollar signs. Jimmy and his partner Claude Fredericks were in Geneva attending the dying 26-year-old Dutch poet Hans Lodeizen when they found themselves strapped for cash. On a Saturday, with the banks closed, whom could they touch for a quick loan? Why the nephew, just down the lake at Rolle. For a 14-year-old, to be projected into the role of family banker could not have been more delicious, and I remember racing off to withdraw my emergency traveler's checks from the school vault. On Jimmy's firm handshake the most charmed of friendships began.

Jimmy was living in Rome later that fall when I received permission to fly down to meet my grandfather who had arrived the previous week from Naples. Charlie was expecting an audience with the Pope, and took the opportunity to check out Father's tailors by commissioning a white double-breasted suit—to be worn with a gold tie clip in the form of a dollar bill.

As a special treat my first night Charlie and Jimmy took me to dinner at Alfredo's. We were all tucking into the renowned fettucine (served with a solid gold fork and spoon by no less than the proprietor) and Charlie was in the midst of a story when, suddenly turning scarlet, he dropped his head and coughed up his dental bridge into his plate. Was I witnessing the start of a heart attack? Reacting quickly, Jimmy paid the bill and whisked the three of us in a taxi back to the Excelsior.

Hours later, I was still shaken by what I had witnessed. "Is Grandpa going to live?" Jimmy remembers me asking as we sat in his room some hours later, dining off a tray on wheels.

"It's nothing serious, his doctor said, just an angina attack brought on by the traveling he's been doing. All he needs is some rest."

"How did you know what to do?" I asked, thinking I needed to be prepared in case I found myself alone with my grandfather in a similar emergency.

"I don't want you to think it's eerie," Jimmy said, as he rose to fetch a black binder, "but I have with me a novel I started a little while ago with the very scene we just witnessed. Only the restaurant in my novel is in Manhattan. You might want to read it, but be careful, it's my only copy."

I remember the pride with which I bore it away—a real manuscript! Of its five chapters, I only recall a scene describing a performance of *Orfeo*, in which the black-tie opera crowd in their tiers of gilt boxes finds itself mirrored on the stage as Hell, that Jimmy was to salvage for his first novel, *The Seraglio*.

THE SERAGLIO

As a writer, Jimmy found himself early. But growing up in that little Versailles which was the Orchard, with the Man with the Golden Touch as his father, could not have been easy. The irreality comes across in the title of his novel, *The Seraglio*, an Italian word for a Turkish harem; a measure of how alienated he felt. Yet if any novel ever changed a life, that one did. My family life, so driven, so illegible, became, overnight as it were, transparent. In derailing me from the track my parents had chosen, *The Seraglio* brought me into the orbit of its author, who would become the key figure in my post-adolescent life.

The Seraglio is a *roman-à-clef* about a series of events that took place in Southampton in 1952, when I was 16. My uncle had just returned from the three years abroad described in *A Different Person*. So much time away required a gift to propitiate his father. Where an earlier prodigal might have brought back an Apollo Belvedere, or a marble Venus, Jimmy had in tow a Paris-based sculptress of Roumanian origin, Guitou Knoop (called Xenia in the novel), whom he commissioned to do a bust of his father. Guitou succeeded in her task so admirably that Charlie, to keep her around, commissioned a bust of my brother Peter.

At the hub of the novel is the vast wealth embodied by the now divorced and sexually restored financial potentate, Benjamin Tanning. Who will land the prize? Briskly, Jimmy lines up the concerned parties: on the one side, the ex-wives and candidate wives; on the other the business types led by my parents. Behind the whodunit of the portrait slashing and the sexual imbroglio lies a serious conflict between the two "sons," the natural one, Francis, and the usurper, Larry Buchanan (my father). Both see Benjamin Tanning (Charlie) as a second Midas. While Larry can imagine no Utopia more fulfilling than a Southampton where everything and everybody can be quantified, Francis resents being turned into an heir to be exploited.

As the novel opens, we learn of the stabbing of Mother's portrait. There are a number of likely suspects, but Jimmy's narrator, Francis, opts for Mother's barely teen-age daughter, Lily; a way of underlining at whose expense the marital maneuvering is taking place; we, the nephews and nieces to whom *The Seraglio* is dedicated. Will Francis somehow rescue us? Or will the novel's last scene, in which the grown-ups merrily consume the chocolate children ornamenting my brother Mark's first birthday cake, demonstrate that theirs is indeed a society that eats its children.

Before Francis can save us, he has to save himself from what he believes his unearned wealth has done to him. With this in mind he descends, as he did in real life, on my father to see if he can renounce his fortune. But Larry turns Francis down, pointing out the unbreakable nature of his trust fund. That leaves Francis determined to do the next best thing—castrate himself. An overly drastic solution? Certainly, in that it represents a fictional exit from a work that resolutely clings to *roman-à-clef* veracity. But not if you want your father to recognize the consequences on a son of his enormous wealth and non-stop womanizing. It does, though, reduce the remainder of the novel to a series of tableaux in the course of which Francis learns to negotiate his way in a new gay life.

I did not appear in *The Seraglio*. Freudian casting required a Buchanan daughter, Lily, to whom the stabbing of Mother's portrait could be initially attributed. But as a reader of drafts, who knew the participants and locale, I had my uses. How the scales dropped from my eyes as I watched the events unfold, in installments, chapter by chapter. In my naiveté, I had assumed that Southampton was all about money. Wrong, Jimmy maintained, it was about sex. In the innocence of the early Fifties, the realization that a mischievous force called "sex" invigorated the better part of adult life could feel rather liberating. To my parents we children were not conceived out of animal need, but were instead dynastic heirs sprung from Charlie Merrill's capacious godhead. It was precisely this myth *The Seraglio* exploded. For my uncle the curse of his growing up had been his father's uncontainable promiscuity. And it would go on haunting him, he felt, so long as its genetic compulsions remained unidentified. We were both convinced that understanding our sexual imperative (from our vantages on either side of the gay/ straight divide) held the key to our moral development.

I feel incapable of re-reading *The Seraglio*. Instead I continue to be distracted or appalled by the anger of the narrator and by the thinly fictionalized characters. And I can understand how others winced. My mother was so put off, less by her own portrait where the cutesy "little" spikes her every remark, than by Jimmy's gratuitous cruelty to Hellen and to my father, that she did not speak to her brother for two years. My father, flayed mercilessly, had every reason to talk about the "hateful novel," but for all his talk, it turned out that he had managed to restrain his curiosity and had not read it.

I can see the attractions of a tell-all novel for one as inclined to gossip as my uncle. But what may have worked for Jimmy's pals, Mary McCarthy and Alison Lurie—Alison's Amherst novel, *Love and Friendship*, even features Jimmy and David—doesn't work as well in *The Seraglio* because the tyranny of facts keeps the fiction from ever generating a momentum of its own. The novel runs out of gas once the incident that gives it its start—the slashing of Mother's portrait—becomes a side issue. And its shocking climax—the castration scene—circumscribes character development by removing the narrator from his role as a player in the marital field.

In a society in which the life-denying forces hold the major cards, the one sane response may be to drop out and not abet them. That was my response as well as my uncle's. Nonetheless the narrowing of focus deriving from an injured son's need to wound gets in the way of empathy. Nor does Jimmy ever explore the lure of power that motivated my father and the other Wall Streeters competing in the Southampton arena. Behind the rounds of golf, the tennis matches, the one-upmanship, what's at stake? Another way of saying that *The Seraglio,* much as it would like to be, is not *The Great Gatsby.*

MENTOR AND APPRENTICE

The motor of promiscuous need may not have drummed quite as loudly in Jimmy's breast as in Charlie's. A sexual subtext, nonetheless, coated much of his presence, from the pronounced inflections of his speech to the hip-flaunting shuffle with the look that never left him of a precocious youth. Jimmy could see a reality different from the dazzling surfaces of gay life, but barely, such was his delight in the ever expanding scene in which he found himself participating. What to another seemed a ghetto could be for him a source of pride; they were the elite. Nor was he alone in this view. For much of the past century the artistic vanguard has been preeminently homosexual. They carried the flag for the rest of us. The brio with which they pursued the adventure of identity, out at the cutting edge, made them our heroes.

As our friendship grew, Jimmy and his partner David Jackson's house in the coastal village of Stonington, Connecticut became my refuge. Not everyone admired his living situation. "There's not a comfortable place to sit in the whole apartment," my mother complained. But if there wasn't much to sink into, there was more than enough to marvel at. The walls on his tin-domed dining room were a bold lobster pink, the furniture lavender. Wherever I turned, from the stained glass street window to the hanging prisms that fired rainbows across the séance table, to the scores of curios, totems, jeweled Buddhas, scrolls and folding screens, all that bric-a-brac became personae to which Jimmy would give voice in one or another poem. The liberating oxygen his rooms gave off was such that I would come away from a visit feeling a new lightness. I floated.

These speaking surfaces formed the backdrop to Jimmy's conversation. Not that extracting anything from someone as shy as he was in those years was easy. That's where David Jackson's convivial talent sustained us all. While David poured and entertained, Jimmy withdrew to his other lab, the kitchen. There as dinner baked and sizzled, an evening's conversation would come into focus.

For conversation to develop you have to maintain a semblance of dialogue. My first lessons went into learning how to address those raised eyebrows reacting to me as I lurched along. What I opined counted, to be sure. Equally important, however, were the images in which I couched them. "Give an example," Jimmy would interrupt. Drawing in a breath—ah, the lure of revision!—I would rephrase the utterance.

Soon I was conversing not in sentences, but imagery, the cadence slowed so I could revise a trope if I saw it drawing a puzzled brow. To call upon authority—if you can't speculate, why converse?—there was the European 'one,' to which we both adhered. Jimmy's own cadences, dropping into sibylline tones, made him someone I can still quote.

He was remarkably present. No one meeting him for more than a few minutes ever doubted before whom they stood. If they did, there was his VW license plate proclaiming POET. Nature was not only to be observed, it was also to be worn. Once, strolling with me in Kew Gardens, a green-barked Chinese birch caught his eye. "Wouldn't you die to have a shirt the color of that bark?" His own taste ran to the hot end of the spectrum: Uncle Zinnia gliding about in his Birkenstock sandals, apricot shirt and pink trousers. The joy he took from his vocation ("If you don't enjoy it," he remarked the last time I saw him, his voice rising with incredulity, "why do it?") must have made him feel it could be, for me, too, a solution. It was not as if the desire hadn't crossed my teen-age mind. The previous summer, walking about Southampton with Ellison's *Invisible Man* in my pocket, I remember thinking what I wouldn't give to be able to write something as compelling. But other than a satire, written when I was eleven, imagining the shake-up of a Henry Wallace presidency, I'd never written anything I liked. Besides, what was I to cut my teeth on—poetry? "But I don't like poetry," I confessed when Jimmy brought it up as a possibility one day. "I didn't either," Jimmy replied, sounding like Marianne Moore, "until I began to write it. But verse does allow one to work on a smaller scale than prose. One is not compelled to know as much. One is not conjuring a milieu so much as a sensibility. Anyway, I promise I'll read whatever you write." With my uncle encouraging me, and my need to escape Father's financial threats, the thought of a breakthrough was promising. All I needed was a catalyst.

THE WANTON CURRENT

I hadn't been to bed for 40 hours and had just regained my room after taking a final exam when I found myself writing:

A naked mariner pitches on the bobbling pillow. Eyes see-sawing, he raises up supple beings, summoning them forth from eider depths to share the vulgar lot. An iceberg discloses herself. Maiden-like she floats, proof to the wanton current that thrashes about her submerged parts. Slowly then the iceberg melts—compelled, like the mariner, to contemplate a dissolution.

In the midst of this evocation parental voices appear:

"Where are Tino's pajamas?"
"In the wash, dear. I hope he won't catch a cold."
"The boy can't go to bed like that. It's indecent. What if Boopsy should come?"
At the sound of the proper name, an eyelid quivers. The Contessa. And a summer afternoon unfolds, the afternoon she first heaves in sight, broad as a barge, breasts tossing in the direction of the drowsing mariner. A bourgeois member responds, beckoning. The Contessa vacillates, swaying like a door waiting for its hinges to slip, or rust away. Then she swings alongside and, after a decent interval, ties up.
The yellow tide advances, swelling in ever-widening stains, across the pillow's wrinkled surface.

During the following weeks I must have rewritten the initial paragraph a hundred times; less to perfect it, than to learn what I had written. All the same I felt compelled to try to take it further. To that end, I invented a scene between the boy, Tino, and his provocative mother set in the Beach Club dunes. An exorcism occurs later that evening when mother and son arrive for what might be a dance:

> They descend at midnight at the Club where the party is still bubbling on. The mariner leaves her propped at the bar and begins to circle the drink-flooded dance floor, wading past the paddling couples to where a woman in pink organdy stands smiling, her face done up in flames. The mariner holds her taut as he can and they dance, throbbing through the crowd like two shadows come together to make light. Then she's at his arm, tugging. "Tino, have you forgotten all you ever learned at dancing school? This is a waltz. Now count after me: ah-one, two, three; ah-one, two, three."

For a kid who likes to think he can dance, the remark cuts. Nonetheless, he is undeterred. He knows other forms, among them flamenco. A while later, catching sight of his inebriated mother enveloped in her usual ring of stags, he pushes his way through and, exercising his filial rights, demands a dance. Heels stamping out a percussive rhythm, he makes her "spin in tighter and tighter circles until she can stand it no longer and topples over in a faint."

Kneeling over her with a damp rag, the boy gently washes her face. Then, as she comes to, she starts, not unreasonably, to curse. "She curses long and loud and she is still cursing when the waiters lead her outside."

For a course, a year later, in Oriental literature, I recast "The Wanton Current" as a Japanese Noh play. In this light, the mother is a ghost whom the masturbating boy has summoned forth. In making the ghost dance and reveal herself the mariner has quite possibly liberated himself from a fatal attraction. But the exorcism, as my fiction writing professor John Hawkes later pointed out, remains incomplete. If the Contessa is the father's mistress, shouldn't the father loom as more than a disembodied voice?

I saw no way to develop that first piece of writing, which may explain my lifelong inability to write plotted fiction. I was too hyper to be able to do more than collage the debris the imaginary current had tossed onto my pillow. In effect, I needed something outside, uncontaminated, to which I could give voice. Without knowing it, I needed something that might be defined as Other.

Where before I could see only an imprisoning family labyrinth, I now had an 800-word thread on a path leading out beyond the thrashing surf to light and freedom. Blind to everything but that compelling necessity, I jumped on that mat, put my head down and paddled. I was, indeed I had to be, a mariner flailing my way into the unknown realm of writing.

In response to that vocational necessity my student life changed. There was so much about verse, prosody and aesthetics, I had to learn on my own. A university as devoted to the past as Harvard did not provide the crash courses in Surrealism and the Moderns I craved. Instead, in the periodical room in Widener Library, I pored over recent numbers of the "little" literary magazines. I combed the Widener stacks for poems about icebergs, coming upon, in the process, John Simon's dissertation on an underappreciated genre, prose poetry. I blundered into a graduate seminar devoted to Elizabethan song poetry for which I produced weekly papers on alliteration, legato phrasing, diction. I also did some translating, one way of absorbing the verbal choices of writers better than I, amongst them Giuseppe Ungaretti's early *Allegria*. What drew me in *Allegria* were the radical line-cuts, nowhere more succinctly placed than in the two-line "*Mattina:*"

> m'illumino
> d'immenso

In bringing across a poem from another language, impossible as that might seem, it helps to veer in on a particular quality. In rendering these poems from the World War I trenches, I found the essence I needed in the razor-sharp, almost Schoenbergian verbal music. With no guidance or encouragement from my professors, and only occasional mentoring from my uncle, I had to proceed somehow on my own.

Poetry can be, as the linguistic anthropologist Bruce Berlin ruefully admitted, a way of "fucking up language." Is the poet, like a mischievous child, trying to get away with something—the otherwise forbidden (unknown or unrecorded)? And how far is far enough? "It's not the precious," my uncle insisted, "but the semi-precious one has to resist."

Parachuting as I did into poetry, it behooved me to try to define what was important in my attempts to write. Metaphor! Imagery! Any New Critic would have asserted. But the "force that through the green fuse drives the flower" struck me as patently auditory. A poet differed in the degree to which he "heard" experience. It was that aural memory which, for me, determined word choice. Sound, not poetic form, was the bedrock under the lyric impulse.

This was, however, not the prevailing point of view. Jimmy's Amherst mentor, Reuben Brower, asked, when I made the mistake of showing him some free verse experiments, "Do you write sonnets? I don't see how anyone who doesn't tackle the sonnet form can call himself a poet. How else can a poet grow into his craft? The virtue of the sonnet lies in that it gives you a means of learning by repeating yourself."

If any writing teacher had insisted on my composing a sonnet I'd have chucked the course then and there. I had little respect for craft at that point. What fascinated me was not the sonnet's ticking box, but capturing something akin to what as a child I had known, out on a mat, endlessly waiting for a wave terrifying enough to ride. That may be why I responded to Freud's image of the mind as an iceberg. If nine-tenths of our mental activity took place beneath the conscious surface, wasn't more to be gained by diving down and exploring the uncharted depths?

It was here that Jimmy and I parted company. The purpose of the unconscious, Jimmy argued, is to throw light onto the waking surface, the only place we can apprehend them. Appearances, viewed correctly, are reality. We are all, willy-nilly, impressionists stringing together our discreet sensations. Jimmy knew as much as any poet of his day about verbal music, poetic meters, stanza forms and their visual aspect, pattern. As a youth he aspired to be a composer, and his Lawrenceville roommate, the novelist Frederick Buechner, remembers him rolling his trousers up over his knees trying to resemble Mozart as a child. But the uncontained aspect of space eluded him and he thought it eluded me too. "Try to find some other word," he scribbled across a poem in exasperation. His solution was to write within the room or stanza of a poem, seen through the controlling metaphor of a prism, a fire-screen, a crocheted curtain. All his reader saw was the extended pattern, not the chaos of "reality" that metaphor and form were attempting to control. In his windows, the colored panes refracted light without allowing a view. His office was a windowless closet. "Wasn't the point," he said, "not to look out, but inward?"

Jimmy's commitment to me never wavered. Whenever I came up foundering, he was always there, verbal lifeline in hand. With other poets' suggestions I've sometimes felt that a poem, however improved, was no longer mine. His suggestions, however, fortified. Even when he didn't solve a particular problem, he could still point to issues I needed to face. One distich, a repository of everything I wanted a poem to be, once read:

> The green dream of things
> Springing into the force of shadows.

"Why not through the force of shadows?" Jimmy offered.

"That's not what I meant!" I objected, aghast.

"Yes it is, only through makes them see it." Has any poet displayed a more scrupulous concern for his readers?

Among my first semi-successful efforts was a poem honoring the Haitian painter Hervé Télémaque. When I sent it to him, Jimmy replied,

> It is too bad that Hervé "painted" in the course of that summer. Between Wilbur and Ashbery, or even Ashbery to Zukofsky, there are so God damn many culture heroes setting up their easels. Perhaps you perversely enjoy joining those ranks, the Poet hand in hand with the Painter (as not so long ago with the Peasant, or even the Prince) but to me—your "he" with his box of oils—simply guarantees the poem will not function on a serious plane, your images will remain images, if they summon up states of feeling it will be stumblingly, pitched forward into the exhaust from the Art Machine. The least touch, I should think, would suffice to make it all right—just don't say that he painted. Mightn't he mysteriously have "dealt with" dunes, a thin strand of businesslike imagery ensuing that would fit nicely with the fishnets and the heavily traveled road? And for the second "painted" coming after the splendid passage of the sleeve, would "stitched" be too cute? Something, anyhow, to suggest work without pretensions. All trades are one, we know, but the others don't, the painters at their worst don't, and your material here is too fresh, one hates for it to have added up to mere "Art."

Jimmy's reproof is forceful and deep, yet somehow also encouraging. If I still couldn't re-imagine Hervé as other than what he was, a committed painter, at least I was brought up short.

Jimmy's admonitions registered the more in that he seemed to know exactly where I was on my road. While I set the sail, he made sure I rounded my cape and reached the next port. And he saw to it that I did not lose sight of where I was heading. "You can't go to a deb party!" he exclaimed when, sorely tempted, I produced an invitation. "You've made a choice and you've got to stick to it. You're a writer and not a socialite." If I consented somewhat reluctantly—the deb party dance floor was one arena I actually understood—Jimmy's line of reasoning was clear. To feel committed I had to make sacrifices.

All the same I knew moments of rebellion. For the apprentice, the master incarnates truth. But it is his truth, that of the work he is engendering; one that resonates powerfully to the extent that the man and the writer are one and the same. It was not just a lesson in craft I was receiving, as one in living.

It was hazardous, of course, to model myself too closely upon my mentor; after all the Merrill I was absorbing remained a foreign substance. Time and again I've struggled to reduce his brilliance to the more modest flame I needed. For Jimmy, any distancing on my part could carry a taint of desertion. In his battle to change the world, he needed every ally he could muster. I didn't mind taking up a flanking role to his advancing gay phalanx. I did mind being jerked about on a puppet's string. But most of the time my strands were so woven that I hardly knew I was being played. To be sure, the exclusivity of Jimmy's priestly art-circle never appealed. But what about the borrowed mandarin tone I affected? Wherever I turned, I was enmeshed. And as long as I remained his creature, how could I discover my own boundaries, and a voice of my own?

WITH LARRY RIVERS AND THE POETS

Visitors to Stonington were regularly stunned by a seven-by-nine-foot Larry Rivers painting of a bucolic Water Mill scene mounted in Jimmy's attic, which had been remodeled to accommodate it. The painting served as a trompe l'oeil wall in front of which the poet and his friends would assemble for cocktails and cigarettes.

The subject was a 19th century one, familiar perhaps from Corot: a central tree, a pair of huge cows on a meadow, late summer clouds and racing Long Island fog. But walking about in front of it—the painting compelled you to move in order to take it in—felt more like looking at a film than a static tableau. Everything—the tree, the meadow, the cows—had been half-erased, wiped with a rag, leaving only hints and indications, a dab of color or no color at all but the charcoal of an immensely assured preparatory under-drawing. Through the vivid gestures and erasures, I felt the excitement of the 30-year-old city-bred painter and saxophonist who was simultaneously discovering the Hampton countryside and 19th century landscape painting. It was almost as if Rivers had foreseen the speed with which the car and its dedicated weekenders would transform the South Fork's cow pastures into acres of mega-mansions.

A tableau of such size and vivacity challenged what my uncle was himself about. The multi-layered set pieces of the neoclassical poets of the 1950s kept the reader at a formal distance with their deft metrics and metaphorical scaffolding; equivalents of the then fashionable four-buttoned suit. Rivers' painting with its scumbled rubbings, its splotchy unfinished look, invited the viewer to participate in the impulsive process of the artist's rethinkings and improvisations.

Jimmy's eventual partner, Peter Hooten, remembers him saying about a small ghost-like Rivers still life (1956) in their 72nd street apartment, how much he had once wanted to write the way Larry painted. Merrill's second novel, *The (Diblos) Notebook,* with its shopping lists, diagrams and scratched-out phrases, its fore-fronting of the compositional dilemma, reads as a direct homage to Rivers' work, as do Merrill's two breakthrough poems of the early Sixties, "An Urban Convalescence," and "The Thousand and Second Night." Like Rivers, Merrill employed pastiche as a way of saluting his sacred monsters; not Corot or Courbet, but Yeats and Eliot. Mockery is but another form of homage.

Pastiche suits a reality as up for grabs as the New York of "An Urban Convalescence" where any building that delighted the eye was likely to be demolished—a triumph of commercial opportunity over civic values. For Rivers and Merrill and many of their wartime generation, modern life exuded a post-Hiroshima impermanence; less a question of if, than when. And as they composed, so they lived: on the go, as if only a speed of footwork could avert the impending disaster.

Whenever I visited, Merrill kept insisting that I look up Rivers in Southampton. "He has a house on Little Plains in back of the high school. I know the two of you will like one another." He didn't say that, after some heavy browbeating from Larry's dealer, he had provided the down payment that enabled Larry to move out of the shack on Toylsome Lane he was renting into the 8-room house in which he would reside for the rest of his life—a generosity that still awed Rivers when he informed me of it—not a loan, but a gift!

Why my uncle wanted me to meet Rivers he didn't say, other than we would enjoy each other's company. In the cultural desert of Southampton wasn't that incentive enough? But he must have known that Larry held the keys to a whole new world: not wealthy society, but artistic Bohemia. Under normal circumstances I might never have followed through on my uncle's suggestion. What did I know about art? In first grade my paint spills earned an F in Art. I was thereafter sentenced to making castles with clay tunnels through which I rolled marbles. My nannies did not know English well enough to read to me and later, after I learned to read, I saw illustrations as distractions to be skipped over. In consequence, I hadn't acquired the visual language by means of which artists illustrate narrative. Nor did it help to be cross-eyed, with one eye far-sighted and the other near-sighted. Even today, despite years of haunting museums and sojourning with artist friends, I feel uncertain about what I'm seeing: the color values, the perspective planes, the way the eye is being led from A to Z. Thus my hesitancy in inflicting myself on Larry Rivers.

It happened, however, that I found myself in Southampton in the dead of March 1956 for an appointment the following morning. With time on my hands, late that afternoon, I resolved to drop in unannounced on Rivers.

"You must be Jimmy's nephew," Larry remarked as he held open the door, appraising me with a portrait painter's hawk-eyed scrutiny. Then this handsome, falcon-beaked man introduced me to his mother-in-law Berdie, and kindly insisted on my staying for dinner. By the end of the evening we had become friends.

Over the next four summers Larry's house, with its eight-foot-tall male and female nudes looming from renovated walls, its blue-painted kitchen floor, its stuffed sharp-shinned hawk on the fireplace mantel reminding me of Larry's animal alertness (eyes that did more than look, that seemed ready to seize with a predatory grasp whatever came into view), became a second home to me. I could drop by whenever I liked, at whatever hour. Strangely, Larry usually seemed glad to be interrupted. If he had work in preparation for a show, he would excuse himself and I'd come back later. Now and then he would take me to a black dance hall where he was playing his saxophone in a jazz combo.

My horizons expanded in 1957 when I met Merrill's close friend and Rivers' dealer, John Bernard Myers, a former puppeteer who helped edit Charles Henri Ford's surrealist magazine *View* during the war. After summering in Venice, this self-styled "tracker of the marvelous" had taken a house a block from Larry in downtown Southampton despite being unable to drive. But Southampton has streets, not canals, and I found myself pressed into service as Myers' occasional chauffeur. A number of artists from his Tibor de Nagy gallery lived, like Fairfield Porter and Larry, in Southampton year-round or summered nearby. With John's social appetite the scene extended into a veritable pantheon of New York's art royalty who, for reasons obscure, had blown onto my native isle.

I relished playing a teenaged Caliban to their shipwrecked *Tempest* crew. That I personally despised Southampton did not prevent me from escorting them to the whitest beaches and showing them where to obtain oysters and dig for choice littleneck clams. On one occasion I even conjured my grandfather's valet Leroy, then in his final summer with us, to serve daiquiris in champagne goblets by the Beach House pool. Some of them still recall the small black man with his brimming silver tray advancing towards them against the pink-orange background of zinnias, tiger lilies, brick walls and copper slide, just as I remember the ample-bodied painter ladies in their one-piece bathing suits, magnified like miniature whales by the sunken pool lights. As for the drunken Trinculos, they too were to be found, prostrate at dawn in the back of my blue and white Bel Air, doing their best to vomit gracefully into the side door's ashtray.

Their dereliction owed much to the recently deceased genius loci, Jackson Pollock. If Pollock could drink, dance and generally spatter his way into contemporary immortality, why couldn't they? In their voyage into the unpremeditated, courage was everything, the courage to paint with the body, piling up the gestural waves until a title emerged, "Blue Disorder," "Pale Rider," "Number 13, '57." At this distance it's hard to imagine how work so stripped of reference could command such prestige. What was memorable about the drips, the splashes, color squeezed un-thinned out of a tube? But those swipes of an elbow, those big arcs of a moving hand, catered to the instinctual self rather than one's visual memory. They painted "like birds singing" for the joy of letting go.

At the parties, the day's work done and the night open to celebration, it was clear how fulfilling they found their spontaneous medium. "You don't paint?" they'd ask me in disbelief, "why you must!" as if I had only to pick up a rag and a set of brushes for my identity issues to be resolved. Although I was at a loss to imagine any scenario in which I might become a man of the easel, their parties provided a welcome respite from the Southampton life. For the painters and their poet accomplices, the gatherings represented more than a social "scene." This was family, an expression of Bohemian solidarity.

Southampton, for me, was home, not simply a summer exile from Manhattan, and my localisms (such as calling old Artie, the Beach Club lifeguard, "the man with the hair") seemed to amuse Frank O'Hara when I showed him "The Wanton Current." I knew Frank mainly as an innovative poet, a small if essential part of the art world figure he cut. At my uncle's invitation I reviewed O'Hara's *Meditations in an Emergency* for an issue he guest edited. What did I make of a poetry so different from the formal verse Jimmy was composing?

According to the New Critics, poetry's power derives from its metaphorical way of saying one thing while implying another; the implication, like a thrown football, gathering weight as it spirals downfield into the receiver's arms. What beguiled O'Hara, Ashbery, Schuyler and Koch, though, wasn't power, but lightness: why compel anything of a reader other than a gasp of surprise and perhaps amusement? They replaced the deliberate scaffolding of figurative language with sensational imagery; the more mixed the metaphors, the livelier, they argued, the verse. Rather than construct multi-leveled propositions, they sought a poetry that hovered on the page's surface with the two-dimensional flatness of a painting. O'Hara's "I did this, then I did that" poems tell us what it was like to be young and poor with lots of pals while undertaking all sorts of things at once, all rather successfully.

The inability to concentrate on a subject for more than a minute does not normally make for a School of Poetry. But imagine being a fly on Larry's kitchen wall when they were all gathered there, the quips flying faster than the ball at doubles tennis. Their "first expression, best expression," mantra came out of the same crucible. All it required was a hand capable of keeping pace with the racing mind. If, for some reason, one needed a certain empathy, there were hangovers. Others, like Larry, resorted to more problematic potions. How Larry managed to knock himself out without descending into addiction mystified us all. But then Larry's experiments, sexual and artistic, showed a remarkable resilience: a man obsessed with the geography of the self, reconnoitering the precipices like a mountaineer. With his life on display in enormous 10 x 15 ft. "ME I," "ME II" paintings, he joined the queue stretching back to "Song of Myself," to *Walden* and Ben Franklin celebrating the Self's mythology.

During this time Larry's mother-in-law, Berdie, provided the domestic stability he needed in which to pursue his art. When she died in 1957, Larry suspected the figurative cycle nourished by this "heroine of the chair" had reached its end. But how justify going out on an abstract tangent that might not sell? Larry's dilemma seemed resolved when he won the then astro-nomical sum of $32,000 answering questions on the history of art on "The $64,000 Question." I recall Larry's growing nervousness as his stake doubled week by successful week. With so much on the line, how prudent was it to trust the promoter's assurances and soldier on? Then came the question of what to do with the windfall: opt out of the gallery rat race, as I suggested, and do "pure art?"

Larry wasn't about to buy my suggestion. "To do pure art," he said in words that still reverberate, "would require moving abroad. The artist who stays in America has no choice but to make an art that fights back. When it's the culture you are battling, you have to be part of it." Instead of holing up by some Walden Pond, Larry preferred to see himself in the cavalcade of cars streaming back to the city,

For Larry, I suspect, the gallery scene held something of the suspense of a tournament. The thrill lay in competing; how far up the art ladder could he ascend? Enough was never enough, there was always a rung more. That may be why in the 1980's, when Larry had become commercially successful, it wasn't my doings that interested him, but those of my Old Man. Whenever I dropped by on one of my infrequent visits, he kept pressing me to arrange a meeting, "It's the zoo-goer in me," he candidly admitted. I hadn't ever viewed my father in quite that light, one of the big cats in the Bronx Zoo whom Larry would visit as a child. Needless to say, Larry's curiosity wasn't returned by my father, who refused to grant Larry as much as a name: "that kike friend of yours."

I lost touch with Larry when I was living in Europe. But in 1999, while in Southampton with my family, I did manage to slip in a visit. I wanted to give him two recently published books as a way of thanking him for the friendship offered at such a young age. Larry seemed genuinely startled. I don't know what he expected me to become, but it clearly wasn't a writer.

Virgil Burnett's cover illustration, "Persian Notes," 1972

As we sat on his studio couch, I couldn't help being struck by a painting, done in the early 90's, of the black saxophonist Sonny Simmons, "Umber Blues II." It was another of those big scale nudes, every bit as confrontational, and gorgeous, as the ones of O'Hara and Berdie. We are in the musician's home, but all we glimpse of it is the bed with its rumpled sheets, a coverlet of clashing stripes, and Sonny's discarded shirt and trousers. Sitting on the edge of the bed, naked but wearing dark glasses as he plays his golden horn, his concentrated face turned slightly away, is the middle-aged saxophonist. Larry has given his skin a tonality similar to the umber Manet employs in painting the velvety couch on which a Spanish maja in a matador's suit of lights reclines. Sonny, thus depicted by the sensuously handled paint, is as much an embodiment of fear and desire as Berdie and Frank. But transgression, too, is what jazz celebrates. In this portrait, rendered from a point as intimate as paint can take us, Larry put all the warmth of his lifelong affair with the saxophone and the African-American spirit jazz embodies. When I said as much, Larry identified it as one of his "Golden Oldies I keep returning to."

Merrill died in 1995, Rivers in 2003. In the time since, I've thought of them both often, two not dissimilar figures whom I caught while they were still composing the masks they would wear. Jimmy's personae were by and large mythic ones: Marsyas, Orpheus, Psyche, Father Time and Mother Earth. For Larry, it was the more well-lighted countenances of politics and history: George Washington, Napoleon, the last Confederate Soldier, the cigar box Dutch Masters. At the time, I was fond of quoting Yeats's lines describing the choice between the "Perfection of the life, or of the work." For Jimmy and Larry there was no such dichotomy: life irrigated the comic take each brought to the adventure of the self. For me, their flamboyant self-invention opened a path they could never have anticipated.

THE MUSKRAT

If my parents were upset by the art crowd I was frequenting, they were far more bewildered by my letters from college in which I tried to share the thoughts, the emotions, and exam time turmoil that had gone into unleashing "The Wanton Current."

"What have we done," Father wrote back, "to merit such treatment?" After explaining the shock my letters had aroused, he proceeded to drum home what he saw as verities. "The very basis of a collective society," he wrote, "is conformity. This applies to manners as well as morals and it includes deportment . . . I have little interest in the intellectual world, or in people who claim to be intellectuals. I hope, personally, that none of your brothers will ever want to take a course in modern poetry." Some six typed pages later he concluded, "I think it is very nice to get such good marks at Harvard, but I can tell you this, Robin: I'd rather they be C's and D's and have you healthy and cheerful in the examination room than lose control of your voice, and part of my body . . . perspiring madly, face half-drunk' etc.—your quotes. I'd like to see the expression on your face if somebody were to read you those last two morbid letters ten years from now! I hope you'll resume communication with us—in simple English—soon."

Obviously, I'd got it wrong. It was not my development they wanted to hear about, but the opposite; to be reassured that I hadn't changed, not one iota. I adapted, of course. I was perfectly capable of feeding them the pabulum they required.

The previous summer, Father had secured me a job in Merrill Lynch's research department, drawing graphs for a chartist delineating the turns in a stock's trading: the frenzied peaks; the descending chasms. Now I wanted to see something of the America I had been studying in my history and lit major. Could Father procure me a job at Safeway to this end?

A rub of the boss's fingers and, presto, I had a market research job evaluating prospective store sites in a variety of western states: Astoria, Oregon, where, trying to read as I drove, I clobbered a parked station wagon; Venice Beach where, swimming without fins or a board, I almost never came up from under rollers that took seeming centuries to pass overhead. In an Oklahoma City bar I stood, a pile of salt on the back of my hand, listening to the sad recollections of men who had gone to Los Angeles and lost it to a pair of blue eyes. Everywhere, as I drove my quarter sections, I saw suburban wives, hoses in hand, rainbow-bright in the light of a front lawn.

Any possible reconciliation with Father failed to survive our first weekend together in Seattle. From then on, I traveled on my own. Soon I was dreaming about Safeway nearly every night. Yet when I tried to give Father my ideas as we sat together over a dinner table—about, say, hiring women store managers—all I got was Father's "over my dead body!" After a while a son gets the hint. Working for Father wasn't for me. Among the remarks given upon leaving my two-month Safeway career was my desk-mate's "I hope you get to do what you want." That he couldn't even name the activity—writing—shows how doubtful that must have appeared.

Back at college I became, at my uncle's insistence, a psychiatrist's patient. He had become alarmed by my haggard looks and the episode of nervous disorder that preceded "The Wanton Current." He was more alarmed by what I might be inflicting on Marcia or any future mate. "If you assume," he wrote,

as I did at 19 and even 24, that a satisfactory, steady sex-life would be the answer to every emotional problem, the chances are you will run the risk of hurting a lot of people and getting yourself into a deeper rut. The point of the analyst, I need only remind you, is that he infinitely absorbs your fantasies and isn't hurt; that he isn't hurt means that you are not, and in a curious way, a habit is broken.

His letter concluded with an appeal to the Delphic maxim. "My real argument is: you are so knowing, how can you resist knowing more?"

With a steady Marcia by my side, and my career anxiety apparently resolved, I had little reason to think I might not be in control of my emotional life. As far as I was concerned those two episodes were just that—blips. I felt obliged, nonetheless, to take up my uncle's suggestion. What did I have to lose?

My parents, perhaps because they were paying, were less than convinced. They viewed psychiatry as a direct affront to their authority. All the same, they contacted Charlie's cardiologist who found me a proper Central European from the Medical School. Three times a week now I sat before this small, silent, forever scribbling, bald-headed doctor. Taking his required notes, I see now. But it could and did indeed look as if he were gathering evidence. About my sexual proclivities—was I straight, bent, or a monstrous new indeterminacy? About the fittingness of the vocation I had so unexpectedly lighted on? Judge me, I implored him, tell me I'm the fellow I want to be: healthy, normal, and despite all that a promising writer.

From the start any possibility of transference was marred by the physical aversion I bore my judge. The feelings emerged in a dream at the end of our first week. It was night and I found myself being swept along in the waters of the Seine. I don't remember the embankment walls and stone bridges I was bobbing under so much as the scary limpidity of the riverbed as I passed over, first, a shoal of raccoon tails (the frontier cap favored by Senator Estes Kefauver), then some middle-European bowler hats.

By now the Seine had turned into an underground sewer and I was growing tired and anxious. Would I ever emerge? Finally, I saw a gleam of daylight. As I beached on the embankment, too exhausted even to drag myself up, there came ambling towards me a large belligerent muskrat—the guardian evidently of the sewer and those beaver tails and bowler hats. I awoke screaming. When six months later I finally identified the dream's muskrat with my analyst, the psychiatry ended,

For most of those six months, the Muskrat kept his lips resolutely sealed, preferring to let me stumble to my own conclusions. Only when I got overly riled at the futility of these exercises in pseudo-sincerity would he bestir himself to point out that my stammering came only when I wasn't telling the truth. On another occasion he had me reinvent a dream I hadn't been able to remember. There's no difference, I asked dumbfounded, between a waking invention and a dream? That's right, he replied, the subconscious exists to serve you, its mission is your continuing survival.

The psychiatry failed because of the antipathy I bore the Muskrat, which kept a transference from ever taking. Then again, with nothing personal at stake, I had no business being in analysis. For the Muskrat, it must have been frustrating to be ministering to a brat more concerned with the imagery he is articulating than anything so banal as "the Truth." That's why he focused on my dreams—the one reality I couldn't doctor. If the Muskrat would not go so far as to pronounce me a writer, then it was up to me. Marcia had secured a summer job in Cambridge. Not anticipating my father's reaction, I decided to sublease an apartment there where I could get started on a piece of fiction.

Given the issues at stake, not least Father's authority, this effort to strike out on my own had to be squashed. What was I intending to write, he asked, not another tell-all family novel! Faced now with this unintended rebellion, he reacted by turning off "the money tap," convinced that, with this one stroke, he had me stopped in my tracks. "This," he wrote, "is a direct declaration that I will not finance any adventures that do not meet with my approval. And if I don't pay for them, I don't know who will—with the possible exception of one of your uncles. If they do that, they risk an estrangement from which I think they would shrink." On my home turf I was not to be budged—not with Marcia radiating courage—and at the last minute Father backed down, restoring my allowance. Why not let me discover what little aptitude I had?

Once again, Father was right. I had begun a story based on Le Rosey, counting on the exoticism of the locale to pull me through. Needless to say, this thing, bereft of any inner life, never progressed beyond an endlessly re-typed seven pages. Those two months of staring at the wall of my ground floor apartment on busy Massachusetts Avenue effectively poisoned the idyll that Cambridge had been until then. For most of my senior year I couldn't wait to graduate.

ENGAGED

For Christmas of my senior year my parents took us brothers skiing in the Austrian Tyrol. I had expected, upon graduating, to take Marcia abroad and have her experience the world that as a youth had so bewitched me. Not possible, Marcia explained, not without breaking her father's heart. Nor could she live with me in a shared apartment. That left me in a considerable quandary. I didn't want to restrict my exploration of the female sex to my first woman; neither was I ready to give up Marcia. I missed, while cooped up with my family, not being with her and wrote, resolving not to be separated again. Was this a declaration of a kind? At any rate Marcia, when I saw her in New York, must have interpreted a new seriousness in my manner. When I put my arms around her in our 69th street elevator, she offered no resistance and brought me to her bed. I must have enjoyed our sex because next morning I proposed. A few days later I bought a topaz engagement ring that went with her skin color and blond looks. Callow enthusiasm and an inability to envision life in separate apartments, had fastened me to her.

As might be expected, the news of my engagement to a fiancée who possessed neither wealth nor the right poise and glamorous personality, and who came from New Jersey, was not exactly welcomed. Yet there must be few parents who would not have tried to dissuade a 21-year-old from marrying the first woman he had bedded. Why, Father asked, if I felt so compelled, couldn't I be marrying someone whose family he knew—a Liz Mellon, a Cindy Rockefeller? Mother felt I was too inexperienced to know what I required in a wife. "How can you be getting married," she asked not unreasonably, "when you have no money of your own and no prospective source of employment?"

Mother was right about not looking beyond my immediate convenience: why cut short an affair before it has fully blossomed? For the good reason, she might have replied, could we have talked frankly, that a marriage was not an affair. A husband was civilly and legally responsible. Did I want a lifetime of alimony hanging about my neck?

I was, I'd like to believe, open to persuasion, if pitched to the one issue that now really mattered—my future life as a writer. To my father, however, a writer's career was an anathema, far worse than an unsuitable marriage. There, at least, I was being socialized, with the good chance that domesticity would teach me responsibilities. If he knew no serious writers, other than Jimmy, there were reasons. It wasn't merely the bohemianism of the art crowd I was frequenting that put him off. Rather it was the different ways writers viewed and conducted the game of life.

Father's way was to keep his cards, marked and unmarked, close to his chest and to play as if his whole existence were at stake, "Challenge my card and you're challenging me." It was by constantly raising the emotional stakes that he triumphed. Whereas the writer has no choice but to expose the nature of the deck the businessman is playing with—whose money? Whose future?—and call his bluff. In this clash of views there was no room for compromise. Upon learning of my engagement, Father had bored right in:

> Your personal problem, i.e. marriage, is complicated by your desire to be a writer. I would give anything to think you have talent in that direction, but I would not be a good father and a good friend if I said something that was not in accord with my belief. There are people with a facility of expression who are natural writers, and I just don't believe you are that kind of person. I thought at one time that you could have fun and satisfaction out of teaching, but here again I think there are limits. A teacher has to be above all things articulate, and you have some defects in that quarter . . . In summary then, there are funds in trust for you to get an even larger allowance than you are getting now. But I have disposition of those funds. I do not want to be tough and arbitrary, but I do want to try and exert my influence so the best in you will come out. I do NOT want another Jimmy on the family blotter.

In his effort to dissuade me from pursuing the vocation of a writer, Father commanded some persuasive allies. Over lunch in Macy's top floor boardroom, Jack Straus told me how at my age he had been discouraged from pursuing a career as a jazz pianist. That did not keep him from entertaining whenever he had an occasion. He just wasn't making an ass of himself pretending he was another Earl Hines.

To me, writing wasn't the performance jazz was to my godfather. Instead it was the one window to personal liberation and self-knowledge that had come my way. In the circumstances, all of Jack Straus's advocacy of the social good he had been able to bring about as head of the world's greatest department store was not enough to dissuade me. To be myself, I told him, I had to forge my own way. If writing provided the one pair of wings I had succeeded in putting on, what choice did I have but to see how far they would carry me?

In June 1958, with a rousing cheer, "No more classes!" I graduated from Harvard, cum laude, though in the lower half of my class. Marcia and I were to be married in September. Rather than participate, like Marcia, in the wedding preparations, it made sense to make a trip I could try to write about. To Haiti, and its voodoo religion. The psychiatry and the "automatic" writing of "The Wanton Current" had convinced me that I needed to learn how to be a poet, possessed by inspiration, "balked and dumb, stuttering and stammering, hissed and hooted." (Emerson, "The Poet.)

Mother as a debutante, 1932

Lack of funds had much to do with my choice. My allowance had ceased upon graduation, one way of making clear to Marcia whom she was marrying: me and not them. With only $500 put aside, there was only so far I could venture. When I told my cousins, Merrill and Alicia Matzinger, of my plans, they insisted on my making a ten day detour to Havana. They wouldn't be there, but I could stay in their house and they would see that their friends showed me the sights.

Under normal conditions, it would be hard to imagine a surer way of not seeing anything. And there were moments in their palatial home, sweating in my sheets and unable to pry open a window, or paddling about under the eyes of a troop of circling vultures in their frangipani-strewn swimming pool, when I felt trapped in another goldfish bowl.

But those weren't normal conditions. A clandestine war was being waged that would end, eight months later, in Fidel Castro's capture of Havana. I was plunged into it my first night when I called on the Merrill Lynch branch manager, Ken Crosby. Crosby was no ordinary Merrill Lynch employee. While working for the Office of Strategic Services during the war, he had manned a fake Merrill Lynch office in Lima, Peru. Father's brainchild—an executive training program modelled on the one he had undergone at Macy's—had come into being for the sole purpose of giving Crosby and his cohorts the expertise they needed to perform their patriotic duty. That had given Crosby a taste for the business and, after the war, he found himself presiding over a legitimate Merrill Lynch office in Havana. But he still remained in the secret service, and my brother Stephen remembered Crosby as one of the business-suited guys who regularly convened in our cellar "safe house" that Father had put at the CIA's disposal.

One of the first things I asked Crosby about was the Castro insurgency. I had read about it, I told him, in the *Times*. At this Crosby bristled, "Castro may have a handful of outlaws hiding out with him in the Sierra Madre, but as you'll see there's no war going on here." To show me just how normal that Mafia-controlled Havana was, Crosby and his wife took me for dinner to their pal Santo Trafficante's casino. I remember the firm handshake and free scotch-and-soda offered by the handsome gabardine-suited mobster. As for Crosby, he was one of the CIA crowd tasked with assassinating poor Fidel. Was the gift of a poisoned stickpin his contribution?

Crosby decided that, among the renowned sights, I would appreciate a tour of the city's better brothels. To this end a young broker from his office, a personable well-educated Castro sympathizer, was deputized to escort me. (He would be among the first shot in the bloodbath that followed Castro's arrival.)

On the urban guerrilla side, there was the curator I met while trying to learn about the Cuban form of voodoo, *bembe*. She told me, after withdrawing to a private room, that she had joined the Communist underground after her lover was killed in Fidel's failed July 22nd assault on the Moncada barracks. That very morning she had witnessed the execution of a comrade by a firing squad. A revolution, Solzhenitsyn remarked, was not something he'd wish on his worst enemy. From the little I saw of this one I'd agree.

The Black Republic of Haiti did far more to open my eyes. True, the mere sight of a colored person did not send me into a screaming fit, as it did my little brother. But my interchanges with my grandfather's servants—they were family to him, not me—or with the few African-Americans I encountered at school had done little to lessen the alienation, not to say guilt, I felt.

Robin flanked by Felix and James

It helped that, upon arrival in Port-au-Prince, I was befriended by a young painter, Hervé Télémaque. Hervé had just returned from a year at the Art Students League in New York and would soon carve a reputation as a witty colorist and Europe's foremost pop painter. Before an African-American I felt I could never ask about the different perspectives that inhabiting a black skin gives; to do so would appear insensitive or condescending. With this African-featured mulatto I could. Color in its many aspects—nationality, politics, sexual skin tones—was his cross, his heritage. As Hervé questioned me about what I had seen during the day and the inferences to be drawn, I began to see some of the range and diversity of the global spectrum. Maybe this is a gift any French-educated intellectual can impart, as easily as he chews his croissant, but it sure was different from the milieus I frequented where conversation rarely rose beyond the staking out of a common ground.

Squeezed into a variety of open-air conveyances, I jolted over much of the hemisphere's most impoverished country and experienced a world utterly new to me. All the same, that burnt marshmallow, a white kid, could not help but feel unwelcome in a country whose flag is the tricolor with the white band ripped out. And the glare of so many diseased eyes, full of such wretchedness, such undisguised contempt, did not make for congenial traveling. Meanwhile, from the other end of my tether, Marcia was bombarding me with daily, "I miss you, why don't you come home if you're not enjoying yourself," missives. By now, after five weeks on the move, I was prepared to see her point. I told her I'd fly to Jamaica for a week and be back by August.

RUMPELSTILTSKIN'S TRAP

In Montego Bay, at the other end of the island from Kingston, I found the calypso equivalent of jazz's Storyville before the US Navy closed it down: Milneburg Joys, Marmalade Rag. Their effect—music, sex—was such that the highly tanned youth in his crimson-flowered Saga Boy shirt who stepped off the plane into Marcia's arms was considerably different from the one who had written her from Haiti ten days earlier.

In Summit, I found the wedding preparations well advanced. Marcia had wanted a small wedding—good friends only. But she was overruled by our two mothers and we found ourselves saddled with a platoon of ushers and bridesmaids along with a seated reception for 250, half of them social and business acquaintances of my parents.

Though my parents were putting their shoulders to the wedding wheel, by no means had they capitulated. Marcia suspected that this Rumpelstiltskin, as she viewed my Old Man, forever about to explode through a hole in the floor, could still play us a nasty trick. That he hadn't as yet tried to buy her off bewildered her; surely she had a price! But so far he had done nothing other than have me apply to Oxford (a gambit that worked more successfully in delaying Peter and Mark from marrying their Jewish sweethearts). At the time, the machinery for landing a Magowan in one of the lesser colleges still needed oiling. The future knight's emissaries could not overcome the evidence of my grades, nor my unwillingness to fly over, as my brothers would, for a personal interview.

Marcia, though, was right in her suspicions. My father did have a plan. Upon my return from the Caribbean he voiced his amazement that I had chosen to visit Marcia and her family rather than avail myself of Southampton's "free grub and booze." With the wedding less than a month away, a duty visit could not be indefinitely staved off. I agreed to meet Father in his Pine Street office and then drive with Mother to Southampton.

I found Father decked out in one of Charlie's Charvet ties and a London-tailored blue pin-striped suit and seated behind a large mahogany desk bursting with family photos: the five of us, a team in identical shorts and sweaters, beaming up from the grass of the Beach House lawn; Mother regal in her Brockhurst portrait; Charlie, in double-breasted serge and clutching, as always, a half-spent cigarette. Beyond Father, two corner windows gave on the harbor, forty flights below.

I took up the chair across from him. "What's up?" I asked.

"Your marriage," Father replied. He went on, "I wish I could tell you the number of people I know who showed bright promise as young men and who are semi-failures today because of mistakes they made at the outset. One of those mistakes, and a frequent one," he added, looking straight at me, "was a too early marriage. The necessity of taking care of a wife and children handicapped the man in making important decisions. He couldn't afford to take a new job to advance his career—perhaps at a lower salary—because he couldn't afford to reduce his family's eating money."

Scratch the threats, the enticements, and there remained his all-powerful narcotic—money. "I don't know what plans you and Marcia have to support yourselves, but if you think you can survive by climbing on my back, you've got another thought coming."

"You act," I protested, "as if I don't have a penny."

"Well, you don't," he said, looking me straight in the eye.

"What about the portfolio, the stocks bought in my name when I was born, I've heard so much about? Whose funds are they," I asked, pausing as I glared back at him, "mine or yours? Or is it all another tax scam?"

"Your trust fund exists, but since the funds derive from me, I can decide when and if you get them. The last thing your mother and I want," he said, fixing me with his small piercing eyes, "is to deprive you of your ambition: the will, the need, to make it on your own."

In our family memorable discussions have often taken place one-on-one in cars. It's our canvas-roofed Buick I associate with Father's decision to join the Navy; the De Soto with his facts-of-life remarks; Mother's Thunderbird, with her accusation that, in getting engaged, I had reneged on my solemnly pledged word. So when, on our drive down, Mother asked how, without a bean, I could be thinking of getting married, I was ready. "How can you prattle on about my not having any funds? What about the famous trust fund

Grandpa and Father set up together the day I was born? Or the account Jack Straus opened the same day at the Riverside Savings Bank? I don't understand by what right, a full year after I've come of age, the two of you can go on withholding it. Do you want me to take my case to Cholly Knickerbocker?"

These remonstrances worked. Back in the city, Father summoned me downtown to announce he was turning over a $60,000 portfolio my grandfather had set up. "But I don't want to encourage any misperceptions on your part," he said measuring his words, "that's the only money you have in your name."

True or not, the portfolio represented an appreciable sum. Enough, I told Father gratefully, to give me a safety net while allowing us a long trip on the continent. And I promised, upon our return, to look for a job.

If Father was unable to consign me to the fundless perdition my rebellion deserved, the family annals contained records of other gambits waiting only to be dusted off. Earlier, when a liaison of Jimmy's with his Amherst mentor, Kimon Friar, was discovered—Jimmy was 19 at the time—Charlie had briefly considered taking out a $6,000 contract on Kimon with the good folks at Murder, Inc. (Was Bugsy Siegel a familiar Charlie could summon on the phone?) Instead, on further reflection, he convened his trust lawyer, Larry Condon, my parents and Hellen, the snoop behind the discovery of Kimon's love letter, for a mid-winter conference in the chills of Southampton.

What did they think, Charlie asked, after they had assembled in the unheated Orchard's great card room, of his hiring a comely call girl to initiate the young man into the nirvana of heterosexuality? He knew of one available for $10,000, specialized in converting homosexuals. Might that be enough to contravene a youth's misguided fantasies? To a worshipper of the Almighty Wad, Charlie's can-do proposal sounded eminently practical and Father said as much. But they were stopped in their tracks by Larry Condon, who dumfounded them with a prophecy Father never forgot. "You may not believe it, Charlie, but this boy of yours is going to be as famous in his own lifetime as you have been in yours."

With me, there was no question of anyone alienating, much less wrecking, a future genius. The problem, rather, lay in coming up with a woman sufficiently persuasive. One can see perhaps the two of them interviewing the various candidates—professionals, *demi-mondaines,* outright amateurs— before settling on a former flame of mine.

I've no idea what form the bait took, but once the particulars were agreed,

I can see the ensuing dialogue. First the Candidate: "How do you suggest I approach him? It's years since we last dated."

"For a starter, I would compliment Robin on his forthcoming marriage." That would be Mother, the mistress of the formal.

"Then?"

"Tell him you need to see him urgently and put that urgency in your voice."

An idiot ruse, but I fell for it. I should have smelled something fishy when Mother, on our drive down, and then Father on his own arrival, made a point of letting me know the Candidate had phoned several times during the past week. Difficult as it was to fathom this renewal of interest, I welcomed the chance of seeing her. "As you know," I told them, "I've always liked her."

I had been in Southampton barely an hour when the Candidate called with her congratulations. How pretentious, I thought, what's come over her? After delivering that bit of the script, she said, "I have something personal I need to discuss with you. Is there anywhere private where we can meet?"

"How about our Cooper's Neck house for a drink this evening. It's being sold," I added by way of reassurance, "and there won't be anyone around."

Some hours later, I found myself seated on the sun parlor's long lemon chintz sofa beside this future Fashion Woman of the Year. For two summers we had met in the dunes outside her family house nearly every night, a sweater of mine under us as we lay side by side or climbed over the wall into the Beach House's swimming pool. But for all the roaring of the waves and the brilliance of the stars, neither of us succeeded in overcoming our inhibitions and making a gesture that would have bridged the chasm between us. Must make up for that now, I thought, coiling a predatory arm around her as I drew her down into the plush depths of the sofa.

As might be expected the Candidate responded with a warmth that soon had me envisioning more exquisite possibilities. I had a paw in her blouse and was starting to undress her when, with a brusque movement, as if suddenly coming to her senses, she swung herself bolt upright and in an offended tone inquired, "How can you be doing this when you're in love and GETTING MARRIED?"

Under the circumstances I had no problem explaining the pull, the priority even, of our unconsummated past. For much of the next seven years, I'm afraid, that summed up my marital code. I wanted Marcia, but if she was not available, I would try to satisfy myself with whoever was. I was not marrying Marcia because she was the one and only woman in my world, but because it was the one way I could take her abroad. Getting married, for me, was little more than a legal fiction, the theater necessary if I was to give Marcia the continental experience she desired. I did not foresee that the fiction might mean something else to Marcia; or that it might take on a life of its own.

Of the wedding I remember Marcia's tiara, her lily of the valley decorated veil and long white gloves; the antique dueling pistol my groomsmen presented at their lunch; and Charlie Merrill's tiny tailcoat and top hat into which I allowed myself to be squeezed, one more item in the charade to which I had consented. All the more distinct, therefore, the crack of doom with which the words of the ancient oath descended: "Do you take this woman ... for as long as you both shall live?" For the first time the awful solemnity of the bond I was taking caught up with me. "I'm really in it now!" I found myself gulping. And I was, no longer in my familial labyrinth, but shackled nonetheless.

These feelings turned to outright dismay when, on our second night on the Ile-de-France, headed for the Europe that so drew us both, Marcia refused to satisfy my lust. Doubtless, she had her reasons. Post-wedding withdrawal blues? A sense that this night I wasn't turning her on?

It was one thing to slip my head into a lovingly plaited noose; another to be strangled. All the more in that the one adult identity I felt sure of was sexual. (I certainly wasn't a writer.) Now I saw my worst fears being confirmed. Why I put up with it I don't know. All I had to do was go to the purser and request a room of my own, then take the first flight home. Instead I was now condemned to drag myself along from one absurd site to the next. When would it ever stop? When would I be me?

More gray days in that floating hotel followed: shuffleboard, ping-pong, badminton. And I had left Jamaica for this?

AFTER THE WEDDING GUESTS WENT HOME

We did disembark together at Cherbourg. For her, it was as if we had stepped onto a stage set. That we were performing it together, finding cheap hotels, perusing menus in which we recognized hardly an item, gave the play something of the feeling of a dance in frozen time, frozen because there was an intimacy that eluded us.

With unlimited time at our disposal, we chose Spain. Marcia's father had worked there installing an international phone system in the thirties, while Marcia had studied the literature and I assumed she spoke the language. I had never been there.

Our plan might have succeeded had we landed in Algeciras or Seville, instead of Cherbourg. By the time we had driven south from Paris by the old Campostela pilgrimage route, we were thoroughly smitten with France. By the intimate, intricately tiled valley villages we wound along; by a vernacular architecture that changed into something different almost every twenty miles.

Spain, by contrast, was still in the aftershock of its civil war and decidedly stodgy. We stuck it out until November set in, staying in the unheated pool house of a friend of my parents while we tried to secure a three-month lease. When that proved impossible, we set off for Rome by way of Provence, my boyhood Rapallo and Stendhal's Parma, checking it all out, three-star restaurant by two-star church.

Marcia made an appreciative companion, eager, fearless, willing to meet anybody, stay anywhere, try anything. Her joy in the still extant past she was taking in could not have been more palpable. Knowledgeable about art history, she retained what we were touring, while doing her utmost to provide the time I needed in which to try to write. But nothing in all the marvels we were taking in set off a spark of invention. Instead I felt a growing unease as I watched my financial lifeline being frittered away.

Wherever we halted there would be an encouraging letter waiting from Father. "Enjoy yourselves and stay as long as you want. You two will never have such an opportunity again." Aware, no doubt, that the longer we floundered on the honeymoon, the easier I'd be to reel in on my return.

The summer in Cambridge, endlessly retyping my seven wretched pages, had been dispiriting. This, if possible, was worse. Maybe Father was right, and I wasn't cut out to be a writer. I remember asking Jimmy upon my return why I had so miscarried. "I could write in the Caribbean, why did I draw a blank in Europe?"

My failure, Jimmy volunteered, had less to do with what I was taking in than the mistake of "traveling with a loved one. One is so intent on having her see that one forgets to look for oneself. In my three years abroad the one site that actually moved me was Ravenna. It's the one place I went by myself."

Perhaps. But in April, on the way south through Andalusia to catch our ship home, we chanced on the little white palace of the last Moorish king of Ronda: an L-shaped upstairs corridor of exquisitely tiled alcove bedrooms looking down on a fountain-loud inner patio. What joy to have lived there! And in the gardens of the Alhambra we found an exhilaration of fountains, arching effects, intimate walkways that quite surpassed the ne plus ultra of Charlie's Orchard. Were these the sparks capable of releasing me from my barrenness? With a week to spare we took a ferry across the nine miles of water to Tangiers. There, too, came hassock cushions, the smoky gold of a musician's cap, or his pair of slippers, ochres that seemed joy itself. If, as Marcia declared, these intimations originated in medieval Persia, we both knew now where at the next opportunity we would travel.

To avoid the humiliation of 69th Street upon our return, Jimmy and David let us stay in their rent-controlled $30 a month walk-up on First Avenue and 51st street. The previous tenant, Kimon Friar, had dropped honey cakes under the plush chairs, attracting a squad of cockroaches. But the walls were painted a beguiling pistachio green, the bookshelves contained the usual Jimmy trouvailles, and we found ourselves well situated for exploring the last ethnic enclaves of the Eastside.

Marcia pursued her own interests reviewing gallery shows for *Art News* and working as a research assistant at NYU's Institute for Art History, while I pounded the legendary pavements looking for work. One might think a Harvard graduate with "Business Success" stamped over both sets of his genes might be employable. But Father warned, laying down the gauntlet, "I'm willing to bet you can't land a job on your own."

As foreseen, I found no management-training program willing to take me up. "Why don't you go to work for your Old Man?" they asked, sensibly. Or, evoking the post-Korean War nitty-gritty, "How do you stand with the Draft?" Efforts to secure more basic employment, as an office temp or a dance instructor, fell to similar mistrust.

My efforts did succeed in drawing distinctions from my parents. A job just wasn't a job, I learned; there were good ones and bad ones. After forking out for the best possible education, they did not relish seeing me, like a beau of Mother's, turning into an airport baggage checker.

In that case, I suggested, could they help me find a job compatible with a writing career? A copywriter in an ad agency? An editorial assistant? But the agencies to which I applied had no interest on hiring a young man who wished to write, and the one way apparently of becoming an editor was to buy a percentage of the firm—not my idea of landing a job. Jason Epstein, after one look at the aesthete I appeared to be, proposed my buying out Miss Steloff at The Gotham Book Mart. His boss, Bennett Cerf, laid it out flatly: "We try to hire women who are less likely to keep pestering us for a promotion. If you want to write, why don't you go to graduate school and become a college professor. They make the same salary as an editor and enjoy a lot more freedom." With no real alternative, I took Bennett Cerf's advice and enrolled in Columbia's graduate school. I saw in it not so much a career, as a refuge to tide me over until I discovered what, if anything, I had it in me to write.

More positively, there was the educational aspect. If the work of the past is the bread a writer feeds on, why not test out on others what you are consuming? In the late Fifties, this was incentive enough to entice a number of us to pursue degrees. Only later, and by then hopelessly immured, would we discover the incompatibility between the demands of Academe and learning your trade as a writer; or realize that our classroom satrapies were the establishment's way of siphoning off the over-educated and non-productive. It's not true, as G.B. Shaw claimed, "Those who can, do; those who can't, teach." Many of us could have performed in a number of influential arenas. But at a susceptible age we had fallen for our professors' self-defensive proselytizing—the lure of a life of the mind. Where could that life be better lived than at a big university with a well-equipped library?

While waiting for Columbia's semester to begin, I returned to a translation of the work inspiring my Caribbean diary, Henri Michaux's *Ecuador*. In a letter from Colombo, Jimmy had brought its sequel to my attention:

> A marvelously good book was just put into my hands in Tokyo—Henri Michaux's *A Barbarian in Asia* ... With the brightest touches he draws the noblest conclusions ... to wit, his advice to the world: Create Civilizations! (like the prologue to *Les Mamelles de Tiresias*: "*Faites des enfants!*") Every page is a joy to read and the style, even in English, contagious, as you will see if you compare my travel notes with it."

Perhaps no one but the author of *The Changing Light at Sandover* would equate creating "civilizations" with fathering children. I've certainly never risen to such ambitions. But it wasn't long before I, too, was bowled over by a reportage so irresistibly personal. The travel writers who had come my way were authorities with a claim to know what they were commemorating. Michaux is an unapologetic amateur and the *Barbarian* represents an on-the-spot recording of 1930–31 trip. Michaux conducts it in essay form, a series of provocative vignettes tossed off without a "when" or "where" that might indicate provenance, perspective, or time of day. "If you can't generalize, how can you claim to have had any experience?" he asks. Its opening works to the same end: "I know some twenty capitals. Bah!" Credentials thus disposed of, Michaux submits us to Calcutta, "the most crowded city in the Universe."

Whereupon invention rises, bristling, to the occasion. "Imagine a city exclusively composed of ecclesiastics, seven hundred thousand ecclesiastics." The sally is one we recognize from farce; everything extends from that first "exclusively." Michaux is not describing Bengalis in their multi-faceted humanity, but a condition of mind so omnipresent it threatens to sweep him away. Cornered, he lashes out:

> The Bengali is a born ecclesiastic, and ecclesiastics with the exception of the very small ones who must be carried, always go on foot ... All of them are self-assured, with a mirror-like expression, an insidious sincerity and the kind of impudence that comes from meditating with the legs crossed.

One can perhaps see something of the aphoristic verve that delighted me in D.H. Lawrence's *Studies in Classic American Literature*. Before setting off for Caribbean, I had borrowed my uncle's copy of the earlier *Ecuador*, intending to translate it as I read it. And it worked. Whenever I was stumped there was this diarist offering a set of lenses, "Defend yourself! Don't be taken in!" With no shame, I availed myself of the voice.

THE BROTHERS DUKE IT OUT

Early in the summer my parents in a conciliating gesture invited Marcia and me to their newly refurbished Beach House for the weekend. They weren't able at the last minute to join us, but they made clear we had the run of the place and could stay in whatever room we wanted. After inspecting the available ones, I picked a bedroom in the front of the house: the only one with a private bathroom, an item essential to my new marital status.

Imagine my brother Merrill's stupefaction upon returning from the movies to find the two of us lodged in his bedroom. You would think before installing ourselves we might have noticed his outfits hanging in the closet and the toiletries in the bathroom. I didn't know it, but he had been there a week. After being expelled from Yale, and arranging to enter the National Guard, he had gone down to Southampton to play golf on its incomparable courses.

Quite reasonably, Merrill protested, "That's my bedroom you're taking over."

"How can that be?" I retorted, equally surprised to find him standing in the doorway. In inviting us, Mother hadn't indicated anyone would be there.

For Merrill, after a lifetime of enduring an older brother's appropriations, this was the last straw. "If you intend to evict me from my bedroom," he said, "you're going to have to fight me first."

Merrill, I ought to have remembered, had his own well-honed notions of territory. Once, after dining out with our grandfather, he had, for reasons of his own, refused to thank him. Put out by what he saw as a discourtesy, Charlie refused to let it go by and badgered him the whole way back. When the Packard finally arrived at 69th Street, the 8-year-old leapt out with his parting sally, "This is my sidewalk and you can't yell at me anymore."

False assumption or not, I was not above trotting it out: "Mother said we could stay wherever we wanted."

Merrill was adamant. "I don't care what Mother said. She's not here and I am. Are you a man or a mouse?"

In all our thousands of fights Merrill had never defeated me. Even when he had outgrown me, I was still fast enough to outwrestle him. This time he was definitely in command. No sooner had I crawled out from under one piece of furniture where a punch had landed me than I found myself pummeled into the next.

One might think, as Merrill stood over his defeated brother, that he would have been satisfied with the threshold he had crossed. But victory is not revenge and, for Merrill, nothing less than my complete disfigurement would suffice. "Don't worry, I know how to rearrange your face."

The remark touched off a proprietary nerve in Marcia. With a shout, she leapt into the fray.

A first victory on Merrill's part might be thought somewhat overdue. But my parents, when they learned about it, were mortified and Father responded by summoning me, on my return to the city, to his office. After a remark about how dismayed he was by Merrill's inhospitality, he came up with a considered atonement. "I warned you that landing a job on your own wouldn't be as easy. Now that you've decided on graduate school, you should have an allowance. I'm turning over from your trust fund $500 a month. In return, I want you to sign this paper appointing me your trustee. The trust fund is something I've set up with my own money. It has grown very nicely and I think I should continue to take care of it."

The moment was crucial. Before putting a pen to that document, at the very least I should have consulted a lawyer. What exactly was I signing away? (Nothing is less trustworthy than a trust fund!) Father would use that legal form to keep me his chattel for the next thirteen years, forced to bow and scrape for each tidbit.

ETHNIC LEAGUE SOCCER

Marcia and I had moved into a two-room $125-a-month walk-up in what is now the expanded 92nd St. YMCA when, one morning, strolling below the large brewery we looked out on, I happened to notice in a bar window one of those front row kneeling, second row standing soccer team pictures. Under it, in white ink, was the legend, "NY Swabians." I had no idea where Swabia might be in Germany, but soccer teams don't necessarily sprout between the cracks of a Manhattan sidewalk, and I obtained the address of the upper Bronx gym where they trained Thursday evenings.

I had played soccer since I was six, learning the game at St. Bernard's. In those days, soccer set a school definitely apart. To find competition we had to travel into alien territory: the Bronx, Dobbs Ferry, Greenwich, or (by thrilling ferry) to Staten Island.

For a kid who had never gotten over being changed from left-to-right-handed, a sport that outlaws the hands had something to be said for it. Isn't our whole nervous system reflected in the soles of our feet? Soccer gives a chance to reclaim some of that lost centrality and balance.

At St. Bernard's positions were assigned by size. Runts like me played forward. So far as skills went, I was a true provincial. I never saw a professional game, even on the box, until I was 22 in Madrid. With no models other than older boys, I had no way up to gain the control and confidence that come to a kid who picks up the game on the street. The Randall's Island fields to which we were bussed were swards of expansive green that didn't require much beyond the ability to suddenly accelerate, keeping the ball as close as possible to our tank-like boots. In a short fall season our coaches had to concentrate on position play. We used the full spread of the field; we cooperated, drawing patterns, advancing triangles, on the chaos of a game. Lift your head, the coach would yell, and look for the open man. When you found him, out on the wing or wherever he lurked, much of your work was done.

By junior year at college enough of the squad had graduated that, in a moment of desperation the coach installed me as a pivotal center forward. Still, being a jock didn't agree with the writer I was struggling to make myself into. In Father's day being a letterman was the beau ideal; in the mid-Fifties it was anything but cool. I talked about the team as "they," I lagged behind everyone running laps, and every evening I drank to the extent semi-sobriety allowed.

When, as a senior, I actually got in shape, realizing it might be my last chance to play this beautiful game, the coach no longer trusted me. I spent much of a game on the bench, trying to convince him I might be of more use than my replacement, a football player who turned over nearly every ball that touched his shoe. But once in a while the oaf, by sheer hustle, managed to thrust his bulk in front of an attempted clearance and score; from our coach's viewpoint, exactly what the game should be about.

However poor the quality, we all accepted that our playing days ended there. That's why you learned tennis and golf, sports you could carry on playing. In the locker room before the season-ending Yale game I remember the coach telling us seniors that in all likelihood this would be the last soccer game we'd ever play. Hearts thumping, and a whole youth's ashes in our mouths, we went out and remedied what had been a mediocre season.

It may seem odd that such a claim could be made in an America which, a mere six years earlier, had fielded a team good enough to knock England out of the World Cup. Those semi-pro players hadn't come out of nowhere. The possibility of playing existed, provided you didn't mind probing the underclass in search of a team. That none of my college teammates did so says much for our tribal mentality. Out on the field we were Harvard. Strip off the crimson jersey, and they were hard put to justify the physical risk.

I had fewer scruples. As part of my American History and Literature major, I had taken a series of courses from Oscar Handlin. The author of *The Uprooted* was convinced that our social history could be assessed solely by measuring the impact of each successive wave of immigration: how immigrants made it, what they did to sustain themselves. It was the opposite, expatriation, that drew me, and to that end I had written a senior thesis on American artistic expatriates in the century preceding the outbreak of World War I. A team comprised of recent immigrants could give me a window from which to contemplate what you did to keep from being melted down.

What made me suppose an immigrant team would welcome me, I don't know. Ethnic teams are naturally leery of adulterating themselves with mercenaries whose loyalties are not to be trusted, and whose presence will inevitably be construed as a sign of weakness.

A Swabia deep enough to field two reserve teams could take a chance and sign me. A few Sundays later we were playing a Lithuanian outfit from New Jersey on an ice-surrounded "oval" out in the depths of Queens. As often happens in a debut I was the twelfth man. The game was proceeding in a scoreless fashion when a little wing of theirs, riled by the clobbering his shins were taking, hauled off and blindsided the fullback guarding him with a single punch that broke his nose. I substituted and minutes later, by pure beginner's luck, scored, a ball centered from the right somehow catching the swinging motion of my foot, an automatic dream clinking into the astonished net.

Such luck could not hold and soon enough I was back where, as a forward I belonged, on the bench.

THE ACCELERATING GRADUATE STUDENT

By September, I had begun my graduate studies. In philosophy, as Uncle Jimmy, speaking for himself, would have had it. No, English, but the modern comparative field I sought was oversubscribed and I settled for the American 19th century that had been part of my undergraduate major. A despised part, I might add, thanks to D.H. Lawrence whose *Classics* had provided an irresistible cudgel. I found I could not high-handedly dismiss an entire corpus—not if I was preparing to teach it. Obliged to be positive, I unearthed some gems, among them Sarah Orne Jewett's *Pointed Fir* sketches, which I made the subject of a master's thesis.

What interested me in *Pointed Firs* was its pastoral framework, an adaptation from Renaissance literature, which provided the structure on which Jewett mounted a narrative far more interesting than the local color for which she was known. A writer has to learn his craft somewhere. I wasn't the sort who could be a know-it-all parodist wrestling with my vaunted predecessors. But a convention system that writes you, rather than you it, had much to recommend to one as deeply blocked as I.

In a footnote from "Et in Arcadia Ego," Erwin Panofsky hazarded that pastoral came out of the same bag as pictorial perspective, both creations of the Este court in Ferrara. A chance *aperçu,* but it explained how a pictorial system of values could come to be adopted into a journey-based narrative form and why some of its most successful practitioners—Fromentin, Jewett, Dinesen, the Hardy of *Far from the Madding Crowd*—came to it from an initial training as painters, or in Hardy's case as an architect.

Columbia's Master's program was conducted according to the continental system: no tests, no papers and at year end—bingo—a two-day exam on which any further progress depended. The whole paperless waiting game so unnerved me that I ended up taking an upper level Melville seminar just so I could write weekly reports, among them an essay on another gem, "Benito Cereno", and the Spenser-derived Saturnalian masque that furnishes its sub-plot.

Because of a generous admissions policy, and the continuing need we males had for post-Korea draft exemption (my stammer and mention of the psychiatry I had undergone to try to cure it were enough to get me exempted), Columbia's graduate program was overcrowded. Those of us wanting to proceed to the doctoral level were encouraged to apply elsewhere.

The year before, on the SS America, I had struck up a friendship with Richard Saez, who was studying comparative literature at Yale with the Czech "critic of critics," Rene Wellek. With Richard's encouragement I applied there. Fortunately Henri Peyre, and not Wellek, was screening applicants. My translation of Michaux made him think I might be a maverick Yale could take a gamble on and he put me on the waiting list.

Robin amidst wedding grooms. Back row: Paul Baum, Bernat Rosner, George Leness, Blaise Pasztory. Front row: Tony Oberschall, brothers Peter, Tulare, Stephen, 1958.

As a subject of graduate study, comparative literature perhaps only makes sense in the way Wellek in his own person embodied it, as a history of literary criticism interpreted from within a polylingual context.

Certainly there were no entry-level jobs on offer in academia. But I had a language background, and was attracted by the more speculative horizon comp lit seemed to offer. The last thing I wanted was to be buried in a period cubbyhole.

I was well taught at Yale. As far as English and Romance literatures were concerned, Yale's was the best graduate school in the country. Marcia secured a great job as the research assistant to the art museum's Oriental curator, describing and helping to date Persian and Chinese artifacts for a catalogue. But the Dixwell Avenue ghetto, next to which we lived in a garish pink-walled apartment, with its biweekly Saturday night murder (often enough a woman disposing of her two-timing man) could give one pause. With some five haberdasheries to the one bookstore, it was clear where Yale's undergraduates were mostly headed—Wall Street. Neither of us wanted to spend any more time in New Haven than we had to.

That I managed to fulfill the doctoral requirements in a mere twelve months might seem surprising. But in a time of expanding enrollment, Yale wanted us out and contributing, and much was done to speed us over the institutional hurdles. Among these were the language requirements. Despite three years of German at Exeter and a summer course in Vienna, I failed the exam twice. Rather than subject himself to a third waste of time, Wellek detected enough improvement to grant me a pass. As for Latin, I had never progressed beyond Caesar at St. Bernard's. The examiners saved my day by assigning a medieval version of the Plutarch passage in which the asp goes to work on Cleopatra's breast.

At Harvard I had not taken a French course; the guiding lights did not seem exalted enough. At Yale I made up for it, taking for my philology requirement Old Provencal and seminars on the Romance of the Rose, Stendhal and Gide. Gide may be an over-rated writer, but thanks to an Exeter tutorial and Peyre's seminar, he became, warts and all, part of me. Stendhal is the real article, a distinct sensibility present in his every sentence, and in a class taught by Victor Brombert, I conceived an abiding affection for the writer as well as his many commentators and disciples.

Expanding on my renewed interest in American literature, I took a seminar on Whitman and Hart Crane given by R.W.B. Lewis. A number of authorities, I learned, had seen Whitman's comic epic, "A Song of Myself," as registering a mystic experience. But none of them had explained how Whitman managed to translate an essentially wordless revelation into a work that marks one of the foundation stones of modern poetry.

Poetic inspiration interested me greatly, and my recent travels led me to think that no critic had ever made it to Haiti, let alone their local Pentecostal church. If they had, I maintained, they might have seen that the experience governing the transformation of self was a voodoo-inspired one of possession. This was outrageous enough to justify a 20-page elaboration: an exposition of what Emerson—the source for much of Whitman—understood by a poetry of possession, followed by a close reading of "Song of Myself." Since possession involves an induced out-of-body experience, I had to name and thus isolate the conflicting verbal rhythms in the initial sections and relate them to the corresponding personae in the poem. Then show how, through a typical process of chanting and responding to a succession of vocal, orchestral and finally operatic music, Whitman intensifies the verbal dancing to a point where, in the "fakes of death," he falls backward onto the floor, his neck held in a vice-like clamp. The totemic spirit mounting the author of *Leaves of Grass* is, appropriately enough, that of a cow. The violation this self-styled animal lover undergoes is clear in the disgust he feels toward the "rest of the herd" gathering around him, the provokers "straining the udder of my heart for its withheld drip," and in his horrified realization that "my own hands carried me there." The possessed dance climaxes in a voodoo-like orgasmic release of "rich showering rain." And the reinvigorated "Walt" sets off to realize the godhead latent in him.

I found myself fluently tossing off semi-publishable essays like this at a rate of three, even five a semester; a pace tolerable only because I knew these were the last courses I'd ever be compelled to take.

The papers were nothing compared to the agony I endured preparing for that September's culminating ninety-minute oral examination. I had picked eight topics in a more or less historical sequence: Old Provencal literature; the *Romance of the Rose* and the courtly epic; Moliere; Stendhal; Melville and Whitman; modern poetry; modern criticism. In this lot there were some real gaps. I knew zilch about the courtly epic (epics take time to read!) and almost as little about Moliere. My one hope was that my examiners, like the three Graeae, would get so caught up passing their one eye back and forth as to forget the time at their disposal.

My plan worked better than I had any right to expect. The Americanist, R.W.B. Lewis, led off first. Back and forth, swifter than a tennis ball, the eye flew: Melville, Whitman, Whitman, Melville, the most finicky questioning for a ripe half hour. By then, inspired by the array of detail I was batting about, they were all in full cry. I sat at our oval table content to let them natter on, now and then stoking the flame with a new name or a date or a rejuvenating mot. Finally, after a seeming eternity, the tiny alarm clock I had been eyeing rang.

One can imagine the consternation. "There are a number of topics we haven't questioned you on!"

"Too bad," I said, "time's up."

I learned, when they reentered the room, that I had received a First, unanimous, "Truly brilliant performance, wasn't it?" Through the chorus of nods, Wellek could be heard muttering, "Not that it matters what we give you, since your heart's set on writing, not an academic career. Are we done then?"

"Not so fast!" I protested. "I still need a dissertation topic, hopefully one that will take me to Paris."

"You don't want to avail yourself of the Beinecke Library and its incomparable research facilities?"

"No," I replied, "I'd rather spend this last year abroad and do some travel, say, to Iran, I can write about."

"I won't argue for the comparative merits of New Haven. Doubtless, we all pay a price. As for a pastoralist, how about Eugene Fromentin?"

"The exotic painter and author of *The Dutch Masters*?" I asked, again out of my depth. "Wasn't he a follower of Delacroix who wrote a couple of books on the nomads of the Sahara?"

"Fromentin was also a protegé of George Sand, a champion of pastoral. Under her influence he wrote a confessional novel, *Dominique*, that is pastoral in the strict way you have defined it. You'd only have to add a couple of chapters to what you've already written on Jewett."

PARIS

In Paris I ensconced myself at the Bibliothèque Nationale, copying out on 4 x 6 cards all that had been perpetrated on Fromentin. Paris in those days was still a city where a couple could walk, arm in arm, down the middle of a medieval street. That we had no Parisian friends other than the Télémaques, and little access to cultural life, helped to concentrate our explorations of the city: the American obligation we felt to memorize in our feet the crossword puzzle of an *arrondissement*.

From our $2-a-night hotel on the Ile St. Louis in the serene traffic-less center of the city we would saunter forth to gawk at the shop fronts and awnings; at the fervently enlaced couples in the wooden metro trains with their magical destinations: St. Lazare, Sèvres-Babylone, Réaumur-Sebastopol, Kremlin-Stalingrad. A city of lights which the rain multiplied into millions of specks of desire: the drops glowing from umbrellas, stockinged calves and hurrying shoes reminded Marcia of how, only in that below sea-level depression of the Seine valley, could Impressionism have emerged with such feminine éclat.

Traveling together on our honeymoon had been a dance of acquaintance. This was more like falling in love. As we drew in the breath of that other life we had penetrated, something began to flow between us. A new closeness, as if we were each other's rapt fingers pointing, each other's dawn.

By mid-winter, though, even Paris had paled and it seemed time to take up our project of a trip to Iran and discover, as we saw it, the folks who invented paradise. To ease the logistics there was Uncle Jimmy conveniently established in Athens in a small house beneath the Lycabettos pine wood. He invited us to come see the "Never on Sunday" style sailor dancing he and David had discovered.

Shortly before leaving, I sent Michaux a copy of my recently published

Caribbean journal, *Voyage Noir*, thinking it might please him to see what his very first book, *Ecuador*, had spawned. The next day he called anonymously at our hotel. I happened to be out, but from the concierge's description, I guessed who it was and stayed in the following afternoon, waiting. As expected, he turned up: a head, bald like a seagull; piercing blue Arctic eyes; and, for a man his size, a sailor's wide shoulders.

For the next two hours, as we walked along the Right Bank *quais*, we talked about travel, about the various journeys that had occupied his life until 1940, and about the trip I had been planning for several years to what I saw as the country of poetry—Iran—that I was about to undertake. Michaux had never traveled there, but he could fathom the attraction of a people so susceptible to beauty, whether that of a horse or a twelve-year-old boy.

A GREEK SPRING

I was prepared for Iran, but nothing could have prepared me for Greece and the feeling it gave of having stepped into the morning of the world: a light so sharp that, standing on the Acropolis, there seemed to be nothing in the whole spread of the city, not a kite, not a bus blocks and blocks away, I could not see. It was easy to understand how, in such transparency, the most rational of civilizations had come into being. For much of the next five years I yearned for little else. Even to descend on its shabby Athens airport caused something to grip and tear at my heart. In this mood I asked Jimmy one evening why such a small Balkan country meant so much more than a great civilization like Iran's. "It may be," he hazarded, "that Iran remains profoundly oriental, whereas Greece is part of the DNA we carry in our bones." For me, though, it was the oriental aspect, the way the culture so precisely straddled the East-West divide that spoke: the honey-drenched desserts and the bouzouki-accompanied *rembetiko* dancing. Seeing such a dance enacted spontaneously, to nothing more than a hackneyed jukebox, or right out on a blazing noon sidewalk, was entrancement enough.

Easter week was underway when we returned from six weeks in Iran and Istanbul. With Athens closing for the week-long holiday it made sense to seek out an island. "Which of the 2,000 would you recommend?" I asked Jimmy when we checked in. "Paros," he said, pulling a white marble name out of the Cycladic hat. "There isn't much to do and, at this time of year, little choice of food, but I was happy enough. And take a cab to Naoussa, across the strait from Naxos. Its little harbor has all the charm of a run-down Portofino."

An island set opposite the Naxos of Ariadne and Dionysos sounded propitious and we took a stormy 8-hour boat packed with island folk traveling with their belongings in rush baskets. The thread-like streets of Parikia held a labyrinth more feminine than I had ever encountered; one that made the pirate in me feel I would never find my way back to my ship, nor would I have wanted to, such was the beguilement aroused with each twist of the head as I peered: through an archway, into a courtyard; over the paving stones daubed in whitewash like hot-cross buns; up a little height to a castle wall set with columns salvaged from a score of temples; the whole so cradled from the winds of the Sea of Icarus that I felt rocked by the echoing whitewash. Then at night, strolling along the esplanade under a constellated sky, it was easy to understand how a great cycle of stories had come into being. Arachne had spun a tight web.

On Easter Sunday we took a taxi to Naoussa. In the taverna to which we repaired for a glass of pine-scented retsina, there was a lamb being turned on a spit. Nearby, on a line of chairs, sat a beady-eyed fraternity. No one was speaking, drinking, doing much of anything but staring. We found the rapt scene so compelling we upped our consumption to half a liter. But the lamb was of a size to feed half of Naoussa. Rather than wait, we decided to walk, while we still could, back to Parikia.

Robin, Tulare, Madagascar, 1969

173

At the time I had never undertaken anything as long as a three-hour walk, reason enough to be stunned by the views sheering downwards, past fields crammed full of poppies—as many poppies as stalks of green and gold wheat—past little blue-domed farmhouses, all terrace, their steps aglow like lumps of sugar, to where in a pot of flame the sea funneled the last oils of the day. Watching the visual legato of the light, as a house reached a tongue of cobbled whitewash towards a cove two hillsides away and drew the warmth back up—how practical on a fuel-less island!—brought home the power of an Orphic flute. In a setting where light assumes a music-like binding, even the rocks are capable of dancing.

Further along, by a hilltop's crossroad, we came upon a woman on a bicycle carrying some freshly cut lilac branches. On a sudden impulse she dismounted and pressed a lap-bright bunch on Marcia; a way of saying welcome, "May you find in our land the joy you seek." A generosity by no means atypical of the Greece of that era. A stranger might still be a god in disguise.

Back at our hotel we hungrily accepted some outer shavings from a spit of roasting lamb. "For dinner?" I inquired. "No, there will be a dance later in the evening." That intrigued me. When Marcia retired, exhausted by our walk, I stayed up, hoping to see some local Orpheus perform one of those hypnotic dances, "part dream, part prayer," I had read about in the Vista Guide. But the dance was a record hop featuring the local line and couple dances; everything but the hypnotic urban warrior dances that the expelled Greeks of 1923 had brought back from Smyrna.

The chance to see what the Vista Guide described came on our first night back from Paros, when Jimmy and David took us out beyond Piraeus to the little port of Pérama and a roadside strip where sailors flocked to dance and flirt with the male prostitutes in suits. The café in which we found ourselves was little more than a few tables and a jukebox. The only food item served was chicken and, if you felt expansive, watermelon. Since the sailors were poor—the average wage was $4 a month—it was not inappropriate to offer one or another table a round of beer. Now and then, in response to a tune, a sailor would rise and start to dance, head down, a priest in a dream of stones. Perhaps after a few steps a tablemate, flourishing a handkerchief, might rise and join him.

I didn't know at the time that what I was seeing was something rather special; that the sailors regarded Pérama as their *scuola di ballo*, what Wimbledon might represent to a tennis player. I couldn't help but be taken by the witty belly dance parodies, the gymnastic flourishes, one whirling set of legs over another prone body, a frank intimacy possible perhaps only on a taverna dance floor. Rather than see it vanish, I jotted some impressions during our taxi ride back to Athens. The notes would become, when completed a year later, my first real poem. The *karsilama* dance, with its sprightly nine-eight rhythm, gave me what my poems till then had lacked—a form to which I could set words, steps. For once, something had clicked.

Two months earlier, before setting out for Iran, I had come upon an issue of *Time* featuring the 1962 Seattle World's Fair, Struck by the provincial cheek—my parents still talked about the 1938 New York edition that had introduced Belgian waffles and the amphibian car—I read an article about the international dance troupes that would be performing there. That intrigued me enough to write away to the University of Washington for a teaching job. On returning from Paros there was a letter awaiting from Robert Heilman, the chairman of the University of Washington English department, offering a lectureship. Would I telegram my acceptance? Heilman's offer left me in a quandary. At this late date nothing nearly as good was likely to come my way. But I had fallen in love with everything Greek and, like any amorous fellow, I wanted to move right in. My allowance did not stretch far in the USA. In a countryside where the average income was $200 a year, I could live on it well enough.

The next evening I took these arguments to my uncle, a very different Jimmy from the one I had known in Stonington. He who had been so shy, so effete, had been transformed by the country of "Essentials: salt, wine, olive, the light, the scream." He spoke and wrote Greek, he cooked Greek, there was little in Athenian life he didn't rejoice in. For the first time he felt joined to people of every class; at one with a culture in which homosexuality was certainly acknowledged, if not necessarily accepted.

Jimmy lived in a little two-story house above posh Kolonaki on the last street below Mount Lycabettos. But I saw little of the house as I was shuttled quickly through the rooms and up, by way of a narrow curling metal staircase, to the rooftop garden which, at the time, commanded a view over the whole city all the way to the Acropolis. As I drew up a seat there, I described the job offer I had received; one I was sorely tempted, in my new mood, to reject.

Patiently Jimmy heard me out, a slight crinkling of the brows showing his concern for what I might come to feel one day, deprived of a career into which I had put a substantial effort. He spoke slowly, "Teaching, for you, may be merely a means to an end. But the confidence that can accrue from it is no small matter. If it hadn't been for the invitation I received upon graduating to teach at Bard, I'd have gone to work at Merrill Lynch. It was that year teaching that allowed me to see myself as a full-fledged writer."

Jimmy went on to say that, from everything he had heard, Seattle was a lively town. David had old friends residing there and he himself would come to visit us at the first opportunity. All that, coming from Jimmy, was reassuring. Next morning, after plying me with a pair of highballs, he and David marched me down to the one open post office under Omonia where I fired off my telegram of acceptance.

SEATTLE

The wound Greece opened was not easily staunched. It helped, though, having Marcia by me who knew from what we had been removed. "You're thinking of Greece," she said as she caught my eyes misting over, "I know, I feel that way, too."

If distance and time can't eradicate loss, they can brush it back, out of sight. Seattle may have lacked the light, the vibrant intensity of Athens, but a city full of parks straddling a series of hills and offering views over two great bodies of water, Lake Washington and Puget Sound within a mile of one another, and the snowcapped peaks of the Olympic and Cascade ranges (not to mention that "watermark on celestial paper" which was vast Mount Rainier) certainly had some natural beauty going for it.

The senior English Department faculty had its burnt out teachers, but at our junior level, morale was high. We read each other's dittoed essays, we helped each other pack and move, and when the first of the month rolled around, we partied, carrying on as if the city were not the Kamchatka it might appear to a less committed eye. Most of us could count on friends from other walks of life: vendors from the Pike Street Market; businessmen and Boeing engineers with whom I played squash at the YMCA; theater directors like Andre Gregory and Ralph Lee; Lorenzo Milam's pioneering community radio station, KRAB, for whom I did a fortnightly poetry gig; Carolyn Kizer's *Poetry Northwest*; and a group of dazzling painters, two of whom, Bob and Fay Jones, became lifelong friends. The spontaneous combustion of all of us exiles, mushrooms, whatever we were, springing out of the rain, could not have been more palpable. Marcia and I were in the middle of it, knitting friends together and doing what we could to animate a community.

Of all the activities, I prized most the ethnic league soccer I played Sunday mornings on the mud fields of Volunteer Park. Upon arriving I found a team of ex-college hotshots who were willing to put up with this converted midfielder. All the same, it was like playing for the United Nations; you never knew who would show up. When our team disbanded at the end of the season, I switched with an Israeli friend to United Hungarians.

In the Fifties, Hungary was the world's premier soccer power. Their football prowess may even have deluded a nation of seven million into thinking it could win a war with the Soviet Union. My teammates, all emigres from the 1956 revolution, had mostly arrived from Canada, lured by the advertisement, "If you play soccer well, we'll pay your fare and guarantee you a job." Enough came to form a team, Seattle Hungarians, good enough to twice reach the national championship finals.

My team, United, was an offshoot, composed of those who had fallen away from, or could not make the more celebrated team. But that notorious slur on their powers of friendship, "If you have a Hungarian for a friend, you don't need an enemy," could result in a renegade squad built around some talented players. Some, like our captain had played only once a year in Hungary, at the annual factory bash. But in America, playing soccer was a way of remaining Hungarian, and they played as if they were still out there with Genghis Khan riding the shaggy ponies and surviving on mare's milk.

In the middle of my second year I found myself, for a four-game stretch, entrusted with a new position, center half. A center half is the last finger in the defensive dyke. To have held out for 90 scoreless minutes against an endless surging tide could give rise to as heady a satisfaction as I've known. When the game was over, there would be the fans' hugs and congratulations raining down while I sat in the mud lapping up a spiked thermos, unable to pull myself away and drive home.

It was their tribal identity I valued. If I kept silent in the locker room, it was less out of shyness than because I hesitated to break in on their Magyar community. But there was more than mere nostalgia drawing me. I remember the painter Aristodemos Kaldis describing his excitement as young man watching Matisse paint in his Nice studio, the canvas coming alive with each daub, a splotch of marine blue here, a balancing orange over there. It was, Kaldis maintained, like watching an explosive end-to-end soccer game. For me, the analogy resonated—in reverse.

The crowning accolade came at a farewell dinner. I had been presented with a trophy to remember them by, when the owner of the Seattle Hungarians called me over to tell me, should I ever return, that he wanted me to sign up with them. Admittedly, the likelihood of his having to make good on his offer was slim. But to me it meant something like what escaping Chester or rural Florida may have meant to my father and grandfather. I could fantasize that, born into similar penury, I might have found a way out from childhood cornfield to illuminated stadium.

In Seattle there was quite a hive of poets. The English department featured a good dozen of us, mostly Bobs or Robins in imitation of our chairman. Thanks to Ted Roethke's long presence, students had a good idea of what we required. They were always dropping off prospective inspiration: a sprig of flowers; mosses and lichens; even on one occasion a soulful gray rock; anything to help me see a very different Northwest landscape, and perhaps themselves, more accurately.

By now I was writing poetry. For the first eight months, in what time I could snatch from my pastoral dissertation, I fiddled with the description of the two sailors' *karsilama* I had begun in the taxi returning from Pérama. In the anxiety I felt upon finishing it—would I ever write another?—I embarked on a second dance poem rising out of our Easter Day walk on Paros. I conjured an Orphic *zembeikiko*, building a legato of light and sea to an intensity where, in response to a jukebox, a lone fisherman could conceivably rise to his feet and, circle by descending circle, dance out his deliverance:

Normal Mallory's watercolor of Robin working in the kitchen of his Brook Green, London, house

> ... the sound a thread downwards
> Through the spool of hisses guiding him as
> He steers over its tilting sundialed frame
> And light pours in swords into him, melting
> The streets into a wax, while the head, dis-
> Membered, floats out over the singing stones.

The poem made a comrade out of Roethke; until then he had not known what to make of me. He even forwarded a copy to an actual Paros resident, the new Nobel laureate George Seferis. We were set to test each other's mettle at tennis, a sport Ted ruined his knees teaching, when he succumbed to a massive heart attack.

Télémacque, cover illustration, Voyage Noir, 1963

"Language is gesture, gesture, language," was a critical commonplace. Add music, as the controlling form, and what did you get? Dance! That's what nearly everything I would write in the next decade would set out to do—dance their way down the page. To what end? What end more lyrical could there be than that of flight, a whole earthbound movement lifting up and soaring into aerial song. On the same behalf I would write about the masters of flight, birds. I would even try, more problematically, borrowing from expressionistic painting, to incorporate the great game of movement—soccer—into a several page poem. Words, alas, are not malleable in the same sense that paint is.

In all this I was in uncharted territory. With no guidelines for what I was attempting, realizing a vision could take years. The constraints I was working within were perhaps better suited to the invention nightclub dancers know, maneuvering on a tiny jam-packed floor. In an effort to give myself more flexibility, I found myself branching out into another unexplored genre, lyrical prose. With more room in which to launch myself I could ascend, however briefly, and still land with a comforting thump back on a slightly changed version of the initial ground.

Much of this lyrical prose went into the travel reportage I was starting to write, initially on Iran, then on Greece and its dance festivals. With limited time, a parachuting writer has to select, if he is to capture the essence of a place. In my case, what drew me was that 18th century ideal enshrined in our Declaration of Independence—the pursuit of happiness—what steps does a culture take to turn itself on? In Iran, that could be poetry as transmuted into a rug, a garden, the calligraphic display of a mosque dome. Or it could be the idea of a garden as realized in a great desert city such as Isfahan or Shiraz. In Greece it could take the form of a line of acrobatic somersaulting shepherd boys, or a single peasant who, having danced with the rest of his family table, stands free to express just who he is, all alone on a moonlit floor. These were the threads I set myself to follow, trusting they would lead to the heart of a distinct culture.

At the time, though, I had written just those dance poems. Their form was basically pastoral. My subjects were in their own space and I was the observing outsider, watching from a secluded table, deep in my glass, invisible. To some, this could look like a cop-out. "Aren't your poems' dancers," Jimmy once asked, "really you? That's what a reader will expect, not somebody else, but you." I remember being taken aback. Much of the admiration that went into their composition came from my witnessing something of which I was incapable. What would happen, were I to barge in? "Everyone off the floor, the American wants to express himself!" All the same, I could see a reader preferring a dance generated from within, the poet with each step, each swipe of the hand, saying, "Here I am, I burn the knife, I cry." To write with the needed confidence would require more than an intuitive leap. It had to be somehow earned, for an outsider not an easy proposition.

FELIX

In mid-March of our first year in Seattle my son Felix was born. Conceiving him had not been, any more than anything else in our marriage, my idea. But from the moment I saw him, something fatherly in me took shape.

Felix, 1969

Felix and I were very close those first years. I'd flip on a Greek record and he would spin around alongside me. I'd go on a training run and he would tag along, wanting to dart down every path but the one I was jogging. Because of the initial vision I had of him, of a being as much dolphin as human, there was this unexpected element of earth which I owed to him and had to make good.

My new fatherhood, the stuff I was finally writing, the diversity of a beautiful city, even the teaching I was undertaking, all helped me get over the Greece I had left. I was, I thought, reconciled to my domestic life such as it was, when Jimmy came by on his long-promised visit. With him he brought an Alexandrian friend, Tony Parigory, to whom he was showing the country: New York, which had fallen rather short; Palm Beach, "Ah! That's more like it," and now the Northwest before descending on San Francisco. We were returning in our car from an excursion to Vancouver when we learned of President Kennedy's assassination. To lift our gloom, Jimmy had us play his new psychological find, The Landscape Game; a good way, he said, of breaking through to the hidden self and finding out where you actually stood.

The player begins by describing the dream house he would like to inhabit, a way of situating himself for the ensuing walk with its sequence of symbolic encounters: a key; a bowl; an animal rushing across the path; a body of water; a wall.

Rather than design a house from scratch—my public self, as it would turn out—I adapted the little L-shaped palace Marcia and I had come upon in Ronda at the end of our eight-month trip. For the dining room—one's social self—the only room Jimmy asked specifically about, I borrowed that of the poet Robert Graves, with whom we had dined in Deya, Mallorca: a rectangular oak table set for six; bare walls hung with old Hispano-Mauresque lusterware plates.

"Are there any trees about?" Jimmy asked.

"Three," I replied, "in the fountain patio." The trees were, I later learned, my friends, "firmly clasped in the walled bosom of your heart."

I was now directed onto a path and told to follow it until I came to a key. A phallic symbol, I suspected, and described an intricately notched tool of tumescent size. "To what," Jimmy asked, "does it belong?" The one set of doors that seemed worthy of so capacious a key were the ones I recalled slanting down to The Orchard's wine cellar. I described a sloping earthen runway wide enough for an ox cart leading to the ten-foot tall cellar that underran the entire length of the house.

Back on my path, I proceeded along until I came to the inevitable bowl—a barrel-sized jardinière of green-and-white majolica. I knew at once what I would do with it once I had trundled it to a place outside my front door—plant an orange tree!

As the key symbolized my religion, of a drunk, possessed, earth-diving persuasion, *"In vino veritas,"* so the jardinière, with its orange tree that would one day demolish it, stood for my notion of art. If winter is the great challenge pastoral's "good life" must face, what could be better than having a planted sun in the form of an orange tree placed outside one's front door?

Jimmy interrupted my reverie, "There's something I should have asked earlier—what time of day is it?"

"Three o'clock," I replied, unaware I was indicating how old I felt. There was perhaps reason enough to feel in the mid-afternoon of my life.

Next came sex and its body of water. "What is it?" Jimmy asked. "The Mediterranean," I announced. I could see it glowing invitingly far below.

"What do you do?" Jimmy persisted, "when you come to it?"

"I'd like to go swimming," I said wistfully, "but it's a little late in the day." Obviously the Mediterranean wasn't in itself a sufficient inducement. Or perhaps I needed to bask on a rock until the sun burned away my inhibitions. All the same I wonder what other response I might have given. True, our love of Greece and Felix's birth had, each in its way, refreshed our union. But for one reason or another Marcia and I seldom made love; certainly nowhere near as often as I craved.

That un-swimmable 3 p.m., looking down wistfully at the nymph-filled sea, summed up pretty accurately my conjugal life. At 27, not only did I feel preternaturally old, but I saw myself living out a replica of my parents' marriage: the same bourgeois amenities; the same lack of any fundamental intimacy. A whole sexual life had, I feared, passed me by. Lack of initiative? Lack of courage? Lack of luck? But there seemed little I could do. I was not about to walk out on Marcia and Felix for something I hadn't known.

Past the glimpse of the sea I continued on until I came to a wall—the hereafter. "What sort of wall is it?" Jimmy asked. "What's on the other side?"

Mine wasn't a proper wall, but a series of fences in a Mallorcan pine forest, sheltering a mixed flock of goats and sheep. An after-life clearly in keeping with the thesis on pastoral I was writing.

The Landscape Game threw open some portals. But it wouldn't have challenged me to reconceive my life without Jimmy's adding it up; the oracle once again setting into motion what has to occur. "What I like so much," he said. "is the consistency of this earth-centered, Dionysiac and Mediterranean self you've revealed." His own bowl, he added, had been a blue-and-green Chinese celadon. Cupping it in his arms, he had carried it down to his river where, kneeling, he had proceeded to fill it. "Just enough sex," he joked, "to irrigate one's art."

We were all humbled by Tony Parigory, a true Mediterranean. "I was out on the dock at Faleron," he related, "it was nighttime and pitch black. But that didn't stop me, I just stripped off my clothes and dove in. Voilà."

DIONYSOS RULES

It seems odd to ascribe to a parlor game the role of a catalyst. But often enough in my life it's the odd remark that has opened a crucial path; all the more tell-ingly when it came from a clairvoyant Jimmy. In naming my Dionysiac path, was he making sure I would not shortchange myself?

While in New York a month later for the MLA convention, I set in motion the Dionysiac design. For Marcia's Christmas present I bought her a set of oil paints; a present she remembers gratefully, as it set her on her career path. The gift, though, was not altruistic. To be sure, I wanted her to develop her talent. But I hoped that a vocation might enable her to see our fraying relationship for the pit it was. Couldn't Marcia think she was the one dumping me?

Felix was two and a half now, old enough to be taken to Greece for the summer and looked after by a Scotch nanny. To where in Greece should we head, I asked the Greek-American painter, Aristodemos Kaldis? I told Kaldis how we had been charmed by the Paros we had encountered two years earlier, but wanted out of curiosity to try something else. Could he recommend an-other island whose landscape Marcia might want to paint?

Kaldis would not hear of the Cyclades. He pointed out that the Easter valleys that had enchanted us would be burnt to a crisp by mid-June. A paint-er, he said, needed "verdura." As for the lime-washed streets and vaulted roof houses, that might be sculpture in Corbusier's sense, but it wasn't architec-ture. If it was culture we were interested in, we should try an island like Samos or Lesbos where education was permitted under the Turks. Of the two, he preferred the variety offered by Lesbos with its 92 villages, mountains and bays. And he recommended that we select as a base Molyvos, the Mythymna of *Daphnis and Chloe*.

Situated on Lesbos's northeast coast directly across from the fish-rich mouth of the Dardanelles, Molyvos had thrived as the last port of call before

Constantinople. But the Turkish victory in 1923 had ended the sea trade. For much the same reason that other towns revive themselves as free ports or gambling dens, Molyvos opted for an art scene. How the word got out, I can't say, but from the far reaches of the globe the "littles of today, but greats of tomorrow" had descended, drawn by the assurance that, however wildly they carried on—painting themselves with yogurt, whatever—they would not be prosecuted.

To the artists, local life hardly mattered. They had come not out of any interest in Greece, but for the chance to perform on an inexpensive stage. They congregated on an algae-ridden shingle beach smack in the midst of the town's discharging sewers. There most of the day they sat, their gaze rising from the rampart cafes to the gaudy pink, blue and yellow painted houses that climaxed in an oversized Byzantine-Genoese castle dominating the hilltop.

Robin, 1975

Marcia did not share my reservations about the foul beach or the dubious scene. To her the artists were fellow pilgrims on a hallowed road. And any beach was a blessing after Seattle, especially one that contained such intense male proximity—beards, shirts, towels, color after color vibrating within a five-to-fifteen-foot radius of her. For her, our jaunt held the purpose of discovering who she was as a painter—and as a woman, not a wife. I had known for some time that I was feeling restless in my marriage. Now I began to realize that perhaps she, too, was drifting away. With each day, it seemed, her enchantment grew. For the first time color was taking her over, saturating her to a point where only a well of red existed, as figured forth in one or another wine or watermelon-shirted man. And woe to him who changed his shirt for a less fetid one. He might as well have turned into a stone. For as a painter picked a dominant tonality, so Marcia chose her suitors. And they clearly admired her in her blue polka-dot bikini, with her wistful enthusiasms, her bursts of shy wit. This Penelope, carefully placing a first toe down in the adulterous brine, must have let on that she would soon choose one of them.

What was I to do: acknowledge this was the liberation I had intended with the gift of her oil painting set and cheer her on? Or go about, as I did for a week, with a rock clenched in my possessive fist? Was unleashing a vendetta with all its escalating possibilities what my "honor" required? No, I had my own Dionysiac instincts to pursue by following those late summer wine harvest festivals that were beginning to draw me all over the island.

The day before the mid-August Feast of the Assumption, Marcia and I had given an end-of-summer party in an idyllic valley café that might have figured as a setting for *Daphnis and Chloe*. With the explosive mixture of Marcia's bohemians and my shepherds and fishermen (I had hired as musicians the town barber and his brother; her friends had brought their rock 'n roll records) it was not a happy occasion. Even worse was to find, when I woke the next day that I had missed the day's only bus to the Aghiassos *panegyri*.

"I may have missed the bus," I told Marcia as I roused myself, "but I'm still going to Aghiassos, even if I have to walk halfway across the island."

"You're in no condition," Marcia rejoined, "to do anything of the sort. You can hardly stand upright. Why don't you take it easy and go with us to the *panegyri* down the coast at Petra tomorrow?"

I was not to be fobbed off. I pointed out that the mountain village of Aghiassos had the liveliest ambiance we had so far encountered and that should make for a festival worth attending. With that, I started for the door.

Marcia called me back. "How long do you intend to be away?"

"Both days," I replied. "I want to see it all."

"All I can say," Marcia said, looking me fiercely in the eye, "is you'd better be at Petra tomorrow, or I won't answer for the consequences."

Faced with her threat I did manage to turn up the next evening at Petra and its famous church of the Holy Kiss. On its steps I found Marcia in a strapless flamingo-pink bit of bewitchery that had her rivals reduced to so much furious sulking paint.

"Won't you come sit with us?" she offered, flashing a pleased smile as she took me by the hand and led me off to their table. But it wasn't well placed for seeing anything but some spirited crawling under the table by her little goat-bearded Moroccan suitor. I excused myself and found a makeshift table of my own. Carrying it over my head through the throng, I plunked it down under the bandstand and right next to a table of screaming whistling acrobatically somersaulting shepherd lads. That's what I had come for.

To dance, however, as the most virtuoso of the shepherds insisted, required fuel—three jugs of retsina. As I tottered back up the hill towards Molyvos in the early morning, I was in no condition to notice Marcia under a bush, a few feet off the road.

I learned next morning about those threatened consequences from a genuinely contrite Marcia. The bushes, it seemed, had made for less than inspired copulation. "I wish," she said, "I hadn't been the first to break our vows. If you had just taken me by the hand and led me away, I'd have come." It was just that gesture I couldn't and didn't want to make.

So we drifted apart, I into the festivals that, in late August, seemed to arrive every couple of days, Marcia into a sexual intensity enhanced by the glasses of effervescent ouzo that spiked their afternoons on the beach. She was only now, she felt, at 28 coming into the glory of her body. While part of her reveled in an appreciation perhaps long overdue, another observer remained standing a bit to the side, as if with a flick of her mermaid's tail she could be safe. She did not want to be unfaithful; it was more that the husband she was counting on to rescue her was himself prey to his own exclusive desire—to behold the dream which is a man, utterly alone, on the round of a moonlit floor, dancing out his very personal *zembeikiko*.

Earlier in the summer, as we were strolling home past the cafes one evening, I caught a glimpse through a doorway of an elegant graying shepherd, George, and his brother Strato, circling, cigarettes in hand, to a *zembeikiko*'s stark, hypnotically pounding 9/4 rhythm. When, some weeks later, George asked if I wanted to rent his mare and make a trip into the hills,

I was able in my halting Greek to express my fascination with his dance, this "wrestling with the eagle" as the Zebeik people of southern Anatolia had originally conceived it.

At first I was content to watch. But now and then, *faute de mieux*, I might attempt to mimic George as he swayed, shifted, stamped. There was no release in it, nor could there be. It was more a rapport we were trying to further. Unlike the so-called butcher's dance or *hasapiko*, the *zembeikiko* does not have steps that can be taught. It requires, in the idiom of hashish smokers, *kefi* (literally "head"), something that wells from within and which you can't let out in any other way.

My breakthrough came in the last week of August when George took me to a *panegyri* in the gangster-exporting village of Magdalena on the far side of the ridge from Molyvos. I was riding past one of the parapet-clinging cafes when the rope holding my saddlebag came apart. I was on my knees, picking everything up when the sound of an 8-piece village orchestra, more prehistoric than anything I'd yet heard, reached my ears. At 10 a.m. that couldn't have been more unusual and, abandoning all my effects, I set off in its direction.

After bursting into the café and ordering a carafe of retsina, I took up a far corner table, heedless of the anxious-eyed townspeople returning by the window one or another of my belongings; or of George when he arrived out of sorts, after stabling his mare. "How did you expect me to find you? What are you doing crashing this private party?" Instead what mattered were the patterns being woven by these absolutely committed dancers. The best of them was the café owner, a portly fellow dressed in somber black-and-white who danced with the grace and surprising swiftness of a great cloud.

On the stroke of twelve they all spilled out of the café and into a single half-circle, handkerchiefs waving, on the steep, high-walled, cobbled street. In the glare, and before a red-eyed assembly of bemused, whiskered faces, they proceeded to weave an elaborate figure-eight around a man saluting them with a tray of prepared ouzo glasses. Then, the last glass quaffed, they were gone. Some five hours later, after waking from a nap, I found them again, a wild Serbian jig shrilling from a roof in the upper town. There was a ladder, so I climbed up to be met by an Australian accent, the son it would turn out of the café owner. "What can I do for you?" he asked. "I love the music these guys are playing," I volunteered, as if that excused my butting in.

"How about dancing something with me—a twist?" A twist, I pointed out, was not part of my repertoire. But I might, plied with a couple of glasses, manage a *zembeikiko*. Whereupon a tall fellow, dressed in an old-fashioned tunic with long rippling sleeves that gave him the look of an elegant stork, asked me to dance. I tried, rather frenetically, I fear. Then the whole party filed down the ladder and, the orchestra leading the way, we paraded from doorway to doorway, greeted by one or another radiant, black-outfitted wife, holding a silver tray and the customary ouzo glasses.

Back at the café, at a long table mounted over the street, a dinner of roast lamb followed, friendly fingers pushing choice chunks into my mouth. Sometime in the middle of the feasting, the Australian brought me into a little den, produced pen and paper, and to my astonishment asked me to write a note to the Australian consul in Athens, requesting a year's visa extension so he could attend to his "dying" mother, she of the bewitching smile and the many ouzo glasses.

We had barely returned to the table when his father asked me to dance a *zembeikiko*. A two-person *zembeikiko* is, as I've noted, not conducive to self-expression. But suddenly, opposite this portly man and his luminous melon of a belly, wings of my own sprouted, and I danced down, from every conceivable angle, into him and his belly. For hours afterwards, in one parapet café after the next, these new wings went on flapping, while across from me, or even over me, George or Stork Sleeves or even the local idiot danced with a fire I helped set ablaze.

Ever since, sufficiently moved by the first notes of a song, I have only to rise to my feet for an initiate to understand what, until then, would never have dawned: that I, this anonymous American with a bit of a speech defect, was a *mangas,* a fellow derelict.

GLORIA

Before going to Molyvos for the summer, Marcia and I had purchased a Rainier-view lakeside home in the central Madrone district of Seattle; an indication, it might be thought, that we intended to stay for a while. Upon our return, our first guest was Father. He had come, he announced, to inspect the local Safeway operation and his first grandchild. His real aim, as it turned out, was to give my provincial complacency a shaking.

The two of us were sitting out on the veranda with drinks one evening and I was trying to describe the fulfillment I felt living in a city of such diversity, when he asked, "Isn't it every professor's goal to teach at Harvard?" clearly puzzled by my lack of a game plan with which to storm the academic heights.

"Harvard," I replied in my professional capacity, "is one of the better appointments, if teaching is your primary career. But I'm a writer first, and not a teacher, and I can't imagine a better situation than the one I have here."

Father was not about to be sidetracked. "How do you make your living," he asked, "teaching or writing?"

"Teaching," I admitted.

"Well, that's your career." With no ifs, buts, or in-betweens, there I was.

Once again the dart had struck. When some weeks later, a poet for whom I had gotten a departmental job (with a wife and five kids) resigned in anger after not receiving an expected summer grant, I felt obliged to stand up and resign as well. Why, with Chairman Heilman away on leave and several hundred vying for every vacant position, I expected anyone in that administrative forest to hear, much less respond, to a lone crashing oak, beats me. It was an impulsive act. Could it be that my father's remark had "spoiled" Seattle for me? But as with Marcia's painting set, so leaving Seattle and the new house she had set up may have been another way of making her question her marital assumptions. Then, too, there was a greener pasture temptation.

In those mobile mid-Sixties a professor wasn't a real success unless he was constantly uprooting himself to move to schools of greater repute. In the chess match I was waging with my father, I may have needed such a move.

I soon discovered that my professional stock, despite quite a number of publications in prestigious journals, had not risen in the three years since I had last thrown myself on the job market. As an Americanist conversant in French, I did succeed in garnering a Fulbright fellowship to Marcia's Romania. But of the forty departments to which I applied, only Berkeley, then in the heady throes of the Free Speech Movement, expressed an interest, occasioned by a travel piece on Iran I published in *The Partisan Review*. While holding out this carrot, the Berkeley chairman, Mark Schorer, made clear that he had a number of more pressing period slots to fill before he could offer an appointment to an "exotic flower" of my sort.

When in April the funding for an umpteenth assistant professor came through, I declined the Fulbright. For me, almost as alluring as Berkeley, was California's reputation as a marriage breaker. Why then didn't I seek a divorce? After some ten years together I ought to have known what I was or wasn't getting. But that was precisely my problem. Apart from one night with a Jamaican prostitute and a few seconds with a Cuban whore, Marcia was the only woman I had known before getting married. And the half dozen beds I had strayed into since had never been given time to release their mysteries. Female sexuality is itself so unpredictable. There are certain furnaces which, no matter how assiduously stoked, seem to never catch fire. Others ignite at a glance. Where in this spectrum Marcia hovered is hard to say. She may have relished only the power of her beauty to attract. At any rate copulation wasn't for her the consuming preoccupation that it was for me.

As I started to come into my own as a man, and as a writer, Marcia had become, like many a Pygmalion, increasingly captivated by what she had every right to think her discovery; one she had no intention of relinquishing. Whenever I attempted to leave, she would let fly with some crockery, or thrust a suicidal vein through a plate glass window. But all her passionate *duende* did little to alleviate the chagrin of my wasted manhood.

I do not know if I ever truly understood Marcia. A girlfriend was what I needed at college and Marcia, with her intelligence and fiery spirit, fit that bill very nicely. But if I did not care enough to want to know her, I could recognize that I feared her. I feared the laser of her tongue, perfectly capable of lashing out at anyone of us who up to then might have considered him or herself a dear friend. Nor did I care for her social pretentiousness, exemplified in the pricey Madrone house, quite a step upscale from the fourth oldest house in town with its lovely wrap-around porch that we had been renting for a proverbial "song." Then again, such abuse might be thought a condition to which I was by now immune, dished out "for my own good" by everyone from Soeur Ami to my father. Couldn't I take, even rejoice in, a "little honesty of expression?" It may be that, in trying to free myself from my parents by marrying, however inappropriately, I needed, to feel secure, another person capable of replacing them. How inevitable then to chafe at the strictures each imposed!

The more Marcia insisted on staying married, the more I resisted, convinced that nothing less than the authenticity of my vision was at stake. Was sex an experience so transforming as to hold the very key to an adult life? Or was it, as Marcia maintained, merely another romantic mirage?

Mother, 1964

It was May and Marcia was about to go into the hospital for a minor operation when I hurled myself into an affair with Gloria, a petite green-eyed Monica Vitti lookalike who was working as a secretary in the English department. Our trysts took us to places of private beauty, a forest hilltop where we picked mushrooms, an actual Warm Beach created by the tide flowing in over the mud flats over which we waded for several hundred awkward yards before hurling ourselves into a channel no wider than a bathtub. When Gloria turned up on my charter flight to London, I managed to spirit her off to Athens and a week on Paros. Wherever we were, like mating lions, we coupled: perhaps not every twenty minutes, but more in any 24 hours than Marcia and I had ever managed in a month.

It's easy enough, looking back at those six golden weeks when Marcia was still in the US visiting friends, to see no more than another instance of the dream that may be all that there is of an essential life. But a man doesn't immerse again and again in life-giving waters without emerging in some way changed. By the time I put Gloria on her plane to Rome and an anticipated summer with a friend on Ischia, I had resolved to ask Marcia, when I met her in Athens, for a divorce.

Marcia's response, once she recovered from the initial shock, was composed. She had, after all, faced my qualms before. "When you left Seattle, we were still man and wife. Now it seems we're not. Have you fallen in love? With whom may I ask?"

I told her about Gloria and the determination she had released in me. Marcia heard me out. Then, smiling bitterly, she walked to our room's open window and, removing her topaz engagement ring, flung it as far as she could into the gritty beyond. From whence next morning, in a less romantic mood, she retrieved it, some two courtyards away. By then we had agreed to meet at the summer's end in familiar Molyvos. I could then decide if I still wanted a divorce.

In reality, I had gained very little—at best six weeks' reprieve. But after so many strangled years I felt, as I set off on the first of two ferries for Ischia to find Gloria, I was finally embarking on a life of my own.

Gloria was more than surprised upon her arrival in Ischia a week later, to find me already installed in a room down the hall from the one she had booked, perfectly prepared to barge in on the beach vacation she had promised herself. Eventually though, we did clamber onto a train across southern Italy and the two ferries to Paros, the one place in the whole Mediterranean, seemingly, where I could be her Dionysos.

For all the island's magic a wider reality kept intruding. And the notion of what we were inflicting on Marcia and little Felix had Gloria climbing the walls. "Your joy," she said, "is so electric and I'm glad I've helped you find it. But what's liberation for you may be something else for them. Believe me, I've been down that road and I don't wish it on anyone."

Our last days together were difficult. No matter what I tried, there was little I could do to prevent the sea of guilt from roaring back in. That left me finally no choice but to return her to Piraeus and the passage on the Turkish liner she had booked. I couldn't see the storm of mascara blackening her face as she waved and waved from its diminishing railing. But even I understood this was our adieu.

Robin, Nepal, 1973

CRIMES OF THE HEART

The morning Gloria sailed was August 24th, the date of the Magdalena *pane-gyri* where I had experienced my initiation into the zembeikiko a year earlier. Gathering together Uncle Jimmy and my honeymooning brother Peter and Jill, I flew off to Lesbos and my agreed rendezvous with Marcia.

It was perhaps too much to expect of Magdalena, when we reached it by Molyvos's one cab that evening, to live up to the unique circumstances I had stumbled into a year earlier. All the same, the first parapet café had two grizzled shepherds dancing atop a table and a chair respectively. Nor was it long before they had each presented me with a bottle of retsina. In appreciation of my clapping out the rhythm? Or was it, as Jimmy suspected, their canny way of putting me out under a table? If so, I still had considerable fires of my own to stamp out first. In one packed shoebox café after another that's what I did, kneeling, wheeling, stamping, slapping heel, toe, thigh, floor.

Across, deep in the gloom of an impending 40th birthday (six months away!) sat Jimmy. Backs to the dancing, oblivious of everything but their next week's confrontation with our parents in Southampton, sat Peter and Jill. Marcia, silent as a sphinx, kept her thoughts to herself.

A month later some quatrains arrived from Jimmy—his version:

OUZO FOR ROBIN

Dread of an impending umpteenth
Birthday thinning blood to water, clear
Spirits to this opal-tinted white—
Uncle, the confusion unto death!

Last night's hurled glass. On the wall a mark
Explored by sunlight inching blindly
Forth from the tavern onto tree-tarred
Heights of gilt and moleskin, now gone dark.

Thorn needle launched in spinning grooves' loud
Black. A salt spray, a drenching music.
Each dance done, wet hawklike features cling
To one more tumblerful of numb cloud.

Joy as part of dread, rancor as part.
Lamplit swaying rafters. Later, stars.
Case presented, point by brilliant point,
Against the uncounselable heart.

Ground trampled hard. Again. The treasure

Buried. Rancor. Joy. Tonight's blank grin.
Threshold where the woken cherub shrieks
To stop it, stamping with displeasure.

In that stamping syntax, those perspiring "hawklike features," my uncle catches something of my pent-up wrath: the frustration of an all-too-young-married youth absolutely determined to dance his way through those tumblerfuls "of numb cloud." Yet "the woken cherub shriek[ing]/ To stop it" is as much the divorced Jimmy as it is little Felix. Doubtless a similar verdict— my family having long since departed in their taxi—could have come from the waiter in a final café, pointing to the upstairs cots. Sign that, even in his practiced eyes, I had breached the permissible limits.

Virgil Burnett, cover illustration, And Other Voyages, 1986

There still remained Marcia to be faced. I had, after all, given her my word that we would discuss what to do about our marriage. I assumed she could use an extra hand in getting herself and Felix and their luggage to Athens and a plane back to the US. Foolishly, I let her persuade me to stay with her. It was during that week our sex produced another pregnancy.

While I failed to dissuade Marcia from accompanying me to Berkeley and carrying on as the academic wife she indeed was, I did manage to return to Seattle and Gloria for a couple of weekends. Such visits could come to seem more than a bit presumptuous; Gloria had, after all, her own life to live. By the time of my third visit I grasped that any embers I might have once lit were smoldering fitfully. But it wasn't until an evening later, when she failed to show up at her house as promised—I waited all night in my car—that the message came through. That ended our tango. All the same, to this day I feel gratitude.

In Berkeley there remained what Jimmy called our "grim final toccata" waiting to be played out. Or was Marcia to pull off another wifely maneuver? Try as I might, I could not gain her consent to a separation. And she refused to consider an abortion; her last chance, she claimed, to bear a child.

That left me all the more desperate and ruthless. To my new colleagues and students I must have looked like one of those drowning swimmers, wildly screaming and waving my arms as I thrashed towards a perceived surface. To anyone stupid enough to hold out a hand I could seem dangerous. But my need for a more authentic life remained. For a man the erotic quest—for the unknowable in oneself—is an inextricable part of his identity. With every scrap of my being I pointed myself to the next incarnation of identity, a love, a poem.

Marcia marched to a different gong. From me, she sought a confirmation of herself as a woman and as a wife. When I refused now to provide it and instead tried to leave, her self-destructive impulse emerged. After one suicidal episode I persuaded her to call a psychiatrist. He told her, "Don't do anything until I've seen you in my office." To her question, the next day, about her frequent hysteria, he rejoined, "If you get kicked in the teeth you feel pain. You don't commit suicide."

In the house and the four-poster we still shared, I felt increasingly marooned. Strange as it may seem, I did not understand that all I had to do was present myself before a lawyer. Instead I saw only the accusation of desertion, if not absurdity, in moving to a motel. Then, in March, as Marcia was entering her seventh month of pregnancy, I began an affair with Mary

Huntington, a 22-year-old ex-model exquisitely dressed and groomed, who was putting herself through college as a part-time secretary in the typing office.

I had to keep my affair secret, lest Marcia react in a way that might harm the child she was carrying. After James was born, healthy and red-haired, the need for concealment lessened. Finally there came a moment when I could not hold my tongue any longer. Marcia had insisted on a weekend together in a Napa Valley hotel. She and I were lying in bed after having made love for the first time in five months. In the afterglow I could feel her renewed assumptions closing in. We were a couple once again. Our new son was going to unite us.

On the contrary, I felt it was now or never. I told her about my affair, making clear I saw no point in staying together. By now Marcia was prepared to accept a divorce. All she asked was, "Do you love her?" When I responded, "Yes," I found myself released. The freedom I had long awaited could begin: dreams, I thought, picturing a horse, on the necklaces of wind.

BERKELEY ERUPTING

The affair with Mary lasted through the summer. I was not immune to her sophistication, which seemed to offer a bridge back into the world in which I had been brought up. Had I foolishly renounced it? At twenty, it is the rare man who seeks his past in a woman. At thirty, the age I was now approaching, my earlier options could seem too summarily rejected. Was my uncle right in insisting I choose between the life of a writer and life in a tuxedo and dancing pumps? As it turned out, I wasn't up to the exquisite tastes that so drew me. And Mary wasn't finally, as she had feared, pregnant. So, despite myself, I once again escaped. A year later I remember seeing her in her white make-up crossing a traffic circle near where I lived and experiencing a shudder. I had come that close to marrying a ghost.

My moving out was confusing to four-year-old Felix. "You are Mommy's Daddy aren't you?" he once asked. And he asked Marcia, after I had removed Charlie Merrill's four-poster, "What was wrong—was the bed too large?" His confusion came to a head one day when I was helping Marcia pack books for her move to a small house near the campus. It was not altruism; I was eager to speed her along. But I must have annoyed her, because at one point Marcia, harassed by the whole sum of her concerns, turned and yelled angrily, "I don't have to put up with you. Just get out of my life."

That was too much for Felix who was helping me stuff her books into carton boxes. Picking up on her words, he said, "Mommy, you get out of my life!" Then, aware of the uncanny silence his remark had brought, he repeated it.

At that, Marcia, forgetting she had nothing on her feet but sandals, gave one of the boxes an almighty kick. Next thing I knew, she was hopping about on one foot and shrieking. Thoroughly cowed, I left the house. Next day I learned she had broken a bone in her big toe.

I had come to Berkeley somewhat reluctantly. The prestige of the university, a so-called Athens of the West, and its nearness to my parents in San Francisco—how some of us long for an impossible rapprochement!—were positive inducements. But for all the beauty of the campus, the magnificent botanical gardens, the old wood-shingled houses, and the setting on a great hill overlooking San Francisco Bay, Berkeley could never be for me the Shangri-la it undoubtedly was for so many others. I just didn't like the Bay area, I'm not a big metropolis person.

I was fortunate to receive the kind of audience and support a young writer needs from a brand-new San Francisco "little mag," George Hitchcock's *kayak*. At the time there was no American literary magazine willing to publish surrealist poetry, prose poems, found poems, let alone work that resembled nobody else's. That precisely was what this one-man kayak of a magazine was about with a wit and illustrative panache that attracted a pantheon of brilliant poets, a number of whom were to become lifelong friends. Hitchcock even selected a collection of mine, *Voyages*, as one of the very first books kayak published.

For most of the next six years, I concentrated on setting down my experience of the *zembeikiko*. The dance itself, that zig-zag of Z's, I could capture in verse with a depiction of an old man I saw setting musical fire to himself on the island of Samos. But my own initiation was not the easiest of subjects to get across. Because of the anarchic aspect of the dance, and the necessity of including all the tension propelling me into its extremes, I hit upon an expressionistic mode: a rhythm present in the prose from the outset and which everything else, Greece, the stark light, each step by dancing step confirmed. Then again, the expressionism—the rage-filled rock I carried in my fist—was not something I could carry any further because it was, indeed as an exorcism it had to be, so self-destructive. Reason enough why you do not dance a *zembeikiko* very often, maybe once a year at your village festival.

I did not arrive until 1965, a year after the Free Speech Movement. Thus I missed the opening demonstrations of the political movements that would consume the next decade and the euphoric mood those participating knew of being part of a joyous volcano pouring its revolutionary ashes over the entire planet. I missed what by then had become a legend: civil rights marches, the campus strike, the Sproul Hall sit-in, the spectacle of a few students, ringed in by thousands, dancing on the hood of a liberated patrol car, the eventual arrests.

By the time I arrived the authorities had the vents pretty well plugged. Not that there weren't almost daily protests, rallies, picketings, and even repeated attempts to burn down the ROTC Quonset hut by attacking it in broad afternoon, several hundred marching strong. (In Berkeley no one ever did anything in the morning, or by himself at night, armed, say, with a box of matches.) But for all the commotion, the revolutionary keg wouldn't catch fire.

My generation, the so-called "Silent," did not possess a group identity. (Has anyone asked of what loneliness, what resentment, our silence was composed? Or what part yearning for a livelier society played in our setting off for our far-flung Elsewheres?) The Baby-boomers did, though, thanks to television. They were the first generation whose collective buying power was actively solicited. And it gave them the illusion of possessing other kinds of power as well. By pulling together, the theory went, they could change the world.

Nor should it have been surprising, given the obvious limits to their experience, that their activism would take a messianic form. We were to be converted. To youth-speak? Rock 'n Roll? Unfortunately no one questioned the assumptions woven into their identity. Why was everyone over thirty the enemy? Because we hadn't grown up suckled to a TV set? Could that be why we found the slogan, "Make love, not war" less than convincing? Or how about the even more thought-defying, "If you are not with us, you're against us?" That same love of jargon may explain why so many were drawn to the Social Sciences. And why they thrived on self-publicity. What did Jerry Rubin ever accomplish? Being on camera was triumph enough.

Where they differed was in their views of the degree of change required. The great protest movements of the era—women's liberation, black civil rights, the various queer and ethnic coalitions—all started out as raids on the establishment in the name of a more just social order. They wanted what I had taken for granted—the same opportunities, the same perks and privileges—within an expanded middle-class America.

Then, towards the end of 1966, a movement emerged, led by privileged youths who sought to replace the constrictions, the drab conformity of middle-class life with something more open to style, surprise, invention. That's what one long-haired satirist after the next proposed as he or she swaggered by in the ubiquitous blue jeans, the flag-striped ass, Uncle Sam hat, fringed "redskin" leather jacket and dangling love beads. Where, in the long ride out west, had the American dream come undone and become a nightmare? And what could be done to set us all on a more life-oriented course?

The movement held the allure of something sprung out of Berkeley's Telegraph Avenue pavement. There was no discernible program, no zanier-than-thou head hippie. It was controlled all the same by the Diggers whose roots were in the kind of street theater practiced by the San Francisco Mime Troupe. Flowing male tresses and outrageous costumes provided a communal stage where we could discover new modes of interaction. Was Truth theatrical? Not who I was, but how I presented myself?

One hippie apogee was the January 14, 1967 Great Human Be-in in Golden Gate Park. It was late afternoon when I and my companion arrived. I remember walking past a stream of returning celebrants for whom the "best"— Santana? The Dead? The Airplane?—was evidently over. My experience of *panegyris* had taught me that even the dregs of an event could bear checking out, so we walked on until we reached a pair of overturned garbage pails by a chain-link fence. Clambering up on them we dropped onto the movement's Champ de Mars, a polo field carpeted, far as I could see, with squatting hippies, spread out like buffalo on the prairie.

Stepping gingerly around and over the blankets, dark glasses and proffered joints, we made our way to the Be-In's electronic heart, a scaffolded platform blasting out rock 'n roll along with prayer chants and panicky appeals for stray children. Here lay a paved walkway where progress was somewhat easier. Those sufficiently high danced, shirts discarded in the mild air, shoulder-length tresses snapping in a syncopated flail across flushed faces. When we stalled, unable to move in the throng, I fixed my gaze on the encampments parked on the far side of the fence: women in mini-skirts seated on the top of a truck, silver boots smacking back and forth in time to the rock beat; kids in old-style vests and long granny dresses playing fiddle tunes beside an aluminum Air-Stream camper whose open windows disgorged a plume of pungent smoke.

The distinctiveness of this Gathering of the Tribes may have lain less in its *Grande Jatte* aspect than in the anonymous community we formed. By Woodstock standards this was pipsqueak, a mere 15,000, half the attendance at an average ball game. Though everyone I knew, or would know, was there, I didn't bump into a single one of them. A few hours later, as we were dining at a North Beach restaurant, I was asked if we wouldn't mind sharing our table. As fate would have it, who should sit down but Marcia and her new beau, the best student from the previous year's pastoral seminar who had become a close friend. They, too, hadn't come upon anyone they knew at the Be-In. Yet here we all were, enthused by all we had encountered, and thrust anew into each other's intimate lives. Perhaps, we agreed, the Surrealists had it right: there is no such thing, finally, as coincidence.

The Be-in's vision of a more communal, flower-powered California was to prove ephemeral. But for several unrepeatable months it did look as if the Bay

Area were about to become a Xanadu. A wave on which each of our little rafts was lifted, ever more wondrously, more perilously, high. In a single week—and every woman of a certain age can still tell you which one it was—all the bras in town vanished.

Didn't the revolution need, as *The Barb* suggested, a leadership and, with it, an agenda? Hardly, when an improvisational spirit seemed to suffice. Not conceptual thought, but vibrations, patterns, rhythms, global change contemplated from within a million molecules of exploding hallucinogens, that's where it was at among us youthfully arrogant, self-righteous dots sitting out there while Big Brother, Country Joe and the Fish, seared our ear drums. A transformation, of both ourselves and the entire planet, as we conceived it from that bend of the Yellow Brick Road, seemed just out of sight, a mere horizon away.

A year later, flower power was another bumper sticker on a Eugene McCarthy for President VW. The wave, like all waves, had crashed.

MIRANDA DELLA GIOIA

Freed from my obligations to Marcia, I saw a substantial bachelor's career stretching before me, night after night by the Bay tossing out my rod to the light of the twinkling waves.

The reality was another matter. Cruise as I did the singles bars, I wasn't having much luck making up for the adolescence I had never experienced. Perhaps I lacked the temperament a one-night stand requires. No matter what I did to reduce the variety to a single sultry type—small, slinky, smoke-maned, mercurial-minded Glorias—there was no way of predicting what might happen. I might even infer an inverse ratio: the better the presentation, the lousier the fit. And my way of backing out of an affair, after an initial surge of intensity, without so much as a phone call, much less a redeeming present, could invite a well-justified response.

I had barely returned from a Christmas holiday in Aspen when I found, lying on my locked office desktop, a black elbow-length glove. In case the sorcery hadn't registered, it was followed in equally mysterious fashion a week later by a length of stout rope looped like a hangman's noose on the inside door knob. Sign of the offense I must have given in some unknown quarter.

Eventually those nights of navigating Berkeley's bachelor minefields seemed to be over. Before leaving for Aspen I had started an affair with a ballet dancer plucked from a concluded graduate seminar. Besides a natural grace of movement, she had the kind of old-fashioned charms not often encountered. She couldn't see without her glasses, nor could she swim, drive, or even light an oven. For an insecure man like me, a palpable treasure.

The graduate student was mulling just when to move in with me when fate tossed up a second possibility in the person of Miranda della Gioia, a freshman enrolled in the second half of a required composition course. The prospect of an affair with a much younger student—the violation of a trust—is not lightly broached. In defense, it is usual to cite Socrates for whom sex appeared to be a part of the mentoring process. But once sex rears its passionate head, it has a way of taking over. And the liaison can never be an equal one so long as the teacher retains most of the power. The resulting guilt, and the inequity in the classroom between the screwed and the unscrewed, can blacken even the most positive atmosphere.

At Washington and Berkeley sexual morality was personal, and no chairman tried to hand down any guidelines. But in view of the harassment I had suffered in college, I made a point of postponing any encounter until the course was finished. By then, an affair could have something to recommend it. After seeing me spill out my guts for nine weeks, a student could have a fair notion of the kind of person she was bent on seducing. That left me the treat of drawing her out in whatever guise she chose to present herself.

But I wasn't pure stone, and on that first winter day as my eyes lit on a voluptuous long-haired Lady of Shalott sitting in the first row, I remember feeling a keen pang about a person from the hippie world of which I had never been a part. I also remember catching, as I stepped in, her gasp of astonishment. I was a reasonably youthful thirty, still required in some bars to produce a driver's license. I learned later that Miranda had chosen my section out of a student guide: a professor who held the keys to the gate of poetry. With two Shakespeare plays, a poetry anthology and a short novel (left to the graduate assistant), my Introduction to Literature could be taught as a course in close reading. By teaching it in the winter term I intended to attract students who hadn't been browned off by the previous composition course.

Miranda was a third generation Albanian Italian from suburban San Jose. Her oval face, with its trace of baby fat, held the lucent inwardness of an Antonello da Messina Madonna—a combination of sensual line and sheer sweetness. Add blue-gray eyes from her Alsatian mother, a full small-waisted figure, and the most dazzling of smiles, and here was a beauty truly unsettling.

Had I been graced with Paris's dilemma, I know which of those three goddesses I'd have picked—the owl child, Pallas Athene. Sex, since Eve, has always been a mental activity. And Miranda was as bright as anyone I've ever met, my uncle Jimmy aside. In class, she was willing to question what everyone else was perplexed by, but afraid to ask. With her mediating between me and the rest of the class, and a teaching assistant of unusual gifts in the person of Jonathan Cott, the course became one of the two liveliest I had ever taught.

Miranda could also write, well thought-out weekly papers set down in a single draft, full of long tumbling sentences as luxurious as her hair. I saw to it that I and not Cott corrected them, writing long comments that treated her with the respect due to a real writer. Miranda reciprocated by staying behind after class and telling me about herself with a freshness I matched as best I could.

Nonetheless I was surprised when, one afternoon in early February, Miranda knocked on my fourth floor Wheeler Hall door during my weekly "office hours". She was wearing a beige silk blouse tied with a floppy bow. After seating her and taking up a relaxed position on the edge of my desk, I asked to what did I owe this pleasure?

"Oh, nothing academic," Miranda replied, "I'd just like to get to know you better."

"In that case," I said without a moment's hesitation, "let's get out of here and go up to my apartment. It's on Panoramic, above the football stadium." I wasn't just my collection of paintings by friends, my Persian rugs, my painted voodoo vessels, and 45 rpm Greek records, but among them, some of my experience might come alive.

"What about your office hours?" Miranda asked, taken aback. "Don't you have to stick around?"

"In principle, but four flights is a climb and it's mostly in the first two weeks or end of term that anyone shows up."

Normally I'd have walked up by way of Fraternity Row. Rather than submit ourselves to anyone's knowing stare, I chose a more circuitous climb past the soccer field on the far side of the stadium. Though I was fit enough to run the six miles of a soccer game, my heart at one point was pumping so that at one point I was obliged to halt. It was then, in an effort to clear the air in the fullest of senses, I told her about the ballet dancer who was about to move in with me.

"I'm spoken for as well," Miranda rejoined. She proceeded to tell me about the high school boyfriend who had followed her to Berkeley, where he was supporting himself in an Ashby Avenue apartment dealing methedrine. "You can always tell it," she remarked, not without a little pride, "by the unmarked narc car parked across the street." Unable any longer to bear the sight of his emaciated body, she had recently moved back to her dorm.

"Why does anyone take speed?" I asked, recalling the episode that had triggered "The Wanton Current." For one who could barely tolerate a cup of coffee, it was hard to fathom the attraction.

"Speed makes you feel so lucid," Miranda replied, "so in control. Since he's not qualified, credit-wise, to attend the university, it makes it easier for him to feel superior. He's always been jealous of me and my parents' wealth."

"What does your father do?" I asked, more than a little curious.

"He heads a ten-man law firm. His specialty is compensation claims, mostly from small farmers whose land the highway people have commandeered. At 50% it's quite lucrative." She paused a moment, as if turning it all over. "At school, I've always been richer than anyone. My dad would be far happier defending murderers, or serving as a judge. He does it for my mother who craves glamour: her Mercedes, the big swimming pool, the five gold-plated telephones stuck about the house. She has red hair, so everything in the house is red. Christ, imagine what that's like bringing your friends home to."

Nets were being spread. We were both children of Midas from ostentatious backgrounds, if not quite the same. By now we had reached Panoramic Way, a single-lane wide, acacia-lined road that snaked steeply up to the vast mystery of Tilden Park. Mine, the second of three descending apartments, lay just below the first hairpin turn. We clomped down the outside staircase past tubs of marigolds and petunias lining the balcony that leaned out on a pair of sixty-foot stilts over the San Andreas fault and a view of the distant Bay.

Giving onto the balcony were two front rooms: a small bedroom that my mahogany four-poster ominously filled and a somewhat larger room with a bare floor, like a raked stage, tilting toward the far balcony corner. Exposed piping added its prominent curves and took over the hallway's dingy bathroom. At this point of the day the kitchen featured a shaded view eastward, across a series of gardens where almond trees were in bridal flower towards the Oakland docks, the scene of much picketing at this stage of the Vietnam War. There, by the breakfast table, with a gallon of retsina for support at my feet, we sat down.

Miranda had said she wanted to get to know me. Which me? The lonely Minotaur gesticulating across from her? Despite my efforts to break free of my family's influence and my marriage, I was still deeply unsure of whom I might be, or become. But there was a masked writer whose evolution I could describe. To a girl whose family had never strayed outside the 75-mile San Jose-Berkeley-San Francisco triangle, I tried to explain the lure of elsewhere and the liberation that can emerge from the disruption of context.

What Miranda made of the journeys, the oversized familial figures, I don't know, but as the shadows lengthened and the retsina drained I found myself more and more captivated. By her fetching way of leaning forward excitedly as she spoke. By the butterfly-like flutterings with which her small round-fingered hands augmented her speaking lips. By the genuine goodness and largeness of purpose she emanated. I couldn't bear to think all this might suddenly vanish back into her freshman life, her dorm, her hippie aspirations. To keep her from leaving, not realizing she might be a strict vegetarian—why are questions so hard for me?—I cooked a lamb stew for which she had to summon all her politeness just to keep poking at it.

Afterwards we retired to the living room couch to listen to a last bit of my constructed writerly identity—some *rembetika*. Finally a *zembeikiko* new to my feet called out, of an urgency compelling me to dance it. In the room's one patch of bare floor that's what I did, surrounding myself in a resonance of clicking fingers and exorcising slaps as I dipped and bobbed and weaved.

I had intended nothing more than a demonstration. In the process someone absolutely new took over; not the seducer who had been detailing certain aspects of his life, but the man I actually was, stripped of everything, naked as the sun. And I was declaring something as well, that I trusted her.

Finally, winded by my exertions, I collapsed panting at Miranda's feet. Everything still hung in abeyance. To take her in my arms and possibly spoil everything, or not to? If I didn't would I ever be vouchsafed another opportunity? And how would she take my inability to seize the day? Skepticism about the possibility of recurrence yielded to impelling need.

Virgil Burnett sculpture of a minotaur

So I sprang. Or rather, since I was the one on the floor, I raised myself and, my over-extended heart pumping violently, put my arms around her and began to kiss her. Miranda's mouth responded with a sexy inviting directness. That left several choices open. Undoubtedly I should have desisted. I had been, after all, accepted. But as the Greek proverb puts it, how do you hold honey in your hand and not lick it?

Moving forward, I reached down and slipped my arms under her. Then, staggering somewhat, I hoisted her off the couch and carried her through the doorway and placed her carefully on my waist-high four-poster. Four years later, after our divorce, Miranda would call the episode a rape. But a woman doesn't submit enthusiastically three times without betraying a certain complicity. And later, she would admit that she had been determined to seduce me or my teaching assistant—whoever might be the more available.

Of that first night, I retain the fierce grip with which her arms engulfed me as she slept. Next morning, after we had walked barefoot over the golden blossom-strewn roadway, I remember dousing her soles in ouzo as she sat on the rim of the tub. (Wasn't there a bar of soap about?) I didn't relish having to choose between Miranda and the graduate student, but if I had to, I knew it would be Miranda, for the promise held in her outstretched arms.

For Miranda, the yoking of our two bodies had preempted the usual dating stages whereby a young woman reassures herself about the rightness of her choice. Instead of her petals opening wider, day by day, she became a tight, closed, defensive bud. What mattered now was her pride—keeping me from dumping her. At our union's inner heart lay a tawdry canker.

Without considering whether she wanted an older man from a different background, she set out to entrap me. To be sure, as conquests go, a poet-professor had his value, if only as a useful trophy in the ongoing struggle with her mother and her peer group. But control exacts a toll on her vulnerability's delicate organ.

After returning to her dorm, Miranda had expected me to phone, just to chat. But my shyness reasserts itself before such a disembodying instrument. I need to see the face I am talking to; all the more if it's one deciding my fate. When, after two days I still hadn't called, she swallowed her pride and phoned and I found myself inviting her over.

As we lay in the dark some hours later, she offered her silken lures. "How," she asked, teasing me, "can you expect me to go on staying with you when you don't want to marry me? Everyone else always has." Then, after a pause reflecting the stunned silence on my part, she acknowledged wryly, "They were, of course, too young to get married without parental consent." I remember her unlikely proposal bringing a decided smirk to my face. Why, with two willing lovers, would I want another marital noose?

Yet the dart took hold and soon enough that preposterous teenage notion became my consuming passion. Perhaps I was no more equipped for prolonged bachelorhood than was Charlie Merrill. And I was now of an age where I could recognize certain longings: for a mate of my deliberate choosing, a satisfying domestic life, and with it a more grounded being. In Miranda I saw a child-woman prepared to dance to that ancient music.

Miranda, Berkeley, 1967

When I informed the Graduate Student of the teen-ager I had fallen for, she made a remark about the quality of such nubile bodies. A sign of acceptance? Hardly. A few weeks later she left out with the garbage the large Télémaque painting I had loaned her. Fortunately, the garbage collector had excellent taste, and I learned many years later that the painting had ended up in a museum rather than a landfill.

Miranda's person, mounted in green, leaflike against me, seemed of a faery delicacy. The face of a deer, with big thoughtful eyes of the blue-gray with which Patinier liked to paint his mountain visions. When I think of them, I see one of those favorite Berkeley days of hers, fog blanketing the hills until only textures remained, the brick of a garden staircase, the leaded windows of a shingle house.

As we lay in bed, Miranda would entertain me with stories of her childhood nights when she would lie awake listening to the train whistles blowing in the distance. Only for her the whistles were ship horns. Someone had told her the ocean was only five miles from her home, which it may have been as the crow flies over the Santa Cruz Mountains. So it wasn't altogether implausible to imagine a fleet of ships that came and went every night. She even thought she knew the shopping mall where they moored.

Then there was the time when her nurse discovered her making up a second bed in her room. "For whom is the other bed?" her nurse asked.

"For me," Miranda replied, "to cry on."

More alarming, could I have realized their significance, were the catatonic episodes she told me about, whole afternoons spent absolutely unable to dislodge herself from the chair in which she sitting.

The temptation, Miranda presented, to realign myself was certainly compelling. How could I, whose life hummed restlessly along, not marvel at a person who had never known an hour's boredom? From what was I trying to escape? Couldn't I too live in the moment and grow from my own internal space? Though I often felt on the wrong end of the see-saw from her, I couldn't help but relish the enlargement of purpose she brought.

It helped that ours was the spring that preceded the 1967 Summer of Love. Hope had become for many an almost palpable presence, high in a branch, singing. And beneath stood our malleable selves, shapes waiting to be melted, molded.

At this acme Miranda suggested consulting the *I Ching*, the ancient Chinese game of fate. With my five coins I rolled—how appropriately!—the hexagram Abundance. It read:

Abundance has success
The King attains abundance

Be not sad
Be like the sun at midday

A welcome turn I learned: abundance, after all, doesn't alight that often. But the rest of the Wilhelm commentary was deeply sobering as it spelled out the impermanence of such bounty. Whether I knew it or not, the well from which I was sipping was poisoned. While making the most of my good fortune, I should be preparing myself for an eventual comeuppance. After a mountain climb, one must master the descent.

With Marcia, there had been barriers of background and class, but we spoke the same generational language; with Miranda, our ties had to be improvised afresh out of the scraps at hand: a Donovan album; our balcony's hibachi stove, on which she cooked an evening pilaf with vegetables I had diced.

Her native idiom came out one day when we visited Marcia in the hospital. Marcia had gone in for a minor operation, expecting to be released the next day. A week later she was still there, the victim of an inappropriately administered medication.

"I knew they were dosing me with the wrong I.V.," Marcia informed us, "but for the life of me I couldn't think of the right expression to make them stop. I'm still baffled."

"You could have said," Miranda told her, "it was against your religion."

Marcia shook her head sadly and sighed, "I guess I haven't been in California long enough."

In our conversations Miranda spoke of Truth as of something actually ascertainable. I was too scattered to hazard such a leap, fascinated by movement in its every aspect, the flux of dots that's a soccer game, a warbler-loud spring forest, the kaleidoscope of a garden. With her more linear, logical cast of mind, Miranda was prepared to see every gesture as fitting an overriding purpose or karma. According to her, marijuana could provide the gateway to this realization. We had been living together a year when she finally deemed me advanced enough to be offered this so-called sacrament. I had tried it once on a friend's houseboat in Seattle, but not knowing how to inhale I resembled an idiot rushing through a cocktail party screaming, "My kingdom for an ice cube." Not smoked, but ingested now in the form of a packed brownie, I experienced a muddy colored vision for which nothing in my life had remotely prepared me.

My first impression, however, was that this could not be real, this large white opossum padding warily, to a deafening roar of leaves, by our kitchen window. But the opossum was real, as was the compulsion compelling me to remove a box of orange-and-green Tide from its longtime site atop our icebox. Other sensations were more painterly: the arabesque of our balcony's arches, transfigured by the pink daggers of the sunset; the circles of light on the overhead steam pipes of our sitting room; even the goddess herself, a spectral Mexican Maria, squat and of a dusky complexion, arranged in a bright red square-cut poncho in the corner of a sofa.

By now the aphrodisiac was taking over. Impelled, we withdrew to the sheets and made love. More slowly than had ever seemed possible, a staccato of fingers painting rash-like exclamations along the inner contours of her thigh:

> asleep, piled, leg over rump, two
> soft pink-
> green
>
> alligators
>
> alligators

MY EDEN UNRAVELS

Before ingesting marijuana I had always performed on a mental see-saw. Reality was, like my doctoral degree, comparative. I might be up or down, but I was never, so help me, vertical. It may have been my lucky star, but I believed with Miranda that what others called evil was merely an illusion. Why, we asked, would anyone prefer the satanic Stones to the enlightened Beatles?

One evening, several months later, I rashly consumed a half lid of marijuana, supposing it mostly twigs and seeds. Twenty minutes later, came the hallucinations. I can still see the tall angular underwater mountains that closed the horizon, the penumbral light beating down like rain, a slanting gray-blue that beat and tore with a diarrhetic speed. It was the speed I found terrifying. Any faster and I'd go bonkers. All the same I could quicken the terror by being foolish enough to laugh aloud. The laughter came in bursts, like a death rattle, or a machine gun. Any more and I'd be a shutter banging in a deserted house.

The wisest, under the circumstances, was to forbid all speech—speech so easily turns to laughter! And not budge from my bed's tossing yacht on which I had taken refuge. Beyond its mahogany planks lay a world of dreaded noise. I didn't dare forsake it to pee, much as I needed to, for fear of the toilet's waterfall-like roar.

Everything, from the intervals between perceptions to their banality, deepened my gloom. The poet of *A Season in Hell* came to mind—ah, a master I could emulate! Then, with more compassion, as I sensed the relief with which Rimbaud had renounced his drunken boat. "It's all in the mind," I told myself. Yet I had only to close my eyes to experience the unconscionable speed with which those jangling chains surged, dizzying, frenetic, as they dissolved me to a tune:

I'm a pig
I'm a gentle antelope
I'm a pig
I'm a gentle antelope
antelope
an-te-lope

At first, the repetitions teased and amused. As they persisted, I felt caught in the earworm I had released.

Afraid to fall asleep, I required a ballroom blaze of lights. I felt an overweening need for space—cool, glassy, grotto blue—while, like the mental invalid I'd become, I squirmed about, seeking a position that would somehow allay the swarming malevolence.

I looked and the light I saw was mine.

With new awareness, I understood how much of my being was predicated on performance. Did I have to go through such gyrations? Was I that insecure? There had to be a way to make myself more direct. Concentration. Absence of desire. Charity. And, at the end, maybe, a man speaking from within, relaxed, integrated.

Alas, any such integration lay far in the offing. The more that night I searched, the more I found myself staring into a muddy pool. Had the "wanton current," the impulses I had once imagined propelling me free, turned into this? Whichever way I squirmed and twisted, I was trapped. Trapped by my father whose financial serf I remained. Trapped by a teaching job that, however glamorous, no longer suited the writer I had become. Trapped, too, by my Omphale and a control that was turning us both into ever more constricted knots of flesh. All the worse in that, as the *I Ching* had foreseen, Miranda had contracted, shortly after moving in, a yeast infection from some misapplied antibiotics. Each time I entered her became a stab, the pain my need inflicted.

My role, as her lover, was to transform her from a girl into a young woman. At first, possibly, I succeeded, but orgasm never came easily. As to what inhibited her I can only guess. For Miranda, as previously for Marcia, it may be that once she had, perhaps inadvertently, snared me, she lost interest.

Miranda did not want, any more than Psyche, a masked Eros; she wanted me. "You're not on some hypothetical page," she insisted, "you're in this bed with me. If you don't feel like being present to me, go ahead and I'll leave. It's up to you."

I felt terrified by Miranda's threat. How on my own was I to pursue the path she had opened? In my dilemma I tried to placate her when I would have done better voicing my fear of the narrowing tunnel into which her goal orientation, the absolute positions behind which she walled herself, were taking us. Moments are to be expanded rather than suppressed. They are what we have.

I had told her earlier about how Father mistook his compulsive ideas for reality. Wasn't I, Miranda asked, doing the same by placing Writing at the top of my private pedestal? This was the idol to whom I had sworn fealty, backed as it was by considerable willpower: the ability to sit six to eight hours a time at a desk, and the panicky fear that, if I ever for a moment stopped scribbling, the edifice would collapse. The concentration, the singleness of focus required, was so consuming I never thought to ask what it was costing. Did I have to be, Miranda asked, so intense? Couldn't I, now and then, let a sliver of light chink its way in, go out, say, and have a good time?

Nancy Ling Perry, 1970

The notion of a developing identity could not have been more fatuous. In reality, I was becoming, as that second marijuana episode suggested, more and more deeply split. On the one hand, there was the fellow who watched birds with Miranda, who played soccer and wrote. On the other, there was the sexual compulsive. One hand could not hear the other clapping.

It hardly mattered that the writer was human in name only. Of the two of me he seemed far and away the more admirable. And that other, that shy, wistful leftie, hands stuffed in his pockets, bustling about in the shadows somewhere, I regarded with professional contempt. "Come on," I'd admonish him, "set yourself on fire, have a drink!" But the guy was like blotting paper. The more booze I absorbed, the more admirable I thought I became: less hyper, more relaxed. I even looked forward to the hangovers. While body shook and temples throbbed, a newly compassionate pen watercolored along, borne on the slowed, heavy rhythms of my genetic inheritance.

Though I had felt strangled by my father and the ceaseless panic he engendered, I never thought to question the straitjacket of overachievement we both wore. It was familiar. Rather than ease up, I scrunched up my shoulders and cranked it tighter, as if an extra notch was all I lacked. Think of those pre-Berkeley years: New Haven-Paris-Iran-Greece-Seattle-Greece-Berkeley. A man in constant orbit, faster! Faster!

In rebelling against my parents and their Southampton life, I was rebelling against the principle that money alone conferred value. All I did, though, was substitute my grandfather's womanizing, as if only her fertile eye could make me whole. And I saw the whole heaving perspiring tribe of us Sisyphuses as forever engaged in the solemn task of pushing that impossible stone of theirs up and over the orgasmic hill.

Long after I went to bed I'd wake to find Miranda curled up with *Jane Eyre*, trying to reignite the bright eager do-it-all self she once possessed. Yet each time I reached out to her now I only ended up undoing another of those first months when we did nothing, it seemed, but hold one another, she wrapping me in her leafy thighs until, deep within her forest lake, she could hear me exploding. Now, some two years later, that interior forest was no more than so many dead leaves and clinging needles where all that resounded was my relentless hammering.

Finally, faced with her evident misery, I agreed to a summer's separation. While Miranda worked in the university library, I would make a trip with my brother Stephen. He wanted to experience the Iran of my "Persian Notes." Why not pick up where Marcia and I had left off six years earlier?

WHATEVER IT TOOK

Our jaunt to Iran in June-July, 1968, did not work out. Feeling my Persian was not up to the responsibility of negotiating for two, I had thrown myself on the mercy of an Iranian engineering student I had known in Seattle. He had brought home a new Impala and wanted to show it off by driving us all over the country. But the point of traveling does not lie in the swaths of terrain being raced over. Cooped up in the glass prison of the Impala's front seat, unable to get out to lounge in a tea house, to shop, to bargain, to talk to anyone but the two of them, I had more than enough time to think of what I had lost in Miranda. In a different way from my uncle, but no less powerfully, she had taken me over. All I wanted, I now realized, was to win her back. I would do whatever it took.

Robin with Michael Beard

When Stephen and I arrived on our own in Isfahan a month later, hoping to secure a safe conduct to visit the Bakhtiari in their summer pasturage, we learned to our shock that their prince, to whom we were bringing a bronze owl of Pallas Athene as a present from our uncle, had died a few weeks earlier of an inoperable bullet wound in his neck. That left little alternative but to fly back to Jimmy's in Athens. There a letter was waiting from Miranda. Her summer, too, had not lived up to her expectations. If I still insisted on returning early (our apartment was rented out), she would find me a "pad."

Miranda was at the airport to greet me. I was so overcome that I did nothing but bawl. I went on sobbing and kissing her the whole of the long clammy taxi ride back to Berkeley. Months later she confided that the man she was kissing with such apparent fervor had become a stranger she barely tolerated. Even my scent proved unfamiliar.

Miranda had found me a cottage in the scorched drylands east of the Berkeley hills. She would remain in her pad, a way of underlining the tenuousness of my reprieve. But a month's silent sobbing in the Impala had brought home how much I had at stake. Chafe as I did under the weight of her expectations, she was the best part of my Berkeley life. My one hope lay in convincing her I could be a changed man.

So a pursuit began, one that to this day in my dreams still thrills with the enormity of the feat I saw myself undertaking; an unlikely couple, but one all the same. With a month before classes resumed I had time to reinvent myself. Hair, of course. On its behalf I sprouted a flopping Fu Manchu moustache. I came to appreciate the soft hedge it placed in front of my long horse-like mug; the possibility of becoming an aware pair of eyes rather than some rubbery-mouthed clown. With the moustache, appeared boots and hip-hugging jeans. In this get-up I attended meditation sessions at the Blue Mountain Center led by an articulate professor from Kerala, Eknath Easwaran.

From the sexual therapists, Masters and Johnson, I familiarized myself with the technique of the clitoral orgasm. I learned of the undersea grotto lying at the center of a woman's body. There below a whole ringing surf, among the anemones and corals and waving fronds, the bright fish of my fingers darted and played.

These ministrations must have succeeded. By next April we were married: a big-hearted Italian wedding with bags of sugar-coated almonds, a black ecumenical minister, my brother Stephen as my best man in a green velvet tuxedo and our friends' old-time hillbilly band who went on playing from two until midnight. (Father, to my surprise, enjoyed it so much that it was all Mother could do to pull him away. She refused to believe that an "afternoon" wedding might not be over by seven and had scheduled a dinner party that my brothers, Merrill and Peter, were required to attend.)

Several months later a still furious Stephen wrote to Mother:

> You've been so full of how brave you were to get through Robin's
> marriage that it has blinded you to what I call the "niceties." Such as
> calling him the day of his wedding to wonder what time dinner was
> because you just happened to have made your own food arrangements.
> Incredible! And the way you look at it, he was shut up from complaining by a
> few attractive checks. The Final Solution!

For our honeymoon we flew to Frankfurt to purchase a VW, intending to find a base in the Dordogne. But it rained for 16 days straight, requiring winter gear. With the rain, though, came a phenomenon you don't see growing up in San Jose—lightning! I remember Miranda standing out on our Paris balcony watching in rapt amazement the zig-zagging bolts crash over the mansard roofs.

In an attempt to outflank the rain, we headed east by way of Provence and Rapallo. But the weather didn't let up until we reached Parma. By then a maniacal gleam had come into my eye, the kind of thing that happens when a character starts taking over a story. Far away in Calabria lay the villages of Miranda's Albanian-speaking grandparents. Further still, in Cycladic Greece, lay Paros. The island held a key to a memorable part of my life and, like any infatuated man, I wanted Miranda to experience its spell.

Game as Miranda was, she found the daily packing and unpacking trying. How she envied those fairy tale heroines who had only supposedly to stamp their foot for the baggage to follow on its own. Epirus, though, reduced her to numb speechlessness when I struck off on a 100-mile long unpaved mountain road. But in Athens, in a cellar tavern, she did behold some authentic dancing, two women up on their tables stomping away. And Paros was still Paros: constellations like a thousand tribal rugs spouting stories; a maze of curling streets along which we strolled in a serenity that came as much as anything from the lack of cars.

With no call to do anything, much less see anything (I had used it all up writing my earlier poem), I could sit out on our hotel balcony and read, with an unexpected relish, *War and Peace*: a work until then put aside because of the demands of teaching. Those demands had begun to chafe. From the outset I had seen teaching as provisional, a profession that would keep me out of trouble if, as seemed all too likely, I had nothing to say. Once I had strayed onto subjects that were, in effect, writing me, then cramming to fill a lecture's hour and a half, the professional need to stay abreast of every new wind that blew by, all that could seem deeply extraneous. It was not critical discourse I wanted to reshape, but the unknown in myself, whatever that might be. All the same I recognized that any opting out would have to wait for Miranda to finish her various degrees. At her rate of a course or two a term—any prospect of a grade less than an "A" warranted a withdrawal—that could take the better part of a decade.

FIRED, REHIRED, AND REFIRED

The spring of our European trip was the spring of People's Park, an event I regret missing as it might have explained what genuine civic agitation could be about: a park rather than a parking lot; a university's responsibility to its community rather than some bureaucrat's bottom line. I wasn't drawn to marching, but I could see myself as one of the "sod brothers," out there with a pick and trowel.

Most of the issues facing us teachers were not so clear cut. Pinched between the student left and the business-dominated Board of Regents, we found ourselves in an intolerable no man's land. Had we possessed a viable labor union and adequate representation on the governing board, we could have played a mediating role. As it was, radicals and regents had every incentive to clash, if only to keep their publicity mills churning.

To the faculty, California was distracting enough already. One colleague quit to become a professional motorcycle racer, another to direct encounter groups at Esalen. Others gave up scholarly work to grind out textbooks for the mass market. More still succumbed to the seductions of politics, using their research skills to compile tracts for the anti-Vietnam war campaign and to defend the university—and their jobs—against the incessant attacks mounted by the Ronald Reagan-led Right.

At stake when I arrived in 1965 was the principle of a tuition-free state university. It was predictable perhaps that shelling out for a free university of Berkeley's cantankerous sort would not sit well with the retired Midwesterners who made up Reagan's Southern California majority. They had strapped themselves once paying for their kids' education and saw little reason to suffer the property taxes that paid for a free education. On the backburner simmered many of the same issues that had produced the loyalty oaths of the

Fifties. If Herbert Marcuse and Angela Davis could be fired for their beliefs, why not any of us?

With each new issue the acrimony escalated. Finally, with the discovery of the carpet-bombing of neutral Cambodia, our outrage exploded, forcing Governor Reagan to employ tear gas and close down the university.

I had followed the insurrection in colonial Indo-China even before my father had gone there on a pre-Dien-Bien-Phu fact-finding commission for President Eisenhower. While in Paris in 1954 I had talked politics at length with Vietnamese of several different persuasions. At college, for reasons unknown, I had dreamed of everything from participating in tiger shoots along the Mekong River with Emperor Bao-Dai to recurrent nightmares in which I found myself pursued by people on pig-size motorcycles and guerillas rising anywhere, at any moment, out of the stalks of a cornfield.

I was in my second year of teaching when my brother Peter invited me to join him on a skiing holiday in Aspen as guests of the Nitze family. Their father, Paul, our chief negotiator in the later disarmament SALT talks, was then serving under McNamara as Secretary of the Navy. Nitze had been a class behind Father at Harvard and had served in every Democratic administration from FDR onwards. With his impeccable credentials and patrician sense of service, he seemed to be everything I could admire.

One evening, as we were sitting around, I expressed my unease (shared with my father) about our country's getting mired in an unwinnable Asiatic land war. Why were we in Vietnam, I asked? For its China Sea oil reserves?

Not at all, Nitze replied. It was to contain a virus, Communism, which would otherwise spread throughout Southeast Asia. And he insisted that, contrary to what everyone in Berkeley was saying, we were winning the war. Why I let this cold warrior con me with his "inside" information, I don't know. Did I so badly need to believe, against all the odds, in patrician competence?

As it turned out, it was not Berkeley's students who were misinformed, but Nitze and McNamara and their on-the-ground sources. Penned in their compounds, untrained often enough in both language and regional history, it would be amazing if any American diplomat understood anything about where he or she were posted. However, it took Cambodia to drive that home.

Up to then I had remained apolitical. But the shock of learning that President Nixon, by personal fiat, had unleashed 250,000 bombing missions over one of the few remaining Shangri-las was more than I could stomach, and I joined in the wave of indignation that swept the university. I lectured in a Palo Alto high school in support of the anti-war Republican congressman,

Pete McCloskey, in his primary battle against Elizabeth Taylor's husband. I pointed out that, historically, the Vietnamese had always posed a barrier against Chinese expansion. And I predicted that the future site of the "anti-Communist crusade" would not be Southeast Asia but Latin America.

It was sobering, in trying to drum up mainstream support, to discover how out of touch we had become. Building a coalition requires, at the least, respect for other people's concerns and priorities. Now, when we needed the trust of these "squares," our snobbery had discredited us.

At the University of Washington, other than basic composition, I had taught mainly American literature; a compelling subject since it was the students' identity as Americans I was helping them discover. At Berkeley, I found myself teaching almost every subject except American lit to anybody from freshman undergraduates to graduate students: Chaucer, the 17th century, the Pastoral narrative, the English lyric, and a course I instituted on Surrealism.

Mother in Parisian evening dress, 1950

For a writer who had almost no undergraduate background in English literature, the education its cannon offered was exciting, as was the stimulus the charged political milieu provided. Students who take ideas seriously tend to take their teachers seriously as well. A number of us had small cults trailing us from course to course. For them, I had become something more than a teacher—a mentor.

Yet for all the intellectual stimulus, I missed the productive camaraderie I enjoyed in Seattle. In Berkeley, for much of the time, I suffered from a wrenching loneliness. Yet I can't help but wonder how others in my situation fared. Those professorial houses tucked away on the steep hill above the campus, with their big decks and picture windows, might as well have been fortresses. At the University of Washington, life was there to be invented, a poem or essay we circulated, a reading we all attended. At Berkeley, the audience was more remote: the New York publishers; the fellow specialists at a conference. We had, in some awful way, grown too big for one another.

Working at home and teaching a one or two-course Tuesday-Thursday schedule limited collegiality. Never more than a small fraction of an over-hundred man department was available for a noonday meal. That may have been why making friends in kindred departments—the whole point, one might think, of a university—was actively discouraged. The priority had to be on getting acquainted with one another. In this Marcia had supported me well. But that made my walking out on this social paragon—for a departmental typist!—all the more unforgivable. And my subsequent marriage to an undergraduate Miranda, who had reason enough to resent being condescended to, only isolated me further.

I was coasting along in my fourth year when, as a result of a mid-career review, I found myself unexpectedly cashiered. The verdict stunned me. Berkeley was notorious for its "publish or perish" standards. It was not so much what you wrote as the sheer volume of publications that supposedly earned you tenure. By those standards I had little to fear. In sheer bulk and range, I far outweighed anyone at my level. I felt so confident of vaulting a mere preliminary four-year hurdle that I gave scant attention to the new item on the departmental questionnaire requesting my views on teaching.

This had appeared in response to the recent firing of a good friend and the department's acclaimed "best teacher," Joe Kramer, for his failure to publish. In the spirit of the day a "Keep Kramer" campaign sprang into being, spurred by the esteem among both faculty and students Joe enjoyed. While the campaign failed, it did succeed in requiring that we be judged by our classroom effectiveness. In effect, a new standard was being promulgated, since none of us had undergone any teacher training in graduate school. Supposedly, communicating your subject was a skill learned on the job.

Still my methods had every right to be called more than a bit bizarre. One 19-year-old during my first term remembers getting back a paper with no grade and the enigmatic injunction, "Please see me in my office." Wondering what could be the matter, she climbed the four flights. In consternation, she watched me motion her to a chair and then, after bolting the frosted glass door, remove my coat. The necktie, I'm told, followed, as did the shoes. As she sat, torn between an amused curiosity and the impulse to flee down the hall, I jumped down from the standard issue oak desk on which I was perched and, to no discernable music other than my clicking fingers, started to dance a *zembeikiko*. (I should add that I have not the least recollection of the incident.) From then on she was not only my student, enrolled in nearly every course I taught, but my friend, one I still possess. As to what compelled me to such an exhibition, I can only guess. New to the university, with my heart still in the Greece I had left just weeks earlier, and still hitched despite everything to Marcia, I must have been ready to explode.

Not every student could be expected to tolerate such eccentricity. My efforts to stammer out a course description were enough to send half the class racing to the registrar's office in an attempt to cancel. "What agony for beauty!" a student confided to her diary. The lack of connecting material between sentence parts could take some getting used to. "I've sat here for 50 minutes and I haven't understood a single word you're saying," was a not infrequent first-week response.

Nor was it only the linear thinkers and diehard note-takers who felt thwarted by this wild-eyed, teeth-baring, foot-stamping professor. Addressing a tenure meeting, my advocate, the poet Josephine Miles declared, "One starts up a conversation with Robin and thinks that, though the words are English, the syntax came in on the last space ship . . . Unlike Monsieur Jourdain," she concluded, none too hopefully, "he will never discover that what he talks is prose."

Miles's "never" seems unduly pessimistic. It might take a few weeks for a student to figure out where on the cognitive dial my blurts and squeaks lay. Eventually some did, discovering a more instinctual cast of mind at the core of figurative language.

So there I was before a mid-career review committee, a diligent scribbler with a student wife. What could be wrong with me?

"His teaching!" I can see a former swain of Marcia's piping up.

"On what evidence can you say that?"

"One of my advisees whispered it to me."

"Me, too," the veteran in the next chair chimed in. "I think we may have found the lamb we need to toss to the baying Kramer wolves."

Canned! My reaction was one of incomprehension. As a teacher I certainly had my defects, but my classroom was not a mausoleum. I was clearly giving my students something unavailable in any other departmental quarter. Nor do I hold with the saw that teaching can't be judged. In the classroom you are being judged, at every moment. The verdict comes from those registering for any future course—the quality they represent. But what was I to do? The nature of the condemnation, based entirely on hearsay, left no defense.

The mid-career decision had come in January, 1969, too late to secure employment for the following September. So I was allowed to stay on for a year while I sought a job. By now the professorial game of musical chairs, funded by the post-war economy, had come to a screeching halt, leaving you stuck wherever you had last landed.

In looking for a job, it could not have helped to have Josephine Miles vouching for me:

Mr. Magowan is a most interesting and esoteric writer, inventive along the lines of Durrell and Michaux, oblique in his theories of pastoral, a good reader of poetry when he gets warmed up, and a good teacher when the students figure him out. He is worth some patience; there is a sweet center within the husk of oddity. His published work speaks for him at his best, and is full of illuminations not to be found in the average young writer.

It wasn't until almost a year later that this "husk of oddity" received an offer from Bennington; all the more welcome in that Miranda could pursue her undergraduate degree there.

Nonetheless the arbitrary nature of my firing, based solely on hearsay, did not sit well with Berkeley's deans. If classroom performance was to be a basis for tenure decisions, a more objective assessment was needed. The department finally produced a form consisting of a single blank page on which the student was asked to record his or her impressions of the value of the course and its teacher.

I was teaching two compulsory summer courses, a freshman comp and the last hurdle before graduation, a history of criticism seminar, when the new evaluations were handed out. Mine, to my astonishment, drew mostly raves. I was, after all, a lame duck with nothing at stake.

As I perused the evaluations in mid-October, a wave of indignation shot through me. My fate was, of course, settled. But there were some misconceptions I felt compelled to address, and on the spur of the moment I dashed off a letter to the senior faculty.

After reminding them of the circumstances under which this recently fired man was teaching, I took up the criticism seminar's one negative assessment, the contribution of a sorority babe who had cut all but three classes:

> When a person is fired, as I have been, by gossip, he has a right to ask certain questions . . . I say this because the one complaint against me . . . seems in so many ways typical: only two or three classes attended in the whole term, an overload problem, etc. But notice the proportions of the class that she is and how the quality of her response differs from those on other sheets. There are mountains and there are molehills. Somebody, somewhere, should be able to tell them apart.

To a highly politicized department my letter offered an irresistible opportunity. A cabal immediately formed. They insisted on having my "candidacy" resubmitted. And for the first time in departmental annals, a cashiered teacher was rehired. The look of triumph on the Irish scholar and future novelist Tom Flanagan's face, as he strode into my office to announce "the start of a new era," would have been reward enough. There were other considerations as well, among them Miranda who had never wanted to leave Berkeley, and my two sons. Not without a certain regret, I turned down Bennington. But the prospect of tenure, of being caged in Wheeler's gloomy asbestos-ridden corridors for the next 30 years, was hardly cheering.

In the wake of my rehiring it seemed appropriate to buy a house. What, Miranda asked, could we afford? I had no idea, since it was not I, but Father who controlled my finances. But I saw no harm in hiring an estate lawyer to examine my trust fund and tell me where I stood.

It turned out that I had a right to what Father had been withholding these many years. A pyrrhic victory. Outraged at my consulting a lawyer—was I contemplating taking him to court?—Father wrote me out of his will to the eventual favor of my children.

Up to then, foreign travel aside, I had lived frugally. I roller-painted my apartment walls, built book shelves of pine boards straddling cement blocks, and drove a VW bug. My father called me a "skinflint." But how else was I to live within my means? When Father showed me the books of my trust fund, I was flabbergasted to learn that my graduation car, my airline tickets, my entire education were items I had been paying for while he pocketed the tax credits and exacted the thanks. More welcome was the discovery that the income my trust fund generated more than doubled my teacher's salary. I could afford to buy a small house with a little uphill garden in residential Kensington just north of Berkeley; a compromise between the rural setting we both wanted and university life. Better yet, I could become a full-time writer, if I so chose.

Between me and any such career change there remained the final tenure decision, some two years away. Time enough, one would think, to repair my social fences and find a publisher for *Narcissus and Orpheus,* a book length study of the conventions underlying a few classics of modern pastoral (*Dominique, The Country of the Pointed Firs, Le Grand Meaulnes* and *Out of Africa*) I had made out of my Yale dissertation.

Instead, flushed with this "new era" of theirs and my equally heady financial independence, I applied for an immediate decision. While awaiting it, I maintained a distinct reserve before my future judges. If my teaching and writings earned me tenure, so be it. I was not about to charm my way into an honorific cage.

The tenure meeting, from what I've learned, was a massacre. Knives were by now well whetted and they descended on the corpus of my scholarship. "Five mistakes of fact on his pastoral essay's opening page," one scholar crowed. Another challenged, "I defy any of you to make sense of page twelve." Nor did it help that most of the lively cabal who had fought to get me rehired were away on well-deserved grants. That left my defense once again to my fellow poet-critic Josephine Miles, she of the Monsieur Jourdain quip. After another gibe at "what he calls his prose," her brief concluded, generously:

> The poems aren't many, but they are exquisite. And that's one reason why I can't think we want to let him go. He works with so much craft to make as he says in his motto to *Voyages*, "le gong fidèle d'un mot." A man who loves words so much cannot be obscure ultimately, if we take the time to read him.

Patience was not the long suit of an overstaffed department beset by falling enrollment. My supporters, I was told, comprised a majority, if less than the two-thirds required. To the others I must have remained, like my writings on pastoral, "all too oblique." For all that I had anticipated and even provoked it, the verdict stung. Yet it was certainly right. I wasn't cut out to be a Berkeley MLA All Star.

I resigned on the spot. One lame duck stint had been humiliation enough.

FAREWELL, MY LOVELY

I have missed teaching at times: the duels with students, as determined to change me as I was to change them, and the friendships, however fleeting, that grew out of it. With the friendships, however, came loneliness, those flocks of migrating youths for whom my class was a mere stopover on the way to graduation. And the performances—the best teachers are inevitably actors—brought its bouts of stage fright, made all the keener by the rows of cool eyes noting my every slur, every tic. Yet the regret my uncle had foreseen in abandoning that career never materialized. Eight years in the academic trenches was time enough.

What I failed to anticipate was the unraveling effect of my firing on the intimate fabric of my life. This came home one evening as Miranda and I were sitting before our fireplace. I happened to be reading Raymond Chandler. His evil alliances spoke to me all the more in that they confirmed what I had witnessed growing up. I was congratulating myself, as I read, on the life together we had achieved—a long haul, but we had made it—when Miranda spoke up, "You know, Robin—or maybe you don't—but I'm really suffering."

"Oh, are you?" I said, failing to catch her drift. "Why don't you call on that psychiatrist you consulted last year about your fear of bees? What was his name?"

Miranda looked at me wildly for a moment and then ran into the bedroom. I followed her, thinking to console her. "I think he's been very good for you," I said, taking her hand.

"Bees, bees, bees," she said, wrenching her hand away. "God, Robin, it's not bees."

"What is it then?" I asked, nonplussed.

There was a long silence, then, "Our marriage. You can't see how shrunken, how fearful we've each become. Why do you think I stay up half the night reading?" she asked, looking straight at me. "It's the one way I have of convincing myself I'm not living with you. When people on the street, or in class, ask why I'm married, I don't know what to say, we're so different from one another."

Poison, Miranda, had said, yes, it was quite a draught I had swallowed. For four years I had lain, consumed in the carnage and atrocity of an ineluctable dream. She within me, I within her. A sumptuous poison and one that, to this day, still leaves me shivering.

Should I have said any of this? Would it have made a difference? Instead, ignoring my own grief, I asked, "You want a divorce?" too aware of her protracted suffering to beg for a stay of execution.

That, amazingly, was it, four years of a close, perhaps too close a union snuffed out in a single question. *One Flesh, Separate Lives*, Robin Skynner titled a book on marital therapy. I certainly could have used such therapy; patterns of conduct do not have to be endlessly repeated. But the time for therapy, in Miranda's eyes, had long passed. Sex, when it clicks, can green over relational fissures. When it doesn't, each word exchanged, each look, becomes a step over an ice ever more tenuous, more withdrawn.

The deprivation I had known in my time with Marcia had rebounded. And I must say I found no solace in the irony. I hadn't delivered the goods—for either of them. Only now Miranda was the marital captive, seeking access to a fuller, more pleasurable life. She looked forward to going out, like others of her age, on dates. And to not committing herself, a proud "Marxist-Feminist" unwilling to serve the male oppressor.

For me, the break-up was a disaster. I wonder sometimes, seeing the way she sometimes haunts my dreams, if I'll ever stop paying for a love doomed from the start, given who she was and who I was. Two worse-balanced playmates on the see-saw to which we were yoked would be hard to find. But what I know rationally doesn't necessarily transmit to the underlying self in which it's still locked. The impossibility makes the oneiric pursuit with its moments of recapture and seeming acceptance all the more exhilarating, "You did it once, why can't you do it again? And again? Despite much later therapy, I still don't get it. Did that lost pair of blue eyes enshrine something so irreplaceable?

I could not bear to watch Miranda's emancipation. And with no teaching obligations it was easier for me to leave. A week earlier I had received a postcard from my Harvard soccer team mate, Tony Oberschall. He was in Zambia studying the post-independence rise of a new class of business entrepreneurs and planning a two-week safari through Northern and Luapula provinces—would I join him in Lusaka in a month's time? On the spot I accepted.

Our last month together allowed us to address the damage we had inflicted with those seductive games of capture and enslavement. With the pressure off I could be honest and Miranda reciprocated as best she could. For her, the generational gap was unbridgeable. Ten years younger and I might possibly have stood a chance. But love is not something you can will. For Miranda, that first determining click never really happened.

Two days before leaving for Africa, I took Miranda to see the Alec Guinness film, "The Man in the White Suit." Towards the end of the film comes a sequence where the sound track goes haywire with workers dashing about, explosions of every sort penetrating the factory yard. Against all the ack-ack there comes a loud reiterating managerial voice. My ear drums felt as if they were being punctured. I left Miranda and took refuge in the last row, hands plugging my ears. Whose was that managerial voice? How much tumult could I take before something barely held together cracked?

In desperation, driving home, I asked Miranda if she would take the wheel. She refused, as it was four years since she had last driven a car. "I want to kill myself," I caught myself pathetically muttering. I still remember the distinct sway of the rear motor as the VW lurched from one uphill bend to the next. Unable to grasp the steering wheel, I remained foetally hunched, steering with my elbows, as if the wheel were located somewhere deep in my chest.

I got the car home, but for the first time ever I chose not to walk Miranda to the door. For a while I remained outside, transfixed. Then I began to walk uphill along the blacktop, King Lear's "Why she, even she!" resounding in my ears. As I walked, taking in the pools of light the street lamps projected in the evening silence, Lear haunted me. Even before divvying up his kingdom, he must have suspected the price he was paying for his monstrous self-indulgence. Was I Lear or his Fool? Then there appeared a response abstracted from the play, "A man who is nothing cannot offend."

WHAT CONTINENT ARE YOU SAVING
FOR YOUR NEXT HONEYMOON?

The news of the breakup with Miranda, whom Jimmy had come to admire, did not sit well with my uncle. "What continent are you saving for your next honeymoon?" he quipped on a postcard, genuinely dismayed by the genetic compulsions he saw me re-enacting, the need to keep recreating myself afresh at whoever's expense. For a blurb, 15 years later, he would write:

> *Vissi d'amore, vissi di viaggio,* might well be this writer's theme song. He travels in order to love, he loves in order to find himself elsewhere. From deep in this or that interior his reader gets postcards: dissolving views, myth-haunted, radiantly dislocated particulars. Their sender is unlikely to settle anywhere except for a season in the next virgin forest. To be touched, even dazzled, by the results is less a reflex of avuncular complacency than a taste for that precisely not familiar self, that revenant stung by rare insects and laid low by feverish embraces, whose prose is collected here for the first time.

From the poet of "The Broken Home," I think I understand. All the same there could be more to Africa than biting off another chunk of the unvisited. I wanted to make a Matisse-like journey of my own.

After a couple of days outfitting ourselves, Tony Oberschall and I set off with an interpreter for the North of Zambia in a rented Land Rover. On our second morning we were given something to think about. We had finished reloading the car when a five-foot mamba—the instantly lethal variety—slithered out from under the overhead rack's tarpaulin where it had been spent the night. Watching us pack must have been fun—would they or wouldn't they? but bouncing about on a humpbacked highway was clearly not to its taste.

The mamba had a point. The driving was everything I loathed. Confined to the spine of a slick, steeply cambered, endlessly straight road, we bounced through bush that seemed interminable, rarely encountering anything but an overturned truck, or a pair of mallards quacking up from a pothole.

After the sexual fiasco of the four years with Miranda, I had needs of my own to placate. Disappointed by the bush, if not the bars, that's what I did, opening myself to a Zambia where the flesh was rhythm, the flash of a pair of earrings, a silver bracelet resonant as the snap of a twig, a thrush call. All this beckoned: bodies, mango-scented, thin as a slice of water, its drops on polished stone; the orange of a shirt that, in accentuating a palm, made the rose-black of a forearm glisten. In that forest of the flesh, hands became stones, skin a river breathing me in where the air hung silver and a pool, bubbling, became breast, the two cones of a moon-drenched sheet.

Virgil Burnett, frontispiece illustration, New Wine, 1994

It is possible to deride the superficiality of such one-night stands. But beyond mere mutual curiosity, there could be something a bar girl and I shared as fellow aliens and parents—so many prostitutes have children. Add the level of danger provided by the thwarted locals and there could be more than enough to carry the two of us through to the dawn.

My three weeks with Tony gave me the grounding with which to strap on a pair of seven league boots and saunter forth. My travels thereafter added up to considerable locomotion: Arusha in Zimbabwe and a bus full of Masai through Ngongoro and the Serengeti wilderness; Dar-es-Salaam, Zanzibar, Lamu, and then Mombasa where I caught a plane to the island of lemurs, Madagascar.

It was on the island of Lamu, off of Kenya in the East Indian Ocean, that my explorations came to an end in the person of a stunningly featured bar girl. I should have been warned off by her protestations of illness. But I wanted to believe her little itch was no more than a little itch. The café she was closing up lay next to the old stone Persian palace where I was staying. But she insisted on a detour to a bench overlooking the port. There in her white dress she sat, back to me, making me take, touch every part in my cold and trembling fingers until she was lit, alive enough to follow me to my room.

I wasn't able to keep her past the first rays of dawn. But when I showed up later in the morning at her café, I had an hour to spare—why not spend it with her? everything shifted into such a key—maybe she wasn't as sick as she thought?—that I even imagined, before the reality of the gonorrhea came crashing in, us taking a cottage on the remote Indian Ocean side of the island. After de Gobineau, Loti and Gauguin, why not me?

ENTER THE DARK MUSE

The Berkeley I returned to in the fall of 1971 was a much darker town than the Berkeley of the mid-Sixties. Everyone I knew now felt powerless: powerless to stop the Vietnam War; powerless to transform the globe; two actions that had looked, only a few years earlier, not merely possible, but inevitable.

The earlier Berkeley offered a safe place in which to reinvent yourself and do "your thing." For suburban kids like Miranda, it was the Mecca to which they escaped to let off steam. They camped out in Strawberry Canyon and read poetry, and even if it was low burner poetry, it was still poetry. Like the hippie movement, Berkeley offered kids a chance to be both smart and sexy— better, as Miranda said, than being dumb and pregnant.

There were all kinds of hippies. Those heeding Timothy Leary's injunction to "Turn on, Tune in, and Drop out" could feel they had "transcended" such mundane concerns as Vietnam and civil rights, let alone voting. Yet their effect on a few of us who had come of age in the Fifties was political. Here was an intensely lyrical cause, born out of Whitman, out of American affluence and optimism, and doffing what we could of our inhibitions we jumped right in.

Before our sparks could gather in a generation-spanning flame, there came the inevitable reaction from all those who felt threatened and outraged. By the sexual riot, the harem trailing every handlebar moustache? By the rumor of somebody's angel daughter who had never come down from a LSD high? For whatever reason a pot and psychedelic-powered culture was driven underground and the illegality bred an understandable paranoia. At concerts no one danced anymore, they sat. The street carnival moved indoors: how blazon it out in your mind-blowing togs when you were constantly being shaken down and strip-searched, or photographed by Big Brother's infra-red cameras? The kids no longer greeted their narcs with cookies and yogurt, but with booby traps. The law was now the enemy and against the threat of two years' incarceration for the possession of a mere joint, they defended themselves: with an impressive arsenal if they dealt, with their front door steel-reinforced if they resented seeing their precious stash raided; with a slow fade into the anonymity of straightness if they had no better ideas.

Yet even earlier, the more prescient were already leaving the Haight for rural communes. Whitman had given way to Thoreau. The crackdown on "drugs," and the commercial appropriation that reduced a visionary cause to a mere youth style, a Haight Avenue freak show, all took their toll. If the same thing had happened to DADA in 1916 Zurich—the cover of *Time* and all that—would Surrealism have arisen?

The underlying cause of the hippie die-out lay in the very generosity of their embrace. Join us, the Be-In proclaimed, "Make love, not war." Was it possible, our politicians argued, let alone desirable to separate sexual freedom from civil rights, People's Park from Woodstock and 1968's May Paris uprising? Weren't we all in the same struggle? Were we? The hippie program was not another piecemeal redistribution of the American pie, but a radical transformation of values. If you can't differentiate, you end up mud soup.

Inevitably, as the politics splintered and radicalized, the intractable elements took over: firebombing our department's Wheeler Hall; roaring, baseball bats in hand, through my class; egged on, or controlled, depending on how you looked at it, by squadrons of visor-helmeted, mace-throwing Blue Meanies being directed from Vietnam-style spy-in-the-sky helicopters. The war had come home with a vengeance.

By 1971, our world-changing tornado had shriveled to a mere electronic blast—rock 'n roll. Not that our Robespierres didn't know exactly how to target us at our most vulnerable. How could we not make common cause with the Brothers whose blues had paved the way for our Stones and Beatles? Wasn't pop culture, at heart, Afro-based? So the hippies gave up Peace and LOVE and took to Action, marching about and getting themselves maced and clubbed. Was it only in those moments of fleeing lemming-like down Shattuck Avenue in a plate glass-smashing horde that there was a genuinely fused Berkeley community?

The Berkeley of the mid-Sixties was not a mob on the run. I could address a stranger on a sidewalk without unduly startling him or her. And it was a community of couples; not, maybe, fervently clasped Parisians, but sybarites who shared a style, heads turned away from the make-or-break of the East Coast rat race. What the community lacked in grandparents and little children it almost made up for in big dogs. They took over the campus, bounding about in the fountains, gathering by the twenties in lecture hall aisles.

Civility is not one of those flowers you can keep trampling again and again. By now the town had become a victim of its far-flung notoriety. You could see the change in the scaffolding that sprang up everywhere as the old shingled houses got chopped into multi-unit apartments, in the bombed and boarded-up shops on Telegraph, in the new fear and loathing on the streets. Where earlier a woman could walk anywhere fearlessly at night, she now needed a car. Add the thousands of teenaged runaways hiding out in Strawberry Canyon to the tripling in a mere 15 years of the city's population—the Gold Rush all over again!—and here was a tableau ripe for Hieronymus Bosch. The Rolling Stones fiasco at Altamont did not, as claimed, signal the end of an era. It was merely the first revelation. There would be others: the Charles Manson murders, and the one in which I was peripherally implicated—the kidnapping of Patricia Hearst.

My involvement had come about as the result of the occupational need I had for a muse. Other writers had known one, why not I? Hardly a month passed now that I was single once again that did not find me backing out my VW to go questing for that Lady of the Lake, all blue notes in a raven-black field. But Ariadnes, alas, are not exactly plentiful on the freeways, waiting thumb out and a ball of red twine in hand, for a twice-divorced, twice-fired, 36-year-old man.

I was beginning to despair when fate tossed up the seeming godsend I needed in the form of a recommendation request. Written in ballpoint pen on red-lined lilac paper, it began with an ominous flair:

time is gone—but if you can dig it—scrawl something on here. Why aren't you teaching anymore? i'm writing and working but i'm going to become a doctor. My name is Nancy Ling Perry. You have taught me all the best things about reading and writing... many many years ago. not having accomplished the Tibetan Ritual of Suicide here i am. i'll see you again.

In less than two years after she wrote this note, its writer would emerge as the principal spokesperson and pin-up gal for the Symbionese Liberation Army (SLA). This inter-racial Berkeley-based urban guerilla group would murder Marcus Foster, the universally admired black Oakland School Superintendent, and kidnap the 19-year-old media heiress, Patricia Campbell Hearst. The mass uprising Ling's urban guerillas hoped to set off never ignited. But their transformation of Patty into the shotgun-toting SLA princess Tania inspired the FBI to assign an unprecedented 550 officers to the case; a media blitz that more than rivaled anything the entire J. Walter Thompson ad agency ever achieved.

At the time all that lay in the inconceivable future. Instead the name called up for me a tiny (4'11") 24-year-old former student who had sparked the most enjoyable course I taught, a Classics of Criticism required of graduating English majors. Their comments on my teaching helped set off the chain reaction that got me rehired.

Brought up in the Sonoma Valley town of Santa Rosa where her well-to-do Irish-Italian right-wing parents owned a furniture store (Ling, the sobriquet by which I knew her, is a Scotch-Irish name for heather), she had attended Whittier College, Nixon's alma mater. There she had supported Goldwater before transferring to Berkeley in 1967.

I saw Ling as more of a hippie than a politico. But she straddled the divide by marrying in 1968 Gilbert Perry, a jazz composer from the Oakland ghetto. Ling was proud of the way she had adapted to black ghetto life—she had continued living at her mother-in-law's after Gilbert walked out on her after a week of marriage—and proud, too, of Gilbert's musicianship. I remember a class report of hers on Blake's songs, enlivened by a tape of Gilbert's setting of "Tyger, tyger, burning bright."

At the trimester's end I tossed an afternoon party for her class in the little house on Panoramic (since swept away in a fire) to which Miranda and I had moved after getting married. It was the first chance Ling and I had had to talk intimately. We discovered we shared a similar thirst for liberation, and, implicitly, for what living together might bring. We were, of course, both spoken for, I by my beloved Miranda, Ling by her impossible Gilbert. But there was the future.

The party was beginning to wind down when there was a rapping at the front door. I answered it to discover a small wiry black man with chisel-sharp features. "I've come for Mrs. Perry," he said fiercely.

I looked at him, this black man, unable for the longest moment to fathom to whom he could be possibly referring.

"Mrs. Perry," he repeated, clearly inclined to make whitey work. In the nick of time, a memory cell beeped—Ling!—and I hustled off to fetch her. That was the one time I encountered Gilbert, but it stuck. A man definitely not to be crossed.

Now and again after graduating, Ling would appear as an auditor in one of my classes, her tiny shoulders draped in a voluminous shawl and her hair peroxided and teased out in a black streetwalker's Afro. Testing the class's demure assumptions? Or, equally plausibly, setting me up? In the light of her list of "Fascist Insects who prey on the Life of the People," one may wonder. The second name on that notorious list, right after Patricia Campbell Hearst, was Merrill Lynch Magowan, my brother who lived in suburban Hillsborough.

Nelson Algren wrote somewhere, "Never sleep with anyone who is crazier than you are." Before Nancy Ling Perry, a woman who hadn't yet accomplished the "Tibetan Ritual of Suicide," whatever that was, alarms should have been ringing. What was holding her back—the lack of a suitable fellow to take down with her?

In my case, the alarm bells were noticeably silent. More pressing was the need to extricate myself from the death threats of the woman I was living with, compared to which Ling could seem merely eccentric. So I wrote back saying I had sent in the recommendation for the lab job she had requested, but could we meet somewhere for lunch? I must also have added something about having tried to invite her to a large party I had given a month earlier.

My note spurred a reply:

1/13/72

Hello robin—dear robin magowan,
perhaps i knew that i was invited to your party altho of course i did not receive an invitation in the mail. i had been living for a year in San Francisco until recently. oh did the ghetto make me ache—at night you lie down and can feel all around the ghetto as it turns on its side and sometimes sighs. So although my husband left me a year and a half ago, i went the day after Halloween and stored all my so many possessions and made an assignation with exile at my mother-in-law's in East Oakland—the exile necessary for the goal of saving $$ which i have a little—& am looking for a pad in which to pursue this impossible goal which the I ching says is possible. With the I ching i hear its secrets, now i must learn to speak its language—and so do i know i am still "not quite foreseeing the chain reaction." Next week i am on holiday, and it would be truly wonderful to see you. What have you been writing? My lungs are filled with some of it from the fresh sea air at the ocean.

shanti shanti shanti

With the letter came a note about a dream "2 few months ago:"

i spent the nite and day with you in my dreams yesterday. You appeared wearing a black and brown Chinese robe. We walked thru a garden down a path to a tea room & drank and smoked & talked together. i cannot remember anything you said. But i can see you still as you looked & moved then, finally we held each other & kissed. It was a vast soft moist satisfying kiss. The dream was freedom and you were love. We were happiness. The tea was water. The garden was bliss. Many thanks to you for being in the air somewhere where my dream went. I wish that i could give you love in your waking hours. i would kiss your feet, for i have always been intrigued by your demeanor.

The stage was clearly set in some magical never-never land. All I had to do was show up barefooted in a black and brown Chinese robe.

Ling appeared for lunch, draped in a flowery black and red shawl and wearing a white, many pocketed, breast-accentuating suit that set off her lively brown eyes and shoulder-length mane of glossy black hair.

"You're looking well," she opined, getting down to basics.

"Nice suit you're wearing," I rejoined, "a real splash of summer."

"Oh," she said, slipping into her husky, black-sounding voice, "this is some curtain material I ripped off a fabric store in Oakland and sewed myself. I have a certain proficiency in the domestic arts."

"And for the unusual in five-finger discount, I see," needing that bit of street lingo to keep my shock-level from showing. "What's this," I asked, shifting onto more comfortable ground, "about you becoming a doctor?"

"You see these hands," Ling said, flashing a bevy of rings, three to a hand. "I ran into this Indian guru, Muktananda, who operates an ashram and a vegetarian restaurant. I have what he calls healing hands. He thinks I should put them to some sort of public service. The first step is that job in the med school lab, for which I thank you. From there I'll go to medical school."

"As a doctor?"

"No, that takes too many years. There's a new short-term program for paramedics. In the ghetto they're needed."

"When does your lab job start?" I asked.

"Either June or September—it's up to me."

"In the meantime?"

"I'll take my two cats and go live in the country. I've got this old van and some money saved from a year's waitressing at the San Francisco Jazz Club."

"The one on Divisadero?" I asked.

"I must take you sometime. It's so revered there's no crime within a block of it. That's where I was living most of the past year. All I need now is to find a pad up by the Russian River."

Going to live in the country by no means meant that Ling had renounced her anarchic ambitions. "I haven't gotten a police record," she told me during that same lunch, "despite the couple of hours they held me at the Women's Penitentiary at Santa Rita. I took advantage of a mix-up to walk away before they got around to fingerprinting me. I'd like to think a clear record might land me a job as a domestic in the home of a parole officer. Once inside, I can off him. There's no worse scum."

Brockhurst portrait, Mother, 1948

A distinct shiver ran though me. That Ling had worked as a street prostitute I was prepared to accept. That she harbored homicidal ambitions was something else. But over our luncheon table, among our many shared confidences, I could not admit to any squeamishness. In winning her acceptance, it helped that I had recently traveled in East Africa and Madagascar (Ling, too, had a *valiha* recording) and that I had known Gloria, a woman of a not dissimilar cigarette-haunted, torch-like temperament.

Eventually I asked about Gilbert. "I can fathom the attraction, but why on earth did you marry Gilbert?"

"There was, I suppose, an element of defiance," Ling replied thoughtfully. "Not only you won't marry me, but I dare you to live in the ghetto—and at my mother's? I must have taken to the life all too well, because after the first week he split on me. Not that he didn't turn up from time to time to make it impossible for me to be living with anyone else. I have nothing against sporadic sex, but sometimes," she said, raising her head and looking straight at me, "you do want something else. Something more."

As a start towards that "something more," I took Ling home to fulfill her dream's prophecy. Afterwards, by way of augury, we threw the *I Ching*. I drew Ting, the Cauldron, an image supposedly of transformation, of what the two of us collaborating might achieve; a cauldron that evoked, as I told her, the engulfing grip of her legs and deeply rounded lower torso, as well as the musky odors in which I was immersed.

"I was," Ling replied, "consciously making my legs into a basket. Usually, making love, I don't see images. You must dance," she added, "marvelously."

Hips were far from her only attraction. "I didn't dare say anything about your breasts," I remarked, trailing off, at a loss for words to describe such wide-slung, deeply cleaved, pear-like magnets.

"That you like them," she said kindly.

"Yeah, that's what I meant. You make me feel intelligent, perceptively so."

Wasn't I doing the same for her shaken self-esteem? Still, after several attempts to turn me into another Joe Husband, I appreciated being taken as the writer I was. I even suggested writing something together—couldn't that be the function of a muse?

All the same, uncertainties remained. Neither of us had a clue where we really stood with each other. Rather than voice such misgivings, Ling showed her understanding of the guy to whom she had just fed a half pie. "There'll be a nice silence and then you'll write. Oh," as she disappeared down the kitchen steps, "about two minutes."

She hit it on the dot. Freed by her "white negro" persona, I scrawled away in assumed dialect for hours. No muse could have come on more auspiciously.

Not long thereafter, from a Russian River postal box, came a special delivery missive penned on gaudy orange-flecked brown paper:

1/23/72

he said that he thought of me as a magician/ did he say that? he said we two should write something together but that was probably bullshit. oh no i'm not a magician, not yet—because you do not really believe that i am. he said to call him sometime when i get a pad. the *I Ching* under "Ting, the Cauldron" says, "at the bottom are the legs, over them the belly, then come the ears (handles), and at the top the caning rings. so perhaps i may not call until i get a cauldron. then will i not be the ceremonial vessel into which you may dip?
one truth is she misses her husband; he loves his wife.

A smart girl, that one. The second part, written over five days, was more of a letter:

1/28/72

dear R—what a lovely lunch we had—you tasted so exquisite to me
1/31

not nails, but talons on my fingertips. i am descended from the owl. I have been listening again—after more than a year—to the valiha. et puis je suis allee au Voyage Noir. Merci.

2/2

Hello, i have fallen into a pad on an acre and a half of slightly inclining hill just above the Russian river. so i have decided to take a holiday trip to the forest by the river and not return to Berkeley until June or September. i do not know what i may say—so all i want to say is that i have missed you a thousand thousand times

shanti shanti shanti

I spent the following weekend visiting Ling in her trailer and exploring with her the surrounding forest. Soothed by sticks of incense, Chinese cooking pots, a library that included Le Roi Jones and *The Serpent and the Rope*, we lay on a cot on the trailer floor. Her letter, penned the following day, shows the alacrity with which she had taken up a muse-like role:

Wednesday 2/8/ 72

Do you believe i have powers of healing? These things take time as the cosmic forces within the body stir to movement. i will greet you then, on the 13th, if you're still going up the coast. i think I should try to call you on Sunday—just a really quick ass call—to ask where, when, and hear if you still wish.

I have spent some time looking at the mushrooms through the Chinese painting we were in, wondering about either writing something about them— write my diary in the language of mushrooms—or eating them. How could this be more dangerous than anything else one might do? i am beginning to see with the third eye. the tree is green iridescence through the window. the nite rings with many bells, rattles like a tambourine, is still, cool as the sea.

as your muse i shall sometimes be foam on your beard. and i love you so i chant for you and i love you.

Not every woman can make herself into a chime for the night's mysteries. It gave her a transparency that made me want to protect her. Like death itself, she rang true.

GREEN DIZZY SCREAMING SUN-ABYSS

We had managed in those first weeks to see each other some seven times. But we had only spent a single night together. If I knew Ling, it was mainly in connection with the heaping pies of grass that spiked our trysts. I had weathered them well enough, why not see, my muse urged, what a more cerebral potion might yield?

So in mid-March, on the day we were to start living together, Ling arrived with a bag of synthetic mescaline fresh from a friend's laboratory. I had already put together an expeditionary basket of wine, cold salmon, sketch pads, a watercolor set and two pairs of binoculars. We set off for Point Reyes, a peninsula situated an hour and a half north of Berkeley which emerged in the late Cretaceous at about the same time as Madagascar and northeast Brazil.

We had been walking on the Palomarin Trail about twenty minutes when, at the end of a sheltered ravine, Ling removed her stash: three powdery piles crinkled on the blade of a steak knife and then and there licked clean. Remorse rising geometrically directed us around two more ravines and, in barely the nick of time, onto a meadow dressed with clumps of scraggly bluish-gray bush lupine.

I had been there once, bird-watching. Taking Ling by the arm, I guided her up, through the clumps of tiny purple-and-gold Douglas iris, to the bluff's fire-mist view. For a vertiginous moment we stood in the wind roar until self-preservation got the better of us: this urge we both felt, before the coming onslaught, to jettison everything superfluous: sweaters, urine, binoculars.

Back on the sheltered meadow, we each collapsed in a separate ball on the ground. "Stay away from me," I heard myself crying, "I want to bail out." But even as I yelled my cowardly plight, she was calmly assuring me that, whatever I might wish, there was nowhere to bail out to, since we'd still be within this imprisoning sky, these chalk-circle clouds tearing us to leather apes in the jungle of our fears.

From one edge to the next I rolled, edge of sword, mouth, precipice, star, as one, then another dive-bombing phaeton unloaded directly overhead its green dizzy screaming

SUN-ABYSS

Electrons the size of golf balls bounced and diffracted against my eyes as I wriggled over to where my Circe sprawled, elbows over eyes, black paint-splattered jeans rotating at washing machine frenzy. Before this woman who had, it seemed, deliberately poisoned me I felt both afraid and vengeful. "Is this what you intended?" I managed to blurt out.

There was a pause. Then, from somewhere within the churn, I heard Ling voice her chagrin. "More TNT here than I've ever encountered. I'm sorry I've done this to you."

I accepted that. Since the explosions were occurring in my mind, it was I obviously who was shaping their content. Not everyone, out in good weather on a spring meadow, has to be so terrorized. I wonder now whether, in submitting, I was seeking a path down into the emotional desolation of others, Ling included?

If so, the catch lay in the growing likelihood of being permanently disabled. Hard to stretch forth a fraternal hand when all you've got left is a stump with a claw. As the rush increased, probing like water from one, then another diametrically opposite point of view, I became desperate. No point wondering, do I think? Is it thinking me? when the issue was nothing less than the blazing asylum halls, I and my fellow inmates staring out from our ever more beleaguered windows.

But those childhood days on the beach playing seaweed, pegged walrus-like to the sand bottom while one wavelet after the next made mincemeat of my ears and, even more, those no-flag days when I'd inch my way out clinging to the barrel rope, had well prepared me. As one monstrous comber after another reared overhead, I put my head on Ling's navel and hung on, arms around her, determined to ride it out. Cocooned in exploding infancy— those stars directing me to our tongue-lost Babel—I lay twined around her, letting only the most necessary

Alahhhhhhh's

shower forth their groaning sparks. I saw myself returning to that mother island where, what my heart once knew, my tongue gave out: the meadow's ring, Ling herself, found.

The change in my feelings towards Ling could not have been more consequential. Where, an hour earlier, I was ready to strangle her, I now found myself enamored of all creation. Ling had brought me this gift and, with her clasping arms, had pulled me through.

We clung to each other until the same instant's grass-light found us sitting up, rubbing our eyes before its huge blue-streaked blades. Yet everything was, I knew, because it all startled so: the beads of moisture on a petal; the chirpings all around. Was it Ling who was pulling me into sunlight, her touch making my legs turn solid? Within the gates of a paradise-blue lupine bush I stood, relieving myself, head in my hands, invisible legs vibrating under me like stalks. Afterwards I tottered back to where Ling was divvying up the poached salmon: cold, fibrous, impossible-to-look-at chunks; and wine; anything that might seal us from a renewed attack.

We had eaten what we could when Ling announced it was time to leave the lupines' paradise gates. With wonder I saw my shoes stand up, laces tied and all. My jeans were sparkling blue marks on the pink gravel road. My arms limped at my sides, but that may have been because my eyes couldn't focus sufficiently to make out my fingers, suspended somewhere below in the mist-prism. Nor could I see the gravel road, though with a somnambulist's instinct, I sensed the seablue at its edge curving away like the balustrade of a balcony. Useless to ponder what was mirage, what real. After all our writhing in wet ghostly meadow grass, merely being upright, heads in the welcoming air, seemed blessing aplenty.

We had settled by a last blue railing above the thousand-foot distant sea when Ling startled me by asking, "Where are your binoculars?" Thinking by her question that I must just now have mislaid them I was on my feet, frantically combing the ridge vicinity. I was about to hurl myself off into the infested chaparral ten feet below—couldn't they have rolled off?—when she added, "The pair you lent me are lost as well."

We concluded that we must have shed them back on the bluff at the onset of the havoc. What should we do: retrace our steps? Return tomorrow with a fresh picnic?

Back, Ling sensibly decided. But there on the meadow, barring our way in the twilight, flared a conflagration of orange poppies. While Ling squatted, sketching them, I sprawled beside her, eyes fixed on her fingertip, as if her next stroke might rouse the meadow's Cleopatra.

The comparison paled in the waning light and I felt newly apprehensive, remembering our still unfound binoculars and the long walk remaining back to our car.

Our groping about on the bluff ledge as we searched in the sea roar confirmed all too well my apprehensions: a rolling glistening of wind; a crashing of assassin waves. Then, through the spray, came Ling's dejected, "I can't find them." It was as if all the trust we had achieved, our bodies pulling each other through, had to be renegotiated. A whole afternoon lay on its back, blown up.

In my panic I heard the first stars ringing "Hurry," felt the ocean damp tightening its fingers about my neck. But in a secluded spot, at the far end of a ravine, we halted, transfixed by a pool the dusk was in the process of transforming into an undersea grotto. At my feet tiny brass-button flowers shivered, glowed. Raising my glance to the far side of the pool, I saw the bare soil merge into the gray of a wind-bent alder. Swaying together over the water, both now rose in a mushroom-like blowing before subsiding. Appalled by the hallucination, yet fascinated, I shot my eyes into a watery cavern. As it gaped open, textures glistened: alder bark silks; bells of a cow-parsley as its spires bent in the glow and my eyes, as if on a reel, spooled from bank to bank.

Where before I felt disconnected from what I was observing, now I felt at one with my sea-anemone arms that, writhing with each blind pulsation, registered it as "night," a purple barrier beyond which I couldn't pierce.

When we reached the parking lot, Ling hopped behind the wheel, saying "I've more experience in these matters." I accepted gratefully, finding it all I could do to open the passenger door, let alone stay seated while she turned us around.

My fears calmed when we reached the asphalted road. As on an aerial cushion, the macadam waltzed us along; so smoothly that, by the time we realized we had taken the wrong turn, the only eatery still open was a tiny pink-painted bar: one of those tacky pine-walled joints with a clattering jukebox and a couple of gals in hair curlers holding forth from their bar stools. The restaurant inside was unique only in that the walls, the lampshades and even the plastic flowers were pink. Against the noise I could hear my heart pounding like a jackhammer drill.

Unable to order against the creaking of the enormous menu, I understood perhaps what makes some prefer their hospital walks and hedges. Life's primal necessity isn't food.

In our motel bed that night, for all our newfound empathy, neither of us felt up to making love. That would be tempting fate. But a pent-up emotional dam had burst and, with the mescaline's guiding spirit, Chief Tomahawk, as I called him, directing me, I found myself hurling bolts of rage at each speck that spoke of a whole incarcerating family labyrinth that had first chained me back there in upper crust Manhattan society.

MY GIRL, TALKING ABOUT MY GIRL

Before the blast of mescaline I was not in love with Ling. We were merely two people on similar wave lengths who wanted to try living together. Now I felt soldered to her by an experience that had brought me into her craziness, her reality. There was no questioning the commitment. I was hers as much as those swine were Circe's.

Next day, on our way back to Point Reyes to retrieve the binoculars, I remember our coming upon a vernal pool that had been taken over by a congress of fire-bellied salamanders: hundreds of joyfully floating, penis-like amphibians. In my be-smitten state I watched as Ling stood under a spring-green willow at the edge of the pool peering down at them. As she stooped forward, enchanted by their orgies, her hair all of a sudden plummeted over her face in a blue-black waterfall. An "incendiary explosion," I immediately jotted in my notebook, attempting to combine the shock of the light with the explosive torch that she carried in her. But of what, I asked, handing her the notebook?

"Chartreuse," Ling wrote. Instantly I saw each inflammable letter hyphenate into the charged, exuberant, light-and-grass-filled liqueur she had become for me.

With the mescaline my psyche had taken a real hit. When I was in Winnipeg a month later, giving a reading, my host Myron Turner recorded the lemur-like way I bounced about his apartment, glass in hand, always on "the edges of things. . .the arm of the sofa . . .the teak buffet, the chest of drawers. . .un-zippering toothy visions of the same bruised rainbow as your stammered elations." ("The drunken prince of lemurs and all small animals").

I had always been able to talk about what I was up to, as a way of trying things out, or imagining works in the making. But now, such options were no longer available, the drugs had altered me somehow. The dragon lady I was living with, the mescaline, the debilitated person I had become, it was all too shameful, too unbelievable. But what I couldn't talk about had to come out and, with Ling poring through my notebooks and starring promising phrases, new work began to rainbow out in a profusion far surpassing anything I had known. She made me understand that I differed from other writers in my vulnerability to female beauty. For me, just as for Charlie Merrill, Helen of Troy existed and those thousand ships sailed. That radiant power comprised a fundamental mystery, and it upset me, much as a striking woman upsets a room by stepping into it.

Yet Ling was never around enough. "Shouldn't I be giving you an allowance?" I asked, early on.

"Taking money from you bothers me. I can make what I need on my own."

Her frank, independent agenda only increased my social guilt. "I don't see how I'm contributing sitting behind a desk."

"Nonsense," my muse replied, taking her cue from Chairman Mao. "Everyone in the Revolution has his role and yours is to go on being one of the Hundred Flowers. In redefining our relation to things and thus altering consciousness, you are actually making something happen."

That soothed my concerns and I was quite willing to look the other way when Ling took off for a weekend to earn a few bucks starring in a porno film (picture the cast, all stoned on acid, squatting in a cabin's rain-frigid silence).

In her last "communication" Ling bemoans the "rather dreadful way I betrayed you." Wasn't that kind of betrayal written from the start into her end of our contract, descended as she was from the lyric prostitute Polyhymnia, open to one and all. Sex was a commodity she could trade for the cocaine that might extend for a few hours a manic high. And prostitution suited an actress who saw herself as an emissary between the kingdom of death and our brief mortality. What is a movie, Godard asked, but a man, a woman and a gun?

All the same, she didn't countenance infecting me with a venereal disease. Upon my return from a previously arranged 8-day skiing trip to Zermatt with Tony Oberschall I found her diary, along with an oval painting, propped on my desk:

The man who lives here has been away for the last eight years. Because I love him I was invited to live in his house. I stack his mail and give water to everyone and chant for him. A vaginal infection, inside, developed in the first year of his absence. I cannot imagine that i am infested with v.d., too many outrageous blatant symptoms. So i wish it to be a private, non-contagious woman's malady. The soreness of the symptoms is easily forgotten over eight years of abstinence; but the worry is an unrelenting fervor of fear. Did I give an infection to the god that lives in this house? (How can that be? Is he all right?) Yeah sure i call it nothing but the blues.

Despite her final warning letter, "i'm a whore...i hustle out of habit," I see her engagement beginning in extremis, as a means of survival. "When a woman's down and out," I remember her confiding as we lay together in the dark, her voice cracking under the misery of the memories, "she can always take to her back."

No doubt her suicidal bent was exacerbated by the hallucinogenics, her equivalent of another's eyeliner or high-heeled boots. Like Circe, she needed these potions to bind men to her, make us forget whatever else we had known. Yet a woman does not head into the Russian River forest to live alone with a pair of cats and the I Ching if she is not intent on deepening her links with a higher power. At the time her identity was up in the air. Gilbert's walking out on her after a week could not have helped, nor could the succession of "one-time sensual experiences" that followed. In electing to become my muse and live-in partner—no grime she couldn't grovel in—was she making an effort to prove she could still be a mistress of the "domestic arts" rather than another bimbo in a pickup truck?

What was Ling's physical presence? Patricia Hearst recalled being guarded by Fahizah, this "girl with the thick drawl," as she calls Ling:

> Tiny, only four feet eleven and slightly overweight, Fahizah sat hunched over the toilet seat, wearing a dark ski mask, a see-through black knit top with her breasts clearly visible, and tight corduroy pants with a gun belt around her waist and an empty holster on one hip...I thought she looked weird, malformed, like a hunchback without the hump, sort of a small female ape.

A few pages later, Hearst again refers to this "monkeylike girl." Strong stuff coming from a woman barely three inches taller. All the same, the description registers, a woman with the kind of hunger in her womb that could slake an entire Symbionese army.

"Small female ape" that she might have seemed, her presence remained, nonetheless, a pulsatingly believable one. Otherwise her airbrushed high school graduation photo would not have graced so many front pages, nor would those fan clubs have sprung into being. My own jottings reveal her "husky, croak-shadow voice, the "coal granite" of her eyes, her "hatchet" fingers. Beauty, maybe, but of a decidedly scary variety.

In my descent into her netherworld I was determined not to be put off by mere squeamishness. Buoyed perhaps by a pie of grass, I would sprawl on the trailer floor beside her, hands seeking out her breasts, the round moans she gave off as I stroked and, as if from a nearby wall, her voice responded, a fire in her throat. Into that chimney I bored, the vulnerability I sensed in her smoker's yellow-tinged fingers, the glossy mane into whose luxuriance my fingers drifted, each strand a potential serpent to tie to my own springing mount until, a serpent myself, I plunged into that volcano where heart labors and screams sing.

For Ling orgasm came in being blasted: that lower-case "i" of her letters: the shoulder-propped legs shortening the vaginal cavity's back wall bull's eye; the ever encouraging, "That's so good, man" as fingers began contributing their clittoral obbligato. All the same such relentless ramming was not my idea of coital bliss.

THE MORE YOU TAKE, THE MORE YOU GET

By early May, Ling was ready to take a break from the "ghost town of the movement" Berkeley had become. I had long wanted to see Death Valley. When she proposed camping out—a new experience for me—I readily assented.

Our week's trip fulfilled the make-or-break test so many couples seem to need to put themselves through. We had each, I think, fallen in love. But for all our intimacy, there was a crucial aspect neither of us had confronted: to what extent could I be relied on to perform in an incendiary role in the "action" she was planning? It was time for both of us to put down our remaining cards.

The high desert offered a plaintive corollary to the moody person she was. As we drove along, I remember her intoning a three-line poem:

> the sad sand song of the desert dune
> the sharp choir of cacti
> and high above the flat drone of the buttes

The lines show her ear for the desolation that drew her.

With each passing day I found myself more in love and, in consequence, more afraid of the domain closing around me of death and criminality. Yet if I could not see a way out, I sensed that, in my plunge into her depths, I had touched something sacred. No wonder that, back from Death Valley, a succession of rhapsodic multi-page rants came cascading out. It was everything I had desired and more than a bit scary. I was a cat high in a tree with no idea how to clamber down. Worse was the indebtedness I felt. What could I give her? Yet even as I bemoaned my impotence, I feared the answer. "There's only one thing you white folk can give a black," I remember Huey Newton shouting at a Panther rally, "and that's a gun." That's where I drew the line; less out of conviction, than klutz that I am, I knew the gun would go off in my face.

My quandary was more than resolved when, some weeks later, I dipped into the mescaline pouch a second time. I had intended no more than a light hit, perhaps enough to clarify the new Hans Hoffman paintings in the university museum. So far they had eluded me. My mistake lay in measuring the powder on a blade broader than the original steak knife. Ling was reading on the sofa as I hesitated after a second lick. "The more you take," she remarked, "the more you get." And there I was, newly embroiled in the madness with only my ambition to blame.

An ecstatic learns to prepare himself for the culminating moment of vision. Here's what I'm about in my inmost core, he exults, as he paddles his *bâteau ivre* into the forbidden waters. Fine, so long as his boat cleaves to the rational surface. But what do you do when the reality is a hallucinogenic one and what you are seeing and what you are transcribing are not one and the same?

Imagine a twilit river at the onset of what one knows is going to be one helluva storm. Only I was the eye in the middle of the river, lit with the storm light's rattling yellows, down which I found myself being propelled. As the waters geysered up under me, hissing in their doom, I realized I had to switch the locale. Summoning my remaining powers, I managed to change the rapids over which I was careening into the silver-pierced eye of a boreal lake.

As I stood on its banks, entranced by the gongs the diaquescent stars were thrumming on the mind-lit waters, I beheld out in the water a chain of revolving, ghostly-gray wave-castles that my pen named

> the silver dishes of the radiators of the soul.

By "radiators," I meant irradiators, a term that encompassed the churning cyclones of the castles and the bone-chilling cold generated by a lake

> whose least wish was ice.

Such a lake could not help but be, by its very labials, Ling herself. In the next instant there she was, in all her romantic enticement, the shining bangs of her hair translated into a brook flashing frog-loud in the black-and-silver setting. By the mouth of the brook there was even a stone lantern. I could be in a

Japanese woodland garden. But was a garden made out of eyes? For it was the eye-like lake's shore-pounding waves that were now drawing me down

    into their dins of silver lather

only in the next breath to release me, by way of a rhyme, into still more supernal

    rims of silver night.

I thought I was watching a stellar ballet, their yellows pirouetting, reflecting, qualifying one another. Like Ling and I dancing, I thought. And I saw us on a little tree platform overlooking the Lorelei lake. Only we in our romantically clasped

    tree-and-tongue-enclenched

unity have taken the form of a pair of embracing cobras. What sort of cobras? Cobras of night

    and, of ourselves!

I found myself scribbling. Carried away on a wave of exultation, I grabbed hold of Ling and together, hands alight, lives in each other's hands, we dove from our projecting bough into the water, fully expecting to be reborn there in a quieter realm of fish-silvery becoming.

    As the letters "d-r-o-w-n" bubbled up around me, I experienced something very different from that breast-of-the-waters in which I had expected to be soothed and transformed. Instead of that mothering tent there were now two tits, or rather temples, in which to rest, however permanently, our now

    twin-parted, twin-brushed
    spreading and engulfed shadows.

The vision might have profitably rested there. But much as the aesthete in me might have relished living out my days in that reflective medium, another 'I' beckoned back from beneath the waters. To have dived headfirst out of a tree into the unlit depths required a certain trust and courage. To remain in that female element, submerged for all eternity, lay beyond my powers as a man, an earthling.

Decisions are rarely unilateral; nor do we inhabit a static universe. As I surfaced, gasping for breath and rightly fearing the vengeance of spurned feminine spirit, at that moment the moon-lapping element turned threatening. The forest boughs now writhed with actual cobras, and the Ling with whom I had been living these past months now took on the attributes of her self-legend: the gangster moll couriering messages to prisons; the topless waitress serving in a Russian River tavern; the dyed blonde prostitute living with her mother-in-law in the Oakland ghetto while serving her black clients. These real life vocations now coalesced in the image of a black stripper-singer; an identity that reflected her aspiration and, much as I regret it, my racist-sexual fear and desire.

As I crawled out of the lake, I found myself in the forest interior, a glade surrounded in boughs of echoing cobra eyes, raised cobra hoods and snaking, forking cobra tongues. As before, the lights and darks of the vision alternated. If in one heartbeat I beheld the forest's hooded boughs, in the next I perceived the spiritual forces controlling them, generously, out of their spidery bodies, spinning me a fiber pathway

a moonlight of the hands

along which quick, like a mat-rider between waves, I scurried fast as I could.

As I did, the hope that held me was the life-line of a path I saw myself weaving, with the help of my spider accomplices, back to my beloved. But Ling was now the woman of her past, a topless smoke-breasted dancer wielding a microphone's snake-like cord as she bumped and grinded about her jazz club's percussive stage, garbed in a raspberry body suit adapted straight from the sheets where I lay transcribing. The sight, and the reminder of the silicone leaking from her implanted breasts, summoned up in me a tide of revulsion propulsive enough to send me zooming away, out into the night sky's satined (if no less satanical) moon shudderings.

I was out in the zodiac at its Spinal Nerve Reverberator Zone, quivering with maniacal laughter, when earth's gravity caught up with me and, yoyo-like, started to haul me back. I saw the earth's core looming, then, directly below, the eye-like lake. But as I infernoed down through its cornea, I found myself on a vertiginous incline. What was to keep me from crashing into the abyss of madness that I knew lay at the end of it? I was approaching the final edge when I glimpsed an unexpected ray of hope—a Japanese cherry tree in full pink-budded bloom, poised to withstand me. But my momentum proved too much as the beauty splintered in my clutching hands and I was now the one

p-e-t-a-l-i-n-g?

or rather, correcting myself, pedaling a brakeless bicycle along the ear-splitting stage of a movie theater. Outside, on its lit marquee blazing neon trumpeted the name of my adventure

INTRUDER IN THE ABYSS

while just below a second horror feature proclaimed

BEAST WITH THE CHOCOLATE FROWN

With my incessant prying, I had offended the infernal powers who were now serving me up, a spectacle for their delectation.

At that moment, to all intents, I had crashed through my psychic walls into insanity.

It was one thing to be zinging about the moonlit lake of a Lorelei fairy tale. It was quite another to be catapulted onto the set of a sleazy horror flick. But the visionary comedown may say something about the weird limbo we insane ones inhabit. It is only people with actual souls who can go about a mythic landscape. Instead, with the dereliction of my sanity, I had entered that realm of the living walking dead to which public spectacle caters: the crowd at a ballgame; the eyes staring from behind drinks at a nightclub show. There, soulless as any man jack, Joe Publick to a 'K,' I found myself.

I had crashed through the walls of a movie theater. Into the show? Stunned, unable for the moment to stir, I lay racked by a bout of coughing that inevitably underlined the coffin my continuous transcribing was perpetuating. "Let it alone, then!" my stricken script quailed, only to be rebuked in turn by a booming Whitmaniacal

LET IT OUT, THEN!

To that behest I struggled to my feet. Insane I might be, but that didn't mean

I could not rationally cope. Like some brick-faced Berkeley street corner prophet, I found myself excoriating this former tender love whom now, in my new blasphemous state, I dubbed

the tendril-vipered goddess

I might have been castigating one of those wooden snake-haired effigies of matriarchal antiquity. Except that this was an overhead billboard displaying a circus's star attraction, a voluptuous dyed-blonde bikini-clad Ling looking up from the sand. Under it I stood, exhibiting the marks of my enslavement as I pointed out to one and all, whether or not they wanted to hear, the unseemly details of her person: the ape-like hairs swarming in their thousands from that nest of vipers; the eyes readying a blast of hot emerald lead over the berserk cheering throng of us fans.

The effect my hectoring produced eclipsed anything I had intended. Not only would I succeed in bringing an effigy to life, but as her outsize movie queen face with its retouched curves and peroxided hair bore down on me and my audience, I realized that I, this ranting misogynist, was still Ling's slave, willing to put up with any humiliation for one last crack at her beauteous lips. Yet the crack itself, the ballyhooed detonation when her colossal face would collide with my own in a momentous kiss could not have been more cataclysmic.

As I braced, from inches away, large as a sun, came this close and closer spreading, expanding voluptuousness. Then, with a searing bang,

the cosmic CRACK!

of her kiss's irradiating megatons turned into her mask's

cosmetic

a molten goo slathering every inch of me in an irrefutable yellow.

Mine, though, wasn't the only mug transfigured. Wherever I looked in the seated circus where her kiss's explosion had hurled me I found these other staring countenances, scary in the sameness of their eyes, their unappeasable aloneness. This was not mere paranoia. I was the one slated for public sacrifice. As the voices wailed and pandemonium rose, I found myself being led out, stripped naked, into the middle of a flame-yellow sawdust ring. There, as within a bubble, I strutted my sun-dance while, from somewhere above, her lips blew a sea wave's diamond curl of cool skittering kisses to our battery of howling fans. At each moment I could feel my knees, my entire being, turning to water. Caught, trapped in that jam of the squares,

the cosmic lances of their cigarettes,

all I had left was the rocket-like capsule of a single word, "final," that I saw enclosing me. I heard the music of ten thousand wrist watches impatiently drumming, while one after another, like mournful bells, my finals tolled:

final breath spraying
final cigarette
swirling

Aristodimos Kaldis, Molyvos, 1964

At the last minute, a reprieve of sorts in the form of a fountain of vapor fumes and breath spray catapulted me onto a trapeze bar. Far away, on the other side of the circus ring, I could see Ling in a snazzy pink-and-white Uncle Sam outfit waiting to catch me. So this was the heralded moment of truth, the final leap of my

    costumed breath

to her "costumed breast." But what the script called for had to be acted out, and, heart all aflame,

    final love shim
        shimmering

I leapt into the floodlit beyond.

That last wild leap was indeed final. Flying past her extended arms, I died forever, not even close. When I came to, I found myself in a quiet, misty, stratospheric sky, where I turned in my pod-like space ship. Everything, my fellow circus sufferers, the insanity fueled by my literary pretensions, had been left blissfully behind. My final memory, as I dissolved in the solar incinerator, was of a flowering gold penis

    circling him in customary light.

In effect, I had become another.

Still, why did I write? Couldn't I, like Ling, have gone outside? The trouble was the nausea that shadowed any attempt to stir. Only when my pen point was starting to resemble an extracted tooth nerve, did I repair to my sprawl of a garden. There, in the waning light, an Anna's hummingbird sang, no mere buzz, but a wheezing pump-like melody, wet as the Amazon. Immediately afterwards, on the brick steps where my poppies mimicked the descending sun, I saw a white-haired, suited, Negro gentleman. Rocking back and forth on his knees, one foot forward, the apparition sang a lilting three-note dirge, ours and that of the hour. Fearing to lose it, I made the words of the song turn slowly.

    swing, swing
        swing with a little style

When the last of the coffin dance was over, there was not a drop of light left.

MY DAMNATION IS YOUR BLESSING

That trapeze leap was final—for both Ling and me. I was a psychic casualty for the next year or so. To a query from my Uncle Charles, Jimmy responded that I did not look at all well and my speech was markedly slurred—a sign, he thought, of brain damage. Worse, though, than the lines down and the broken glass strewn all over the lot, was the uncertainty. I never knew when the ground under my feet would open up and plunge me back into madness.

Before my life had always supplied me with a well into which I could dip and find renewal: the well of a foreign encounter, of birds, a sport, a woman; wells that were all, in some way, connected to the writing to which they would give birth. Now the words that mattered came fixed in an inalterable glue. It was as if I had touched the skin of death.

All the same the vision brought a phenomenological clarity. If the lake was Ling in her role as a Lorelei, a transparency enticing and consuming me, it was also, an eye, a means of perception. For a man who confused inspiration with diving, one may see the magnetic attraction a Lady of the Lake offered.

To my dismay, upon diving in, I discovered that water was her element, not mine. In ordinary life a man can usually negotiate an exit from the sexual waters; he has something of himself he can return to. But for me, whole-heartedly committed as I was, there could be no way out. I was Ling's slave, this thing at the end of her attraction/ revulsion yo-yo. No sooner had I been enticed into the nightclub where she operated as a jazz-singing sexual magnet, than in the next reel I was being ejected into the equally terrifying mental stratosphere. At the next flick of her wrist, as I re-entered the lake, there I was propelled into the kind of Front Page circus spectacle with which Ling and her SLA cronies would fascinate and appall us a year later.

To cooler heads it might look as if I had been catapulted onto the set of a sleazy horror film. But I was the sacrificial figure being held up to public ridicule, and the sight brought home, as nothing else previously had, the reality I was living with. There had to be another end awaiting me than that of a bourgeois fool.

For Ling as well, the second blast was our *coup de grace*. She had only to read my "Take me, I can't survive, I'm here with you," to realize the pall she cast. And the fear she inspired as I lay next to her must have been palpable. Within a week, to my considerable relief, she had moved back to her mother-in-law's in the Oakland ghetto.

All the same, our four intense months together must have added up to something more than the "business relationship" by which she was overheard explaining me to her accomplices in a Berkeley café. She had needed to get away from the ghetto and recharge. And I had provided the necessary space and distance. Just as one can discover one's native roots from abroad, so Ling, while living with me, had come to see her life in the ghetto as more than a sordid failure. One of the Sixties' better achievements was to attack, at least temporarily, the myth of inherent racial-sexual boundaries. You could be whomever you wanted to be so long as you thrust your whole person into the role and acted authentically. Ling had attempted precisely that. When her marriage failed, she had stuck it out in the ghetto, determined to make herself into a person Gilbert could forgive one day for being white.

While living with me, Ling missed the ghetto's street vitality: the broken bottles and vivid language; the hawk-eyed addict following her home from the Safeway, intent on making off with the shopping cart she had taken. The ghetto appealed to her sense of irony in the way it mirrored the governing WASP hierarchy, where gangsters and not businessmen, like my father and the Hearsts, held the power. They, and not I, were her people.

I suspect that Ling and I both suffered from a similar need for excess, which we confused with imagination. In Ling, the excess took a kamikaze turn: she wanted to be the anarchic spark that purified the air by making things explode. Her trajectory from the mescaline she planted in our two heads to the public firestorm of her demise seems clear enough.

For much of our affair there were few boundaries between us. For some reason of her own she 'came on' to me and wanted to participate in my life before she went all out in a very different direction. As individuals, however, we remain, as Lily Tomlin put it, "in this thing alone." To think otherwise is to succumb to those black moonlit waters described in so many tales. There's nothing, of course, to deter one from plunging in: man into woman; woman containing man. But I finally saw that this so-called muse was, as a friend remarked, "a BAAAD, BAAAD BITCH GODDESS who will come out of the grave to eat you, to close your eyes to the dawn and inveigle you into that blank cave where albino plants whirl in the dead current."

At the time, the two of us could not help but mourn what we had lost:

i fell asleep while waiting for my brother to come & dreamt that we had our heads shaved & went swimming on angel island. i love you (maybe we went swimming in a pool of tears.) you are beautiful.

After Ling moved back to Oakland, we continued to see each other once a week. She knew I needed the sexual reassurance that she was still there for me. Afterwards we might drive up to Tilden Park and clamber onto an outcrop, taking in the view. I must have looked more than a bit forlorn as we were perched there one afternoon, because she asked, "What's wrong? Your eyes look so sad."

"The view?" I hazarded. "It's the light, the smudged low-ceilinged sky that bugs me. Nothing has any edges, any definition. Perhaps that's why we leap so easily into our all-encompassing abstractions? When was the last time," I asked, turning sharply to face her, "you saw a shadow?"

Ling cackled, "If that devil with the bag of gold were to come by, he'd better pick the morning after a storm. No one otherwise would have a shadow to sell." She paused a moment, taking a puff from her hand-rolled cigarette. "They make all that smoke over there in San Francisco and let the winds carry it towards us. Then they wonder why in the East Bay we've got all these drawn blinds—why we're so unhappy. There are reasons."

"That's part of it," I replied, "then there's Berkeley."

"All those students!" Ling exclaimed, "No old people and few children. The ghetto has all kinds of people, but you wouldn't care to move there?" She went on, suddenly serious. "It's not the light that disturbs me. I've known, after all, nothing else. For years I've wanted to travel and see what's out there. Not like you've done, but a couple of months in India or Japan would suit me just fine." She paused, as if waiting for me to say something. "Much as I'd like to split, I'm afraid it's not to be—not in this life. What I've got to do is right here."

From the wistfulness of her tone it was clear she did not see herself surviving any fuse she would light. But I was too disheartened to believe I could in any way influence the fatality looming above her. Instead I asked, "Would you mind if I write up our mescaline experiences?" "Far from it," she said, "That's something that needs to be out in the open. But please leave me out. It's not the kind of exposure a guerilla needs." She didn't elaborate further and I knew better than to ask.

Life at her mother-in-law's didn't pan out any better this time around. Whatever high smoking local garden poppies brought (I remember Ling's wheezing on the phone, her voice so husky as to be barely intelligible), she now found herself faced with a carless commute to her lab job. A Berkeley pad made sense, and I gave her a rental deposit, glad to have her back nearby.

Shortly thereafter Gilbert must have reasserted his marital rights. A note came listing an "expensive ass" pad in the flatland below the campus. That afternoon I appeared on her doorstep, a large housewarming box held awkwardly between my knees as I knocked. There was no answer, but through the blinds I caught her silhouette moving about. I kept rapping away until finally she asked who it was and peered, as if unable to believe there could be such a fool about. Then in a horrified voice, unlike anything I knew, she pleaded, "You mustn't come here, please." I dropped the carton and skedaddled, convinced I had done enough to earn an explanation.

Sure enough, at 7 a.m. banging on the kitchen door, was Special Delivery:

July 28, 72

trillium—you goddam tender flower, i guess i have no real basis for saying i thought you knew what i am—a whore, a dope addict—i hustle out of habit. . . you'll probably really despise me for saying it's a good thing that last nite was the second day of the new moon for surely nothing else could have saved you. dig, baby, i have clap—not to mention that Gilbert is living at that pad. he wouldn't have killed you; he would have cut off your penis. he controls the mailbox & doors & everything else. i wish i could say with complete assurance, "i'm sorry when you offered me yourself i took it." I wish there wasn't this anguish. it's very dangerous for you to come near me—that's the truth. don't please. the last point of irony is thank you for the box of things. i open myself to whatever spirits may come from it . also thank you for everything. can you dig that my damnation is your blessing?

Seeing Ling always came at a price, but the chill of Gilbert's threat echoing through my vitals made the glimpse of Ling outlined behind blinds the last I'd see of her.

Scared as I was, I still cared about her and, before leaving Berkeley for Katmandu, I wrote informing her of my plans. Ling replied the next day:

Friday, February 9, 1973

dear robin—hello—hi hi hi

finally after one year i feel like i have the privilege to write to you. i don't want to keep living in this world without seeing or hearing your poems sometimes . . . i feel like that's too much.

after about 7 weeks of the fall quarter i was just finished—spent a couple of hundred on cocaine, went through an acting routine, & took an incomplete, and the fellowship at the lab ends in a few weeks.

things with Gilbert in our expensive ass flat went from worse to worse. i tried every kind of old routine to make him leave until i finally got the guts to leave myself did on the first of the new moon this january, renting a room with a refrigerator, sink & hot plate in Oakland by the lake.

i was a mad invalid—frequently—from november till january.

oh my newest goal is to travel to Brazil, which is why i'm still hanging around—to save money. and my most rare fortune recently has been to purchase a several months supply of hash oil.

i feel very out front & for real now that i've walked out on Gilbert. Course i've been trying it one way or another for years, but shit this time at least it's very direct—like i didn't say i was going away on business or nothing—i just said i'm leaving.

Berkeley's good for one time sensual experiences—that's what my love life consisted of for most of the time i was with Gilbert.

oh, i'm actually very very happy to have heard from you & hope you come to have dinner before you leave Berkeley? or should you phone me? or make a deal to write sometimes? or drop by the orange juice stand at college & Bancroft any weekday afternoon?   Shanti

Included on silvery flower-leaf paper was a warning:

> Far greater the poet's obligation
> To Crime
> Than merely to rhyme.

On still another page—from the same "mad" period?—came another of those all too cosmic images:

> and sometimes i'm the ocean
> on which float

A Ling infinitely older and sadder than the jaunty 25-year-old who had written me a year earlier. William Blake, I'm afraid, had it wrong. The road of excess does not always lead to the palace of wisdom.

I did not turn up for a meal on her hot plate. Nor did I call on her at Fruity Rudy's stand. Something about her letter's tone put me off. It's not the rhyme in crime that makes it poetic. But Ling felt otherwise. 18 months later I learned of the list of Fascist insects she had drawn up.

AN INFRA-RED BEAM IN THE SNOW

By now the only obligations compelling me to stay in Berkeley were my two sons. Marcia had married the theater director with whom we had shared a table in North Beach after the Be-In. He would remain a real friend and, for my sons, a warm and protective stepfather. He made it clear they would be leaving Berkeley at the first opportunity. Rather than stick around, savoring my custodial pittance (one afternoon and one morning a week), it made sense to go where I might see my sons less often, but for more sustained periods, such as summer vacations.

Berkeley may have been an aberration in a life that sought a more intimate grounding, but it had a spirit I could not have found anywhere else. Political reality, I now knew, could and had to be changed. You just had to work at it and persuade others to get behind the wheel and push. But after eight years I had all I could take. Nor did the re-election by a crushing majority of "Tricky Dick" Nixon and Ronald Reagan as governor bode well. If ever a year cried out for travel, 1973 was it.

Where to go? The opposite side of the globe from Berkeley, the rawest mountain air, the highest shrines. I had made plans to fly to Katmandu, Nepal, the starting point for a projected reconnaissance of India and southeast Asia, when over dinner one evening my doctor, a veteran of the first successful American Everest expedition, announced he would be leading a month-long trek in April along the seldom visited Rowaling Valley and across 18,800 foot Tesi Lapcha Pass to the Everest area Sherpa highlands. Would I consider linking up with them in Katmandu?

After my admission of never having trekked, much less climbed, the doctor did his best to reassure me. All I needed for Tesi Lapcha, besides a broken-in pair of hiking boots, were knee gaiters and high altitude goggles.

Porters would handle my personal effects. Here was a chance to learn how to live on my feet in the open air, and I signed up.

Nonetheless I was daunted by what I had undertaken. Was I really ready to step into thin air? And what would my life be like on the far side of Tesi Lapcha pass, when and if I got there?

In Nepal, I couldn't have been farther from the familial and collegial worlds I had occupied. For the whole of April, the walking claimed my complete attention. I had expected a leisurely stroll, with time to stop and raise my binoculars to a wheeling lammergeyer, a flock of startled thrushes. But there was never time: we had to keep pressing to reach Tesi Lapcha before the first monsoons forced an 8-day detour.

I learned this lesson the hard way on our first day. After a mid-morning tea break I had struck off on my own, wanting to put enough distance between me and the other people on our expeditionary force so I could do the bird-watching that, for me, was the point of the trek. Unfortunately, at the very first fork I managed to take the wrong path. By the time a Sherpa had located me and we had finally caught up with the group, he had dinned into me the difference between a stroll and a trek. And the hurrying in boots far from broken in developed a set of blisters that I solved, if that's the word, by resorting to a spine-tilting combination of boot and sneaker.

I found the Himalayas awe-inspiring. Every time I raised my eyes to a snow-capped divinity I felt elated. Nor have I ever encountered people more vibrant than the Sherpas in whose villages we camped. But before leaving Berkeley I had torn the ligaments in a knee trying to demonstrate a sliding soccer tackle—clearly, not my forte—on a student's carpet. With a bad knee, on terrain that rose or fell with nearly every stride, the walking was painful. I would regularly limp into camp a half hour behind.

Throughout the first sixteen days there loomed the disquieting specter of Tesi Lapcha. In Bedding, near the top of the Rowaling Valley, we parted with our barefooted Thamang porters, hiring in their stead the booted locals. After a brutal hike up to their summer pasturage, and another day spent acclimatizing, we set off over the final stretch of glacial moraine.

It took a while to get the hang of the quick-striding scamper moraine requires; I was never sure when a rock would blast out from under me like a woodcock. On the narrow cliff-edge paths our porters had a tough time of it and twice boxes of our gear went tumbling down a slope while we stood about, afraid even to talk for fear of launching an avalanche. Without such stoppages I would have been left far behind. My blisters hadn't healed and I couldn't risk donning a second boot before our ascent of Tesi Lapcha.

That evening we dined in falling snow at 16,000 feet. Everything, from the kerosene we now cooked with to the doubled gloves with which we ate, made it seem as if we were on another planet. Earlier in the day I had had an ineffective shot of cortisone and my limping had our two doctors worried. But with only a single day's supply of kerosene left, we had little choice.

It was still dark when we rose, so many pieces of stamping expectation. I was impatient to be off on the several mile walk along the valley floor while we still had crisp snow underfoot. The earlier, the better our chances. In reality, I had no need to be so worked up. Snow, after all, is a soft substance and the walk, in the rising light, could not have been more awesome, the eeriness broken here by a massive powdery rumbling, there by a turquoise shimmer of icicle arrows. I needed no pretexts to extend breath to a still unlit earth held in sky whose walker was but seeming mist, hope under a cloud.

At the valley's end, coughing, heads rising, shoulders pulling, we scrambled up over a forest of red and tan boulders, careful of what we might dislodge on those below. The ice in places was steep enough that our Sherpas had to cut traverses with axes. At one moment came a more perilous groping along the inner face of an open cliff. But if my knee was problematic, there was nothing wrong with my arms and shoulders, and I climbed with the freedom of a child shinnying up a tree.

Despite heelless boots and a great crate secured by a forehead-held tie, our porters performed better than we. I watched them as they stopped in a huddle to gossip, or to encourage one of us sunken onto our knees. Their tongues protruded and their heads bobbed as they climbed, necks bowed, goggled eyes lowered against the glare, bodies spread out under their burdens like turtles. I looked at the wide-set eyes in their fire-stained faces and prayed that the shifting black-red-and-green carpet of their boots would see them though.

By now my own eyes were burning and each foot felt like a planted stake as I struggled to shift them forward in the howling gale. When I could no longer see where I stepped, there were red-beaked choughs no more than ten feet away piping their encouragement. Spectral in the rarifying gloom, I made out an elderly porter, his long arm draped protectively around his woman. A few more steps and I found myself on the ice of the summit rim. I had made it. The electric howl of the gusting currents so affected me that merely watching a pair of guides hopping about like foxes on an overhang had me in tears— zest so surpassing my own.

The ice on the descent proved hard on our porters. Twice rope lines had to be set up. Even so, the valley below was a-tumble with runaway crates. For me, with my great boots, the descent was a dance in which I had only to balance arms to the side and, feet together, hop in a dipping flight through the forest. Something in me had taken wing.

Just past the last of the snow, in a wind-shrieking dell on the moraine, we set up camp. Later that afternoon, in accordance with the grant that had helped fund his trip, our other doctor, an eye specialist, checked our pulses by shining an infra-red light into the back of our eyes. In a verbal flash, as the infra-red flooded me, I saw my deliverance: from the "stocking of moonlight," the sexual-visionary temptation I associated with Ling; from the "dripping, red sweater of the dawn," one linked in my mind with the terrors of menstrual blood and Larry Rivers' portrait of Marcia. With these images came the realization that, in crossing the feared pass, I had done it: tunneled my way out of a life-long incarceration. Imagine the amazement of the child who, digging in the sand, actually reaches China on the far side.

The labyrinth I had escaped was fear. The fear that I could not do things on my own. The elements of that fear were diverse as the silver bonds of patrimony, the icy cords of matrimony, the quixotic quest for myself in women. I had looked to others to accomplish something only I could do. Now, over on the other side of the pass, if not the world, I was my own master with my own life, my own life, to achieve. I could fly, I could jump, I could shout. And no one was going to take that breath, that cry of joy from me ever again.

FATHER REACHES OUT

That night on Tesi Lapcha, while winds ripped at my tent flaps, for the second night in a row I saw my father in a telepathic dream. It was apparent from the recurrence that he was reaching out with all his remaining will to those he loved. I learned later that, while in Germany for a board meeting, he had developed rheumatic myalgia, a painful debilitating disease from which he never recovered.

Kaldis, 1964

Father's brush with death left him an enfeebled man, hanging on by the slenderest of threads. At any point, he knew, the sword might descend, and in the face of that threat, he changed. Life now interested him—the roses he dead-headed, a dragonfly on a pond. Despite swollen ankles and difficulty breathing, he took his male relatives on a safari to the East African highlands. He sold the Beach House and moved to a less prominent residence on a creek opposite the Shinnecock Indian Reservation. And he bought a Boston whaler in which to putter about at high tide. You must come and see the birds, he would write, genuinely appreciative of the tern plunging like a coin into a ripple off his jetty. He who had been a Reagan-style conservative could be heard muttering his incomprehension of the folly of our Central American interventions, at the Cold War's never ending brinksmanship. He didn't want to see the globe explode; not while he was still on it.

How deep any of this went is hard to say. There were interludes of returning health when he would let fly with the old vitriol. Probably his net estate of thirty-three million expressed whatever it was he had achieved, and like any man reduced to a single testament he was forever tinkering with it, lopping off a divorcing brother here, restoring him two years later. For those excised, there would be the odd hand-out, a $1,500 check in his enfeebled script given with a hug in his London hotel room, or the $100,000 cabled to each of us brothers on the night of his final attack.

I saw him for the last time in September, 1986, three months before he died. Mother had a World Wildlife Board meeting in London to attend and, sick as he was, Father insisted on accompanying her. As he said, he might as well expire there as anywhere else. His week at Claridge's Hotel was not easy. He seemed to spend every other day flat on his back, rising for dinner only by a supreme effort of the will. On one of his better days, I succeeded in inviting him out for a farewell lunch. If he was up to it, we could go afterwards to The National Gallery. As always, there were memories of his growing up in Chester I'd have liked to probe. But this didn't seem somehow the occasion for biographical testimony.

At the meal's end he reminded me of wanting to be taken to the Gallery. Was there anything he wanted particularly to see? No, he was in my hands. Gambling a bit, I steered him to the Dutch rooms, a Vermeer or de Hooch interior, and finally a room of Rembrandt portraits. Nearly everybody on those walls, I pointed out, looked even older than he. For a few rapt minutes he looked at those wizened, gnarled faces, as if suddenly grasping what a real artist could achieve. Then he asked to be taken back to his hotel.

Now that Father is no more, I find myself missing him dreadfully. That he loved me in the end I don't doubt, but I wish that he might have understood me as the person I am. But a man in whom I could rarely confide was hardly the person to discover me in my work. I see now that the rift between us was one of truth. His life, the achieved version he paraded, was his confection and no query of mine could make him revise it. Put another way, he did not trust me—nor I, him.

Doris in the receiving room of her 2100 Washington St., San Francisco house

MONTARNIS

For years, I had allowed myself to be pulled this way and that: now towards my father, now away from him and his devouring family. Come what would, I told myself, I had to be my own creation. Once across Tesi Lapcha, in those mountain villages in which we now found ourselves, that waffling ceased. The air filling my lungs was breath enough. I did not have to go on, as planned, to India and Southeast Asia, nor was I capable of doing so. I had lost a lot of weight on the trek and my efforts to put it back in Katmandu only further disrupted my digestive system. Instead I used my return ticket to stop off in France—a good place to fatten up—and stay at the home of the writer-illustrator Virgil Burnett in the walled medieval village of Montarnis in the Auxois.

When I arrived in the second week of May, winter had barely receded. Each day as I walked under the apple blossoms, I felt a frosty threat at my heels. But the fragility brought something with it, a burgeoning forth of my own.

On two previous occasions I had visited the Burnetts without succumbing to any enchantment. To a turn of mind bowled over by the combinations of wine-dark seas and sharply rising coastlines, by the incitements of clarinet and bouzouki, all of Montarnis' remarkably intact heritage—convent, abbey, turreted counting houses, gates and fortified walls—had not seemed vivid enough. Now, after the Himalayan screes, I could appreciate the solace offered by an ancient hilltop village surrounded in steep mist-laden greens.

Here was a once substantial town—the religious heart of imperial Burgundy—that had reverted to something like the 330-person subsistence farming community it had been when Julius Caesar had camped there during the siege of Vercingetorix's fortress of Alesia just across the narrow valley. Unlike most such "preserved" towns, Montarnis remained unspoiled: no yellow parking lines, no hotel or souvenir shops, and only once in a while a tourist bus pulling up at the little promontory outside the gates.

The town was so perched on its hilltop crest that I could walk out by one or another gate and discover new pieces of an ever mysterious puzzle: a purposely placed druidic bench, a votive sculpture in the niche of a wall, a new moth or damsel fly. Monks, magi, druids, had all contemplated here, bringing an attentiveness I tried to emulate.

The more I sauntered about in the steeply pitched countryside, the better I came to see the fields and hedgerows, the grays, blues and pinks of the dry-laid walls, as a distinct creation. If it was a soft, lingering countryside, it was because those working it had contrived to keep it full of cows and wooded hilltops and intricately maintained hedges. Their tender concern for the landscape they had molded could influence a visitor into thinking he had been flying all his life towards their still center.

When the long May sunset finally dropped, moonlight took over, lighting turrets, gates, and ramparts with the spectral authority of another age. Cobbled squares and bare ruined cloisters sang. Blood throbbed. To write I had only seemingly to listen. After being for much of my life on the run, betwixt and between, here I was where I needed to be, if I was to make anything of what had befallen me.

In coming to Montarnis, there is no question I was fleeing, for my sanity, if not my very life. I had no wish to wind up nailed to a wall. Or if I was, then I was going to be the one doing it and in own manner. That, it may be argued, is what life writing involves, and in that choice there is, as I keep finding, real freedom. In becoming more focused, I was more alive. And my fate was now in my own hands—not a parent's, a lover's, an organization's, each exploiting me for what I might symbolize.

It was not as if I wanted merely to write about what I had undergone; I had to. Everything about the life I had lived compelled it. Provided I could see myself, I could see the world. It's the dancer who, alone on the tavern floor, gives back to those watching their space, their freedom.

James Merrill, Salisbury, Christmas, 1995

I was beginning now to see how foolish I must have looked throughout my younger life. No sooner had I extricated myself from one predicament than there I was enmeshed in the next. Lacking any perspective, my life was my writing; my writing, my life. Whichever way I wriggled I was trapped. And, given my coordinates, all I could do was keep repeating myself. The "wanton current" was eternal and I was being sucked into its maelstrom.

At the time I didn't see my labyrinth in so dire a light. It was more, I thought, that I hadn't descended far enough? To reach that fabled palace of wisdom down in the muck at the bottom of everything, all I lacked was a guide. And I approached each new woman as if she could deliver me from the vortex in which I found myself.

It hadn't occurred to me that those depths might be dangerous, or that the pursued might become the pursuer. Violence and sex are not casual bedfellows. Nor can one traipse from one would-be muse to the next, taking everything from her—all the inspiration she has to give—without incurring some response. Does it seem surprising that, with nothing left to lose, or give, she should pull the trigger, feeling that, at the very least, she is doing her sex a favor? Along the scale of violence how much of a leap was it from Ling's suicidal inclinations to her becoming a murderous terrorist?

After the second thunderclap of mescaline, my obsessive pursuits came to a convulsive end. Staring insanity in the face on the one hand and, on the other, a drone's life in a proto-revolutionary scenario, I had to admit something was drastically wrong.

With that admission came the possibility of emerging from the wanton current that had pulled me along. Then the recognition I experienced in the windblown tent on the far side of Tesi Lapcha—that I did not have to be beholden any longer to anyone or anything—effectively helped me see how I could live the rest of my life. As the Mexican proverb puts it, "You can't take from me what I've danced."

CODA: THE SYMBIONESE LIBERATION ARMY

In mid-June the Burnetts arrived to reclaim their house. Shortly thereafter, I left for Athens, where I would meet my sons and convey them to volcanic Santorini for a month of island life. After they left, I lingered on, journeying to the temperate forests of Mount Pelion to check out what might remain of that first of the mythic rock bands, Pan and the Centaurs.

I returned to Montarnis in early September. Up to then I had resided in rural settings only sporadically: summers in Southampton, or on Greek islands. Here was a chance to experience the long undressing of a Burgundian autumn and a spring that, beginning in mid-February, would still be tossing up flowers when I returned to Mendocino in June to see my two sons. I had no idea what shape my life would take thereafter. Find a job? Resume my travels? Everything was up in the air.

That fall my thoughts kept circling back to Ling. I was putting together an account of our mescaline experiences when a last bulky packet arrived from her. It contained, along with a letter, a 25-page prison diary kept by a "young white male." The letter began awkwardly:

i wish i could come up with whatever could disguise itself as the correct manner and right words to present what i am about to say; it would really be a disguise, though right on, and so i won't even consider trying.

1. because certain things i was doing mentally while staying with you last year brought me here to this; i remember (among so much) that you once said to me something like you hoped i would be able to actualize my militancy both by being more verbally clear as well as make some kind of tangible connections.

7/9/73 11 p.m. BEGIN AGAIN? and for the last time so bear with me.

Yes, another writer who could not bear to throw away a first draft! How ironic to learn that I, of all people, may have radicalized her far differently than she had me. Affairs can take on an uncanny power; we don't walk away from their fires unsinged.

dear robin, greetings

realizing, perhaps more than i can make you believe, the rather dreadful way in which i betrayed you, realizing this because i've been betrayed so many many times myself:

i am very intense and serious these days and when i do just take it into my mind to relax i get higher than any drug has ever taken me—ANY DRUG— and for that reason i have finally come to the place—as i'd heard and seen so many others do—where i don't touch NOTHING i even kept a lot of acid, oil and weed around for the 1st month cuz i just couldn't believe it until finally i threw most of it away—along with the handmade sterling silver coke spoons—and then gave the rest away—and all i wonder now is why it took me so long to get here?? i mean, you dig, i had this outrageous intake due to the fact that i thought i needed to blur the miseries of this reality we all live in. Now I've found in these last months a way to direct my rage and work at ending these miseries instead of trying to alter them all around and accept them. So there are some of our brothers—white, black, and brown (not too many asians it seems just now) with whom i correspond and visit and send money orders and work at legal aid with AND THEY ARE ALL IN THE PRISONS OF THIS STATE OF CALIF. FOR ONE YEAR TO LIFE. And there it looks like they will stay unless i can generate more financial support than the $400 a month i make at this orange juice stand.

And then now HERE'S THE HARD PART (i'm sure you've seen it coming); naturally there must be 2 reasons for everything including letters to you. This man whose letters i send is in desperate need of a retainer to get his lawyer on his job and i, as usual, am in desperate need of a little assistance to keep me on mine (i mean hitching up and down the street soliciting blow jobs at $10 a shot just isn't making it). So how much to ask you for??? Let's just say anything from $50 to $500 would be welcome (not that i expect you to believe me, but i don't do drugs no more, and i'm really sorry—maybe even more than a little—that i whipped so many onto you, really...)

Hoping that you'll get this soon—and really wishing you well even if i never hear from you you you

No doubt I should have seen Ling's desperation and coughed up the needed $500. But the notion of a lover's alimony bothered me, as did the threat of blackmail. So I responded with a $50 check. I added that I would buy the beautiful pastels she had painted while sitting out in the garden during my second overdose for the remaining $450—a way of suggesting other lines of work than soliciting blow jobs. But my check was never cashed and to this day is probably lying in some FBI file.

Ling's is a fascinating letter for the disconnect it reveals between her private and public selves. The middle class jargon with which it begins, strains credulity. Who is peering over her shoulder as she types? What do they hope the letter will accomplish?

Whereas the second part, written in her nitty-gritty slang, brings out the woman I knew. Even so, the warmth of her response has to grapple with the "RAGE" of the addict struggling to kick her habit cold turkey. What Ling in her condition really needed was the support of a halfway house, not some gun's magical cyanide bullets.

From the I Ching to the Koran may seem more than the hop, skip and jump of a few months. But these "children of the wind" were as much a mystical brotherhood as they were anarchist assassins. To show their revolutionary commitment they needed blood on their hands. But why Marcus Foster, the much admired African-American Oakland school system superintendent?

I suspect the school board's proposal for a photo identity card must have struck a raw nerve in a woman who saw her anonymity as her criminal trump card. What she didn't know was that Foster himself was opposed to the ID card, or that on October 9, in the course of a stormy board meeting, he had succeeded in getting it scrapped. Nobody, unfortunately, had informed the SLA.

Ling was one of three masked assailants who gunned down Foster and his deputy Bob Blackburn in an alleyway. Somehow Blackburn survived two barrels of 00 buckshot despite 23 wounds. Pronounced dead on the operating table, he happened to coincide with a brilliant young resident who was able to restart his heart. Years later, Blackburn treated himself to a few jazz piano lessons from "a sweet guy by the name of Perry. The lessons were going well enough when he realized just whose ex-husband this Perry was. "He couldn't go back there," a friend told me, "it was too painful."

The gunning down of Foster and Blackburn was one of those acts that, no matter how you looked at it, made no sense. When this action, as Bill Harris admitted to Patty Hearst, "sort of misfired," the SLA became pariahs. To relaunch themselves they needed something really big. Why they chose body snatching, I don't know—for the relative ease with which it could be pulled off? If America was a sham democracy controlled by a corporate oligarchy, one way of striking back could be to target the ruling elite.

Ling was, among her various organizing roles, the SLA's archivist. She kept her trove in a cabin-like house in the El Cerrito hills north of Berkeley. When, shortly after midnight on January 10, 1974, two of the backup crew to the Foster assassination, Russ Little and Joe Remiro, were arrested while driving a van nearby, Ling panicked. The prospect of a police search so alarmed her that she tried to burn down the cabin. In a tinderbox landscape where not even July 4th sparklers are tolerated, the arson attempt attracted immediate attention and Ling herself barely made it out, zooming in her stolen gold Buick Riviera past the incoming sirens.

Among the scores of incriminating boxes lay Ling's green spiral notebook with its list of prospective targets. The second on the list, right after "Patricia Campbell Hearst—nite of the full moon," was my brother, Merrill Lynch Magowan. (My father figured on the list as well.) With this information now in police hands, the SLA's revolutionary timetable accelerated. They needed bodies they could trade for the imprisoned Little and Remiro. And among those bodies may have been my own.

The SLA's decision to try to find me was prompted by Rob Wilson's article, "Berkeley Inscape: the Poetry of Robin Magowan," which appeared in the *Daily Californian* Arts magazine the day after the bust of Little and Remiro. Why, they must have thought, would the student newspaper have run such a piece if I wasn't part of the local scene? Ling left the business of phoning Wilson and the English department to find my whereabouts to the SLA's other actress, Angela Atwood, and her more plausible voice. Had Ling betrayed me enough already? Or did she fear having her cover blown?

It may be that the tale the SLA fed Patty on the night of her kidnapping, of hers being but one of a number of similarly conducted snatchings, was no more than wishful fantasy. Yet it seems unlikely that the two-million-dollar ransom doled out "to the people in need of food" (PIN) was conceived only when the feds thwarted the prisoner exchange the SLA sought. For what it's worth one may speculate what a Safeway-managed food giveaway might have achieved, conducted without the foul-ups that bedeviled the Hearsts (Patty's father approached mine to ask Safeway's help with the distribution. Father turned him down.)

While Angela Atwood was manning the phones, Ling was actively spreading her nets. She wrote a postcard to the poet-painter-bluegrass musician Norman Mallory, with whom we had spent a couple of days near Pyramid Lake on the way back from Death Valley. (Norman recalls my awed admission, as Ling plunged headfirst off a canyon bridge into an icy green hole, "She has powers no man would contemplate"):

dear brother,
     i am sorry i can't tell you who i am or what i am doing. if you can get this to robin or know where i can get in touch with him just mail this postcard so i'll know. It's very important.
     I love and remember our days together warmly and am sorry i have to stay so mysterious.

your sister

The intercepted postcard brought Norman a scary, guns-drawn investigation from a huge well-muscled FBI agent in a blue shantung silk suit. The first thing he wanted to know was whether Ling and I were "cozy." When Norman looked baffled, the agent proceeded to illustrate his meaning by forming his left-hand thumb and index finger into a circle. Then with his right index finger he thrust repeatedly in and out. After his visit, Norman's phone, like so many others, was tapped for months.

On February 4, 1974, Patricia Hearst was kidnapped. From the moment I read of her fiancé's description of the break-in, and the white woman's voice on the apartment intercom, I knew Ling had struck.

The kidnapping turned me into a latter-day Actaeon. I had seen the Huntress naked and was I, for the crime, to be turned into a stag to be devoured by her baying hounds? As revolutionary history keeps demonstrating, the former sympathizer is dangerous precisely because he incarnates doubt. In a cause as beleaguered as the SLA's, nothing less than the blindest adherence would do.

It was not only the SLA with whom I had to reckon. There was also the FBI. I had come to their attention when Ling listed me as her reference in renting the tract house at 37 Northridge Avenue in Daly City where Patricia Hearst was to spend 52 days in a two-foot closet. If I was offering such support, couldn't Ling be holed up in Montarnis? A Laurel and Hardy-sized pair from the Sûreté were dispatched to check me out.

While Laurel rummaged about the Burnett house, Hardy asked questions that would inspire my subsequent dreams of Ling: turning on a landing to shove something razor-sharp against my throat, "Now you're coming with us;" or, machine gun in hand, from the top of a double-curved staircase, mowing down this loose mouth; or, in a more poignant reminder, appearing as a fugitive, naked under a tattered fur coat, a blue prison-tattooed NANCY LING still visible on her nape despite strenuous efforts to efface it.

The kidnapping of Citizen Kane's granddaughter has been called a "metaphor of America," of its new post-Vietnam vulnerability presumably. If so, it may explain why the authorities over-reacted: from the Attorney General who, for the first time in a kidnapping case, instructed the police to shoot on sight, to the FBI, who assigned half the Bureau's manpower to the case. Why, when the police had the SLA surrounded (but not, as they supposed, Hearst and the Harrises), didn't they wait them out? Did they so fear a public trial?

Instead the authorities blasted the hideout with some 9,000 bullets and lord knows how many firebombs. The police claimed that the wooden structure caught fire from the ammunition poured into it. From one of the newsmen present Norman Mallory learned that the house had been sprayed with gasoline from a point outside the range of the television cameras. A charred corpse is no phoenix.

By the time the firemen were allowed in, all that remained of the person I had loved was her charred hand, about to reload from the bullet bag that contained her makeup kit and perfume—a cheerleader to the end. After learning of Ling's death I happened to be in the Montarnis convent getting some papers Xeroxed. The nun assisting me knew about the Hearst kidnapping and remarked, after hearing me out, that Ling struck her as a genuine saint. The ways of the Lord, she told me, precisely because they can't be foreseen, exist to astound us.

Astound me, Ling did, as much by the manner of her death as by all that had preceded it. Yet it was not a throw of the dice that brought Ling to the SLA and the SLA to Watts, but something intensely willed. Death, for most of us, cannot be completion. There are too many unturned corners, unfinished chapters, flapping about. For Ling, pausing to reload, I think it was.

With Ling a quest ended; one that had enlisted the deepest part of my psyche. By the time her personal cyclone had whirled by, I was in a different sphere, determined to make for myself a different life. Sure, I still had a lot of work to do. But the lonely, desperate groping around, the destroying of myself and whoever I touched in the pursuit of an overheated illusion, was over.

The issues we didn't talk about nonetheless haunt me. Her suicidal yearnings, for one. How many attempts were there? What had gone wrong?

The affliction of the ghetto was not the source of her pain. A mood disorder was, and it could have been treated. Likewise I could have expressed my feelings about those masculine street values of hers—guns and the poetry of crime and all the upside-down dead end rest of it. As for helping her "actualize my militancy," well, no; robbing a bank and kidnapping and killing people was not what I had in mind. Nor would I have wished on anyone the torture inflicted upon Patricia Hearst in that tiny airless coffin of a closet.

All the same, the satiric comedy of the Hearst kidnapping threw off some potent sparks. The unlikely transformation of Patty into Tania, the cussing, vindictive, rifle-toting Symbionese princess certainly spoke to me; it was what I had narrowly escaped. So too did the food ransom "to the people;" a cruel fairy tale the SLA visited upon the Hearsts. Yet it was eye-opening to behold, in supposedly the richest country on earth, a hundred thousand citizens braving public ignominy and untold hours in line for a ten-dollar frozen fish handout.

Five years after she was kidnapped and then convicted, Patricia Hearst, the daughter of an influential media owner, would receive a presidential pardon. In 1976, after 40 years of marriage, the Hearst parents divorced. My father could not imagine why anyone would want to ransom a semi-retired 71-year-old man—didn't we all want to inherit?—and carried on the same as ever. But both the new Safeway chairman and president took so personally the threat posed by Father's name in Ling's green spiral notebook that they sold their lifelong Oakland residences and hired round-the-clock bodyguards.

POSTSCRIPT

Write on what you know, the ancients advised. What else but my life, I thought? Well, as it turns out, nothing is darker, more finally resistant, than the self. Fortunately, I've benefitted along the way from the advice of those who either knew me and what I had been through, or were simply better read. A bald list cannot acknowledge the nature of each contribution, but here it will have to do: Virgil Burnett, Andree Abecassis, Richard Howard, Murray Ross, Michael Beard, Norman Mallory, Lorenzo Milam, Gerard Van der Leun, Laurie Lister, Ed Smallfield, Walter Perrie, Julia Casterton, Victoria Wilson, Ron Silliman. All generously provided their comments.

John Ryle saw my work shortly after I moved to London in 1978—not an autobiography, but a vast collected ME. He suggested I make a separate book of the travel contents. That became *And Other Voyages*.

Some years later, *Maya Revisited*, as I then called it, turned up on the desk of an agent's reader, Robert Mabry, a former chief editor at Putnam and Dial. Bob could have merely delivered his report. Instead he was kind enough to call on me. In the process he explained that an autobiography, which is what this had to be, as opposed to an oversized prose poem, needed a consistent voice. Better, he was willing to show me how to make myself over from a lyrical writer into a disciplined chronicler.

By the time I returned to America and a domicile in rural Connecticut in 1991, Mabry had moved to St. Paul, Minnesota. A few years later, while visiting Berkeley, I happened to show my work to a former student and friend, Susan Hesse, a professional writer and editor. Susan knew much of my milieu first-hand, and seemed to know instinctively the insights, portraiture, and expansions my story needed. She made the whole process come alive.

Story Line Press published a first edition in 1999. Since then a number of new materials have come my way, enabling me to revise significant portions of what I had written. This then is a substantially new version.

APPENDIX

THE HERDSMEN
after Claude

Their lightness rends, breaths of clay
Gathered in the cool of a mountain-
Lit dawn. Watching them in that thin
Morning of the world, I note less the sheep
Or temple than the threads of light
Binding them to pipes and staffs, the echoing
Ravines and secretly one another.
Day becomes opaline.
Their earth is not only olive, salt, wine,
But the echo and response
Of birds and pasture and trees,
The clarity of unblemished distance.

NOON TAVERNA

Secrecies
of air—

wine
and flies

SAILORS AT PERAMA

The two move, circling,
as on the rim of a glass:
hands, soft-spinning flowers;
feet, spokes in a cycle of prayers.
They speak in a tongue of rain
sensing through the jukebox's din
hands breaking like plates.

PAROS

The road spins, high on a waist, threaded
Through transparencies of sea-
Whitened olives. Fields ripple, tiers
Of green and gold speckled with poppies—
As many poppies as stalks of wheat—
Maybe in a corner the lone cube
Of a farmhouse binding fields and sea
In a white flowing salve.

The roadway glimmers, the eye sheering
Down past little blue-domed houses,
Terraced, with steps like lumps of sugar,
To where in a pot of flame the sea
Funnels the light's last oils, houses
Reaching whites down to it like tongues
And up, over the cobbles, the lime
Drawing it, skywards, like a first breath
Promise of infinite accession.

Soft smoke is in the voice, honeylike
Reaching over the bay with that flat
Even insistency of serpents
Over grass, until some fisherman
Gets up from his table—hissing—his arm
A mast moving in a white vortex
Over the floor, eyes down, the slow circles
Descending, searching, the sea with him
Naming her, the sound a thread downwards
Through the spool of hisses guiding him as
He steers over its tilting sun-dialed frame

And light pours its daggers into him, melting
The streets into a wax, while the head, dis-
Membered, floats out over the singing stones.

TAPESTRY

Midday's olive trees salaam,
beaded blues,
grays, fountaining
over a tinder of bright
basket yellows, stitched
thick with horses, goats,
fig trees, small rooster-
colored houses,
under an oak the bell
of a herdboy, crumpled.
The hours wait, unseen, heavy.
Only blueness, a far
harbor writhing, oyster
in the still
pointed sun.

KALDIS, PAINTING

Each touch marks an explosion
of cypress & thumb-
pressed olive trees
against which the red
and blue house stands
atilt in a splatter of lime-
hued steps.

Out of this his mountain rises
cap of gold, brows
of curling knee-high juniper
afloat in a dream of lava,
slopes gathering meadows
of tubeless down, cut,
& poppy-singed
where only the breadth
of a cypress sways
& invisible
among almonds
a ploughman whistles.

ZEMBEIKIKO

An old peasant gets up   turns
Takes   steps on   makes with his hands
Fuse of a cigarette   crackle   sing
In the ash of his glass dancing
The floor   a round white   over which he stoops
Hops twice   JUMPS!
Sizzle of browns
Blacks   flash
Of a horsewhip
Stubble-bright falling

Z

Zembeikiko
Says it!   His is
Hisses!   He takes something round
Shape of a palm and with it
Hits/smashes: floor   trousers   shoes
Scoops   slices   spins
Is manna is hands is sunwhip & stone
Is the man who says   NO I'M NOT
Old Coocoocoorooooo
Who suncaps shoes & washes the stones
In the verminous oxides of night
& stands   tongue of crow   floorblack hands shouting
I HANDS RAIN COME
LOOKING FOR YOU   DADDY
WHO GAVE ME THIS NAME   WORM
A giant fist   dances   sings
As a tray of ouzo glasses descends

Shoes   plates   hair   glittering phosphorescent shirts
Through which he   mosquito bright   glides
White   dipping

Moving all over the floor

                              moving
                              sowing
                              threshing
I am me   he says   I burn the knife   I cry

Wings soar and melt
The fire
Is the globe   I am

FELIX'S BIRTH

Knots of light speckle the hospital wall
as day like a grove of oranges
begins to dawn. Attendants
drift in & out, but nothing can be done,
nothing that won't stop your coming.
16 hours later you come
bearing the wand
& as you strike
the screams
sing
& dusk
is cut in sandwiches
of green & gold. Threads
wind out of your eyes
where you lie stretched
across her belly's amber
as in a vial of oil:
mouth wide & twisted like a harp
eyes the color of
distant firs & mountains
corners tilting up like small pontoons.
Behind your nursery glass
blue mittened hands stir
in their tidepool sleep, starfish
searching, and with blind eyes
you wade
seeking your length of gum-
green water like the answer
to some dream of distant raft and
sunlight
thistle & thigh-white cloud.

CONSOLATIONS OF BOURBON

Appalled at our four-year charade
too few, not at all, counting them,
the minutes left
before I leave our house of glass,
the sword-points of your eyes
locked in our double jail's
too few, not at all.

I want to leave you doors
that close when they don't open,
the house I put up for my bird friend
the pasture where you dropped
the lazy silk of your behind
and I fondled it, *too few, not at all.*
I want to stopper my sink to your despair
and clench a hand bright-fisted again
to sheathe my every bone
in the crying banks where I yaw
helm in the green sand, grinding.

Suddenly I hear:
you don't want, you are
this stick wanting night,
a hen to clobber, a cloud
to burst in that dripping wilderness
where I take you to my breast
and the stars murmur
and the rains
descend.

MESCALINE HOPSCOTCH

O joy, jumping up with lead
O joy, mounting all my veins
To cobra a forest, cigarette ash my brains
O joy, o joy, neon crimson cigarettes
O joy, o joy, I'm jumping up in smoke
O joy, o joy, hooks in-finite
O joy, o joy, what prongs have you me on?
O joy, o joy, jumping matchstick cigars
O joy, o joy, jumping funeral parlors
O joy, o joy, anything you can imagine
O joy, o joy, I-I-I cannot
O joy, o joy, jump any longer
O joy, o joy, come to the end of my rope
O joy, o joy, jumping out of the moon
O joy, o joy, what will it all come to?
O joy, o joy, how can it all go on?
O joy, o joy, jumping, jumping
O joy, o joy, jumping funeral parlors
Jumping, jumping, all along my mind
Jumping, jumping, jumping funeral parlors

IMAGES

BIOGRAPHICAL NOTE

Born 1936 in New York City, Robin Magowan received a BA from Harvard, MA from Columbia, and a PhD in comparative literature from Yale. During the 1960s, he taught at the University of Washington and the University of California at Berkeley. He moved to France in 1973, then to England in 1978, where in 1986 he founded the transatlantic review *Margin*, which he edited until 1990. The author of ten books of poetry, Magowan has also published a translation of Michaux's *Ecuador*; a study of the modern pastoral narrative, *Narcissus and Orpheus*; two collections of travel writing, *And Other Voyages* and *Fabled Cities of Central Asia: Samarkand, Bukhara, Khiva*; and two books on bicycle racing. He currently lives in Santa Fe, New Mexico where he copes with a large rock garden.